Country Counseling

Country Counseling

Barry Keaton, Ph.D.

ISBN 1-4141-0727-7

Country Counseling
Back to the Basics of Christian Counseling
by Barry Keaton, Ph.D.

Proceeds from sale of the book will go towards the furtherance of helping those who are hurting. You may order additional books by writing Comfort Care Ministries, Inc.; 248 Coppermine Rd.; Buchanan, Georgia 30031 or call 770-646-9686.

∞The paper used in this publication meets the minimum requirements of American National Standard for Information Sciences—Permanence of Paper for Printed Library Materials, ANSI Z39.48–1984.

Library of Congress Cataloging-in-Publication Data

CIP applied for and is available from the Library of Congress

Contents

About the Cover

It is with grateful appreciation that I acknowledge Mr. Jeff Abney for providing me with and allowing me to use the art work on the cover of the book. The following information was also provided concerning the print:

Alabama Baptist

A Brief Biography of Rev. J. A. (Jimmy) Welborn

The man in the print *Alabama Baptist* represents a universal character - the country preacher - but he is not just a character: he was a real person who lived in the real house shown in the artwork.

Rev. Jimmy Welborn was born in August, 1896 in Carroll County, Georgia. When he was a child his family moved to the small community of Hopewell in neighboring Cleburne County, Alabama. "Brother Jimmy," as many knew him, later recounted memories from his childhood including the coming of Halley's Comet in 1910, when some in his community, and a number of scientists of the day, feared doom and destruction from the comet.

As a young man, Preacher Welborn worked at farming and sawmilling and, at one time, served as a policeman in the community of Fruithurst, Alabama—a "walking policeman" according to his niece, "before they had cars." He did later own a T-model but gave up driving for good after a trip with his sister Carrie to visit family members on Christmas (possibly 1937). During this trip he wrecked the car, breaking his sister's false teeth. That was the only injury, but Jimmy never owned another car.

Preacher Welborn was a World War I veteran. He was never married, and he was largely self-taught. Despite a lack of formal education, he was a scholar who could articulately discuss just about any issue. He was especially a scholar of the Bible. He pastored Pilgrim's Rest Baptist Church in the hills of north Cleburne County for twenty-six consecutive years, beginning in the early 1940's. He walked several miles to church most of those years, and finally gave up being pastor because of poor eyesight. The church is located on a dirt road on the edge of the Talladega National Forest and just got electric lines in the 1980's. Although he pastored a very rural church, he was never a loud, "fire-and-brimstone" preacher, preferring instead to deliver thoughtful messages in an intellectual, almost genteel manner.

He lived alone for many years (after his unmarried sister Carrie died) in Edwardsville, Alabama. His life was solitary and simple. He often walked the six miles into the county seat of Heflin, Alabama, doing so even into his eighties. He said that he walked from his home in Edwardsville down the train tracks into Heflin at age 87 or 88, rather than taking the highway, because he knew that if he walked on the highway someone passing by in a car would be sure to stop and give him a ride. He wanted to prove that he could still walk all the way - hence the railroad route.

Preacher Welborn was well known in Cleburne County and was loved by everyone who knew him. It is impossible for those who knew him to imagine him ever being visibly angry or expressing a negative word to or about anyone. He spent time in his later years with nieces and nephews in Heflin. One great-nephew even took him along on a trip to President Reagan's second inauguration in Washington, D.C.. Preacher Welborn died in July 1993, one month shy of his 97th birthday. He is depicted in the print as he was—from the band-aid on his finger to the thirty-year-old calendars on his walls. He lived a truly devout life of quiet purpose and devotion.

Should you wish to order copies of this print, the address is: Mr. Jeff Abney, 7 Lookout Avenue, Rome, Georgia 30161. Or you may reach him by phone at (770) 234-1644.

Dedication

This book is dedicated to the Counselor of Counselors, The Lord Jesus Christ. Only through Jesus is there effective Counseling. Only through Him can we effectively counsel. It is with great hope that Jesus will be glorified as this text is being used to help hurting people.

Acknowledgments

It is with grateful appreciation to the following that I am able to present this book. Without their help it would have been impossible.

and enthusiasm when it looked as though things were going to stop. For always being the person we could count on.

Mr. Jeff Abney

Thank you for agreeing to do the art work. For the many hours of drawing, reviews, and redrawing. For allowing us to use your art and talents to glorify God. For taking time out of your already busy life to help others.

John Wasdin, Atty

Words could never express how much I appreciate your friendship. Your wisdom and counsel have enabled me to tread paths I thought impossible. Above all, I appreciate your love for God and your fellow-man.

Mr. Robert L. Steed, Atty

With grateful appreciation for all your assistance in helping to bring this work to publication.

Warren P. & Ava F. Sewell Foundation

In grateful appreciation for your financial support to Comfort Care Ministries, Inc.. Your gifts have made a difference in the lives of hurting people. It is our prayer that God will continue to bless and guide you as you continue to help others for the glory of God.

Ms. Elizabeth Plunkett Buttimer

Thank you so much for your financial support and assistance in helping to bring this work to publication. Your concern for mankind is no secret. I consider it a great honor to have you as a friend.

Ms. Carol Walton and Ms. Lou P. Treadway

With grateful appreciation to my two childhood English teachers, for the inspiration and positive influence you had on my life.

To my wife Linda. My children Haley, Cass, and Justin. My Son-in-Law Dwight and Sister Annette.

Thank you so much for the hours upon hours you listened while I expounded about this book. For always believing in me when deep down inside I did not believe in myself. For loving me unconditionally and lifting me up with your smiles and encouragement. For being the kind of family that I believe everyone needs. Most of all, for tolerating my absence that I might be present to serve God.

To Haley Keaton Taylor and Linda Keaton

For the many hours of editing and re-editing. For your assistance in bringing this work to conclusion.

To everyone in my life who ever said "you can do it." THANK YOU!

For as he thinketh in his heart,
so is he:
Proverbs 23: 7a

Focus of the Book

The main focus of this book is to provide a counseling resource for the Pastor of people who are located away from conventional counseling resources.

It is consistent with God's instructions that the Pastor is the first person to whom Christians should go when they need help with problems. Whether he is a full-time or bi-vocational Pastor, he has to make decisions about how to minister appropriately to needs encountered. This book is designed to help him do that.

The rural Pastor is less likely to be able to easily contact persons like professional Christian Counselors for help in making basic assessments and rendering fundamental Christian Counseling Services. This book will help him do those things, but it does not eliminate the use of the professional counselor when the specialist is needed. When that day occurs, the Pastor who has used this book as a guide is prepared to make a proper referral.

While the goal is to assist the isolated minister, no Pastor can fail to profit from the assistance this book provides. It is unique because this book, when used as a resource, becomes specific to the area you minister in. You become the partner in the book's completion. You are co-author, therefore it is custom tailored for you.

The book is designed to allow you to reproduce resource sheets and fill them out so that you will never run out of space to put new information. If you move to an entirely new area, you still have a fresh resource book to take with you. But just imagine the wonderful gift you might leave the fellow who comes behind you; a starting point for a successful ministry from the heart of the previous Pastor. That's a way to love your people in absence.

If all previously said were not enough, an additional benefit is that the material will preach! It is enlightening and scriptural. Some material has teaching curriculum and could be used for church seminars.

Counseling Concerns

Some Pastors are concerned about whether to counsel or not to counsel in this day of litigation. We need to get real in our understanding of the situation. The Pastor really does not have an option when the question of counseling arises. The very act of preaching, if it builds the church, includes how to live the Christian life. You are counseling! The question is whether you are going to counsel well or not.

We often preach from I Corinthians 12, when we want to encourage;
(1) unity in the church,
(2) undertaking Christian work lacking in recognition,
(3) reaching out to people beneath the social norm of the congregation.
But what does it say to us in church leadership?

Nay, much more those members of the body,
which seem to be more feeble,
are necessary: (vs 22)

We should acknowledge that which is necessary cannot be dispensed. Water and food are necessities of life. The people who are hurting are necessities to the church. I did not say there are not problems at times, but God's Word says they are indispensable. Without them, the whole church suffers loss.
Verse 23 tells us:

upon those we bestow more abundant honor;
and our uncomely parts have more abundant comeliness.

How do we bestow honor? By showing the members they are important. How do we show they are important? By meeting them in the area of their need. Yes, it takes time, but that is what pastoring is all about, isn't it? Investing time in being a guide to the flock. And some of it we have to do one on one. Chapter nine of First Corinthians speaks to the minister on that one point. Paul said,"...I made myself servant unto all, that I might gain the more (19b)."

Please notice a promise is given to those who take the time to follow the Christian prescription of bestowing honor. The uncomely parts have more abundant comeliness. When you take time to work with people, they start looking better all the time. Allow me to suggest the whole church is elevated by that.

Someone is probably saying, "That's great, but what if I get sued?" Every church has a building. Every building needs insurance. You get insurance. If you are insuring your building with a company that specializes in church insurance (if not, you are probably paying too much), more than likely the company carries a rider for counseling coverage that can be added for a very small fee. Just because you are not formally counseling does not guarantee you won't be sued the way you are now operating. So you might as well do it all the way.

If you are going to counsel well, you will have to invest time in people. This requires discipline, so a good plan is essential, even to a full-time pastor. If it is essential to a pastor who does not have to hold a second job to live, it is even more important to the, so called, bi-vocational pastor.

There is nothing wrong with utilizing the expertise of others. God gave it to them so they could share it. The less time you have, the less time you have to be original (This could be a blessing for it should encourage dependence on the Holy Spirit.) Incorporate the expertise of others into your plan for meeting your responsibilities as a caring pastor. Use resources. Don't be afraid of doing the wrong thing. Anything you do that is contained in this book will do no harm. You are not going to harm the person. It is a positive input when you are doing something to help them. Sure, we all sometimes feel ill-equipped to meet the challenge, but that has its good side. It keeps us humble.

Does your church have a budget for ministerial supplies or a church library? This book recommends other materials. You will want to have them on hand. It costs money. One way to solve the cost problem is by using the ministerial budget or church library to fund them. However, some books and booklets you will want the counseled member to have permanently. If they can afford them, ask them to reimburse the cost. It's fair, and most will be glad to. They are getting help. If you see cost would be a problem for some people, those expenses should be funded in the church budget, like the rest of the ministry.

By the way, don't recommend a book you have not read!

One of the great fears of people today is the fear of involvement. You may feel that fear, but you are fighting back. That is obvious. You already have this book in your hands. In truth, you cannot help being involved if you are true to your calling. A pastor who disregards the counseling needs of his flock and community sees the flock go somewhere else to have their needs met. He also sees the respect of the community wane. First he loses. Then the Lord Christ loses.

Finally, you should be careful of what you read and, consequently, recommend in the field of counseling, just as you will be careful of who you use to help someone who comes to you. Everything recommended in this text is believed to be both Biblically sound in its assertions and recommendations. Many people, even some calling themselves Christian, are basing their philosophy of counseling on the ruinous assumptions made by worldly men. Granted, insights are offered by worldly psychology and psychiatry sources. What is fundamentally true is always of God, whether it is perceived by a lost man or a saved one, and what is true will not conflict with biblical precepts. If

there is conflict, it is not of God. It is wrong. Men may be wrong, but the Lord never is. The word of God is always the final word on the subject.

Where no counsel is,
the people fall:
but in the multitude of counselors,
there is safety.

Proverbs 11:14

Why This is Called Country Counseling

The text is called Country Counseling because it is essentially a common sense document, seasoned by experience in pastoral ministry and counseling. It has suggestions that may be received, rejected, or adapted to meet the user's particular situation. The glory of rural America is common sense, experience, and adaptability with some other important qualities thrown in. Among these are a genuine concern for one's neighbor and confidence in the faithfulness and power of the Lord God Almighty. This too, is the basis of our ability and willingness to serve our fellow man, particularly those of the household of faith, but excluding none. This ethic is fundamental to the strength that first made our nation great.

Country Counseling recognizes that specialized training is very good. In fact, the minister who fails to try to improve his abilities is a poor minister and will not be found reading this little dissertation. Country Counseling recognizes a greater factor than specialized training, one that defies refinement into a secular test tube. Some will call it natural ability, others refer to it as some type of built in insight into people that produces a successful counselor. We call it dependence on and surrender to the leadership of the Holy Spirit in order to be enabled by Him. It is our contention that every Godly man has the ability within himself to minister to his brethren as a counselor. Why? Because within him dwells, with power, the Spirit of the Holy God who designed man and formed him to begin with. (I Corinthians 3:16)

God that made the world and all things therein,
seeing that He is Lord of heaven and earth,
dwelleth not in temples made with hands;
...For in Him we live, and move, and have our being...

Acts 17: 24 & 28a

For they that are after the flesh do mind the things of the flesh;
but they that are after the Spirit the things of the Spirit.
But if the Spirit of Him that raised up Jesus from the dead dwell in you, He that raised up Christ from the dead,
shall also quicken your mortal bodies by His Spirit that dwelleth in you.

Romans 8:5 & 11

Therefore, brethren, we are debtors....

Romans 8:12a

The Spirit itself beareth witness with our spirit,
that we are the children of God:
....For the earnest expectation of the creature waiteth for the manifestation of the sons of God.

Romans 8:16 & 19

It behooves the man, having already been empowered, to study to show himself approved unto God. As in any other Christian endeavor, the good servant does not say, "I have arrived.", but rather he says, "I must become better prepared for the next phase of the journey."

We believe the Holy Spirit not only brings scripture back to our memory, but also brings to mind what is good in the things we learn about Scripture and Christian principles. He also makes the synaptic connections to enable correlation of principles, too! (Matthew 10:19-20)

Not as though I had already attained,
either were already perfect:
but I follow after,
if that I may apprehend that for which I am also apprehended of Christ Jesus.
Brethren, I count not myself to have apprehended:
but this one thing I do,
forgetting those things which are behind,
and reaching forth unto those things which are before,
I press toward the mark for the prize of the high calling of God in Christ Jesus.

Phillippians 3:12-14

But, to bring back to memory, the information must first be put there. Those who established this country had great respect for knowledge, and, most particularly, that drawn directly from scripture.

The rural spirit of the Country Counseling is one that says we do all we can ourselves, but if push comes to shove, we know who we can call on to help. Just as the rural man knows who his friends and neighbors are and their relationships to him, Country Counseling has a plan for discovering resources that the pastor can call on in need.

Country Counseling is also optimistic, like the rural farmer who plants in expectation. It pre-supposes that no realm exists where the

Lord Jesus cannot prevail. It believes, as a central doctrine, that no situation exists where the Lord cannot have ascendancy. The law of the harvest must prevail, and we will reap the product of our endeavors, ultimately, abundantly. Absolute victory is assured in the lives of all who genuinely are interested in victory and are surrendered to the authority of God. Uncertainty is left at the door, believing the Prince of Glory can come in.

Like the best of our country's forefathers, the central focus of what we do must be the Lord who gives the increase. As in sowing and reaping, He has appointed times and seasons for what we do.

To everything there is a season,
and a time to every purpose under the heaven:
Ecclesiastes 3:1

Why, seeing times are not hidden from the Almighty,
do they that know Him not see his days?
Job 24:1

And of the children of Issachar,
which were men that had understanding of the times,
to know what Israel ought to do;
...and all their brethren were at their commandment.
1 Chronicles 12: 32

We feel the rules for counseling were established by the God we serve, just as He established the rules of planting and reaping in other parts of His creation, and that He reveals these rules to those who will harken to His leadership. Therefore, humanistic and other philosophies of man are to be rejected. At the same time, it must be acknowledged anything demonstrably true about man, from whatever source it is gleaned, is to be used for his benefit.

Like the rural craftsman of yesterday, we must build to last, by raising up spiritually sound men and women who will pass the judgment of the Great Building Inspector.

For other foundation can no man lay than that is laid,
which is Jesus Christ.
Now if any man build upon this foundation...
Every man's work shall be made manifest:
for the day shall declare it,
because it shall be revealed by fire;
and the fire shall try every man's work of what sort it is.
1 Corinthians 3:11,12a,13

Finally, as in rural America of a bygone era, the highlight of Country Counseling is the church and the man of God as he stands to proclaim the Word of God. The best counseling is done from the pulpit by the expository preacher. This given, the issues that require personal attention are understood to be more challenging than those that sometimes make their way into the counselor's office where no such preaching exists. Counseling is pastoral. A shepherd knows that sometimes sheep need individual attention. A pastor who neglects individual needs loses sheep. Christ's under shepherd must tend carefully what the Lord Jesus has entrusted him.

....for they watch for your souls,
as they that must give account...
Hebrews 13:17b

The Lord, Himself, lost none but the one born to that end. Herein lies the challenge of our service. It is clear the Lord has high expectations of our usefulness in His absence. (James 3: 1) And why not? We have all the power of God backing us up.

Many have remarked how close God seems to us while in the country setting. With the lights of town and the hustle and bustle of the city excluded, we can observe the vast canvas of creation all around, even overhead. Country Counseling knows the importance of being still and knowing God. Not just to be commended to those we serve, but for our own sakes.

The Theology of Country/Pastoral Counseling

In a sense, the entire text is both theological and doctrinal, for it embodies the philosophy of the founder of Comfort Care Ministries and those who are part of that ministry. We believe this philosophy is grounded in the Bible, supported by scripture, and validated by the number of lives that have been changed.

No doctrine is valid when it is held in a vacuum. The expression of true beliefs find their confirmation when openly displayed and discussed among the Saints. Since others have given able expression to the doctrine of counseling, we hold, and have expressed that doctrine well, we for the most part, defer to their statements. Our comments given here are only to add a little of our insight to what is already apprehended by many. Country Counseling does not exist in isolation. The statements contained herein should find acceptance across the broad diversity of doctrinal statements that find expression within the boundaries of true Christianity.

The summation of what the scriptures have to say about counseling is in 1 Thessalonians 5:12-24, the core passage being verse 14:

And we beseech you, brethren, to know them which labor among you,
and over you in the lord, and admonish you;
And to esteem them very highly in love for their work's sake.
And to be at peace among yourselves.
Now we exhort you, brethren,
warn them that are unruly,
comfort the feebleminded,
support the weak,
be patient toward all men.
See that none render evil for evil unto any man;
but ever follow that which is good,
both among yourselves, and to all men.
Rejoice evermore.
Pray without ceasing.
In everything give thanks:
for this is the will of God in Christ Jesus concerning you.
Quench not the Spirit.
Despise not prophesyings.

Prove all things;
hold fast that which is good.
Abstain from all appearance of evil.
And the very God of peace sanctify you wholly;
And I pray God your spirit and soul and body be preserved blameless unto the coming of our Lord Jesus Christ.
Faithful is He that calleth you,
who also will do it.

To help illustrate what is being taught in the scripture, we have prepared the graphic on the next page. Here is where the life in the spirit meets with knowledge and experience, so the counselor might correctly discern what is needed by an individual at a given point.

This illustration, like all others in the book, may be reproduced or made into a transparency for teaching, as the need occurs. We do not consider anything good and useful to be our sole property, but rather the gift of God to be used for the edification of the Saints. Therefore, as it has been freely given unto us, so we share with you.

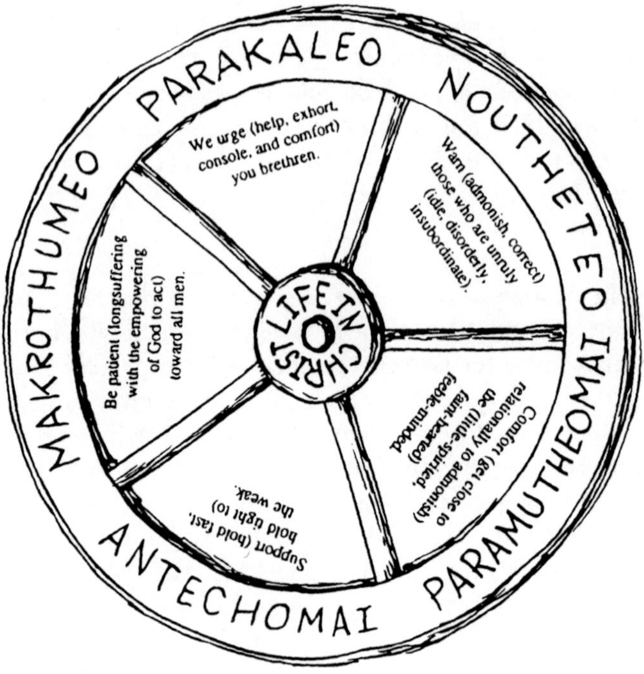

For a good short story study on the Theology of Counseling, read the appropriate sections from Healing Relationships by Stephen Grunlan and Daniel Lambrides, published by Christian Publications, Inc., Camp Hill, Pennsylvania.

Most of the text of Country Counseling exists to give you the benefit of accumulated experience and knowledge. *But the Holy Spirit you must have within you.* Country Counseling provides basic help and refers to where you can find resources consistent with a Christian

Counseling belief system. But, what makes the difference is having the power of God backing up the work, just as you must have it in other aspects of the ministry. Ministry that is successful requires three things of those practicing it. We call this The Three S's or Three Step Solution:

(1) Salvation
(2) Scripture
(3) Surrender

The first step in Country Counseling is that counseling must be practiced by a saved man. It is only saved men who can follow the leadership of God in ministering to others. The second step in Country Counseling is that it must be practiced by a man filled with the Word of God. The Scripture must be finding application in the counselor's own life. And he must know the scripture so that the Holy Spirit can bring it back to memory when it needs to be shared with others. And, the third step of Country Counseling is that it must be done by a surrendered man. A surrendered man is one who pursues the will of God in his life. A man who walks by faith, and in faith, and will therefore not come under condemnation.

You will notice that the statement concerning counseling, found in Thessalonians, coincides with the statement concerning the use of scripture in 2 Timothy 3:16 & 17:

> *All Scripture is given by inspiration of God, and is profitable for doctrine, for reproof, for correction, for instruction in righteousness: That the man of God may be perfect, thoroughly furnished unto all good works.*

Counseling is uniquely suited to the Man of God, for no counseling can be truly effective if either the Lord or the Word are left out of it.

Country Counseling works to clean up what is dirtied or sullied in people's lives, but it is not working just to clean up exteriors, but rather, the whole person. When a hurting member comes to you, they need to get clean. They need to have three baths. The first, testifies to new life in Christ. We refer to the Baptism that takes place after conversion. In making sure of their salvation, you know the basis for a journey to victory is established in their lives.

The second bath is the bathing of the client in the Word, which makes them aware of possibilities, as well as, responsibilities in Christ.

Some people view with incredulity such an assertion. I have been asked, "Do you really believe God's Word has the answers to all problems people face today?" The glad answer is; You had better believe it. Try counseling without the word and see what happens. Better yet, don't. Enough people receive bad counsel. Country Counseling must utilize the verses of scripture that speak to specific needs. Fortunately, several good books that correlate scripture with the needs are out and can be found in most Christian book stores. (The minister who touches many lives may wish to order these in bulk since they can be had inexpensively.)

Respect the Word of God. Teach those who come to you for counseling to respect the Word. Tell them what the Word has to say regarding the issues in their lives. The Theology of Country Counseling is that people become whole as they become conformed to the image of Christ, as He purposes to be revealed in them. That image to be revealed in them is always consistent with the Word.

The third bath is the bathing of the hurting member in prayer. This third bath is the basis of the remainder of our comments in this introduction to the Theology of Country Counseling.

The pastor's counseling preparation includes prayer, prayer, and more prayer. Prayer, under the authority of the Lord Jesus Christ, is the means by which God has chosen to unleash all the power of Heaven to come to our aid. As soon as the pastor discovers a member hurting, he should be remembering them in prayer. When a member requests counseling, he should directly and specifically approach the throne of God about the issue, asking for insight into what is the source and solution(s) of the problem. Before the counseling session, the pastor needs to pray for wisdom, not only regarding what has been heretofore mentioned, but also in his speech as he communicates with the member. You see, both the counselor and the counselee need Divine intervention. Many a pastor has been robbed of knowing how to assist a hurting member simply because there is no request made to God through prayer.

James said we have not because we ask not. The Lord Jesus said in John 15:7; He gives to those who abide in Him, and He further commanded persistence in intercession. Luke 11 was given to be a continuous action, and His example to us as our High Priest is one intercession.

We recommend many books. But in seeking solutions to hurting people's problems, we categorically and emphatically state that if you read a thousand books and neglect prayer you will fail. Counseling without prayer is like a Big Mac without meat. In other words, it just ain't no good.

Counseling sessions should begin and end with prayer. Pastors are Men of God. It should not be surprising to a client if God's man prays with Him about problems. If the client is surprised, even if he is unsettled by it, he will get over it. Pray! If you need to stop in the middle of a session and pray with the member, that is okay, too! You are, after all, seeking God's divine intervention in lives.

Country Counseling or Pastoral Counseling is counseling on God's turf. And God's turf is saturated with prayer. There is no way to under express the importance of prayer. God's Word tells us that prayer can move mountains, heal the sick, raise the dead, and set captives free. The power of prayer has no limits or bounds and is, therefore, essential to counseling.

> *And He spake a parable unto them to this end, that men ought always to pray, and not to faint....*
>
> ***Luke 18:1***

Section One

Getting Started

Getting Started

The Pastor's Preparation

Pastoral Counseling does require preparation. Too often, pastors tend to define counseling in their minds as casual chit-chat. That attitude is about as far from the truth as you can get. Counseling is more than just a few moments after Sunday morning worship services casually discussing means of coping with crisis such as divorce, separation, or loss. It goes far beyond that. Counseling also reaches beyond a pat on the back, or a quick prayer and a statement of trust in God. It is not enough to say, "Read the Bible, pray, and everything will be all right." Counseling has to offer those who are hurting more than just a few superficial words. Over the years, I've watched as members entered pastor's offices time after time, with no obvious results. Why?.... Lack of preparation.

The average pastor is usually in a state of unpreparedness when it comes to counseling. This is not talking about a formal education in psychology, either. That does not guarantee success in counseling. But three things are always present when successful counseling for serious problems occur. These three ingredients are organization, structure, and thought.

Organization begins with being prepared to invest some time in listening, exploring the causes of problems, and searching for resolutions. It recognizes this cannot be done in fifteen minute sessions, once a week, where there is no refuge from intrusion. How many times have individuals tried to express their hurts to the pastor only to be interrupted by other members saying their Sunday morning hellos and good-byes. That time is not organized for counseling, neither can it be. Being organized can mean that an immediate arrangement is made to get together in a timely manner and setting, appropriate to meet the need. When you are prepared to respond quickly to get the ball rolling when the need is presented, you've accomplished the first step of being organized to counsel. In this book you will find much to assist your organization in what is intended to be helpful hints. But, organization is something you must establish and be in a continual state of establishing if you are to have it. Pastors very often find their ministry limited by the servants within the church because the image they present testifies they are lacking in organization.

Structure begins with having a proper place to counsel. As mentioned earlier, the proper place to provide counseling to the hurting is not standing in the doorway of the sanctuary. It's not off in the corner of the church building, or out in the parking lot. The proper place to counsel must be free of distractions and interruptions. A counseling environment is a place of privacy and safety. Whether in the church or home, the counseling setting ought to be a place that provides no interference in listening, talking, and praying. You cannot explore the causes and solutions to problems with other things going on. In fact, it is downright discouraging to a hurting individual to have a series of interruptions like telephones ringing, people knocking on doors, or even conversations going on outside the room.

A proper counseling setting provides peace and quiet where full concentration can be given to the problem at hand. The lighting of the counseling room is one of those oft overlooked key elements. Nothing can contribute to an already depressed person's downward mood swing like a dimly lit, or poorly lit room. Everything about the counseling environment should convey hope and caring, from the paint on the walls to the comfort of the chairs. Bright colors, comfortable chairs, in a well-lit but not glaring room seems to lift the mood level. People having mood problems need a mood boost. Coming back to your counseling room should provide an anticipation of something good.

Several years ago, many pediatricians and other medical doctors did away with the white hospital look and converted to multi-colors for their uniforms and offices. Why? Because colors do make a difference. You want good color combinations, and you can usually have them by appealing to one of the best resources in the church. That's right, the ladies. Ask the sisterhood to come up with some color scheme ideas for you. While they are doing that, get with someone able to improve dim lighting or break-up glaring lighting in the area where you will be counseling. When it is all put together, you will be amazed.

The side benefit of developing the counseling setting is that the people who participate in helping you with your ministry will feel good, too. They will feel they are part of their pastor's work because they helped him in getting it set up.

Once the counseling setting has been prepared, it will require constant attention in two areas if it is to be useful to you. The first of these is temperature control; the second is neatness or cleanliness. Attention to these two areas are where organization to counsel and physical structure intersects to produce the comfortable environment that effective counseling can occur in.

A person who is emotionally healthy is adversely effected by heat and cold. The individual experiencing emotional problems frequently finds the slightest uncomfortable variation greatly exaggerated in their perceptions. The counseling setting being clean and orderly conveys an unspoken message to the visitor. A friend of mine once said, "Cleanliness is a sign of character." He may have been partially right. The area does not have to be show room clean to convey a sense of order to someone whose life is in disorder, but if it is not clean and organized, you won't convince many that you can help with their disorganized lives.

You must not forget odor in maintaining the organization of your physical structure either. People will come in for counseling who will leave behind distinct odor when they go. People's bodies sometimes reflect the stress they are under by giving off unpleasant odors. It's just the way our bodies work, but it must be combated to keep the counseling room from deteriorating. Investment in some pleasant smelling room deodorizers would be worthwhile. This might seem a point that's not too important, even a little strange to belabor, but it's the little things that sometimes mean a lot. No one would want to be counseled in a pig sty. So remember the importance of environment to your being effective in your work. As you observe the benefits of attention to these details in your counseling ministry, you will wonder why other counseling books made no such points. The reason is simple. Those books are written by people whose main focus is centered on counseling instead of pastoring. Much of what goes into the maintenance of environment is done for them. They give it little notice until an obvious problem occurs. In fact, they often did not initiate the original structure set-up. They relied on a professional with expertise in that area. If you can afford such luxury, then you are a very well blessed pastor.

A final word on the physical structure must be made before we can move on to other matters. Everything done to develop the counseling setting has been done to convey that there is hope for the hurting and a light at the end of the tunnel for those in recovery. The entire effort put into establishing this setting can be destroyed by an often made error. This may seem irrelevant, but when the pastor considers how the same condition effects him as he goes about the areas of his work that are sedentary, he will realize the importance of what is about to be said. That is, you can destroy the environment you have worked hard to develop with bad seating.

It's not a joy to sit for an hour on a chair that feels as if it has a rock for a bottom, or for a person to feel they have to fight to keep from sliding off, or a dozen other things that make chairs uncomfortable. You are not operating a fast food restaurant where seating is designed to hold people while they eat, yet encourage them to move on and make room for the next customer. Do not encourage your clients to be thinking about leaving while you are counseling.

Doctors are notoriously poor at choosing waiting room seats. It is amazing that some of the most uncomfortable of doctors' waiting rooms are often ones that belong to those who treat problems like bad backs. These people may get away with poor seating. In the case of a doctor who is trying to assess how bad a person's condition might be, poor seating might prove enlightening. It will not help what you are there to do.

It used to be thought rock hard pews encouraged attention to preaching, piety, and worship. Instead, it probably discouraged attendance, especially among those with physical ailments. (Some of the people you see will be experiencing physical problems for one reason or another.) Finally, some people got smart and started padding the seats. A few "liberals" even pad the backs of the pews now. A pew may still not be the greatest seating in the world, but we learned that making them more comfortable did not drive people away. At least, I never heard anyone say, "I won't go to that church! Their seating is just too comfortable!".

If the individual is expected to attend a one hour counseling session, he or she should have a comfortable place to sit. The very best seating is where chairs are so good, the counselee never gives them a thought. They just use them and focus on the counseling process. When you have selected that kind of seating, you've done well. Surprisingly, you may find that when you have made your selection on seating, what you have gotten is not necessarily the most expensive that you looked at. Don't equate comfort with expense. Sit in what you are considering. Financiers often talk about the bottom line. To make a pun, getting to the bottom of your seating dilemma by testing the options is the only way to make the right choice. That way, poor seating won't cause your counseling sessions to bottom out. Seriously, if you wouldn't want to sit in it for a session, don't expect the hurting member to want to.

Organization for counseling involves seeing people by appointment only. This works best for the counselor and counselees. In this manner, the pastor's casual interaction with the member is separated from the more profound delving into people's problems that requires time and privacy. The appointment assures the counselee your undivided attention during the meeting, and it assures the pastor that they are serious, to some degree, about dealing with the problem when they arrive to keep the appointment. One thing that the appointment also conveys to the member is your professionalism. This is a reassurance to the person who feels desperate in need.

Of course, every pastor must sooner or later encounter the crisis situation where no appointment may be scheduled. But after the genuine crisis has been dealt with, the appointment system must be in place when follow-up is called for. Do not let people turn non-crisis situations into crisis issues simply to get immediate attention. Discourage people from just coming by or stopping in at will. This presupposes that your time is not occupied or valuable. It abuses the pastor and even robs him of or takes up time that he might spend with his family, because he is forever trying to catch up. There is a line that must be drawn between availability as a pastor and the scheduled availability of the pastor/ counselor. Experience is a great teacher. You will become more adept about handling people with consideration and firmness, while managing time given to God's service, if you keep in mind as you go forth, only so much time is available.

Something else to remember in scheduling appointments is not to overload yourself. Remember that you must have time for leisure and family, because they are your first responsibility before God. Separate a time that belongs to them. Structure your working day so that being a spouse and a parent is not neglected. This schedule will, no doubt, change as children grow older. But, spouses and children both need to know they have a time when you belong solely to them.

Develop a policy concerning appointments. When two or more appointments are missed or broken without legitimate reasons, you may want to consider that as a signal that there is a lack of genuineness to the individual's request for help. Requiring people, who are having problems, to keep appointments and be on time, not only helps in organizing yourself to counsel, but also gives them structure in their daily living.

Sessions that go for more than an hour to an hour and a half are usually non-productive. An hour is probably the norm for effective adult counseling. This is not an inviolate rule, but certainly is generally true. Timing sessions provides an additional impetus to stay focused and on target. It saves you from wasting time, and encourages the client to strive to communicate to you early what they want you to know.

Children should never be in counseling as long as an adult. A thirty minute session is more than adequate for what you will need to accomplish during one meeting. Their attention span is shorter, but it also doesn't usually take children as long to open up, if they are going to. But it surely is true that they will quickly lose focus and become impatient. If you are going to have an ongoing communication with a child, you must be really sensitive to how they are actually responding. You be the judge about the time, but please consider these suggestions carefully.

Adult issues should never be discussed in front of children. Sometimes moms bring children to counseling due to the lack of a sitter. What are you going to do? Be prepared for that to eventually happen. If you have a church secretary or other staff member at hand, they might help out, but it would be at the expense of what they are really there to do. It is very easy for moms to get in the habit of relying on such a service. So, enlisting a church staff member at the last minute is really a bad idea. Besides that, most pastors don't have the luxury of full-time staff to misuse. If the child is old enough and responsible enough, having them wait in another area with a few age-appropriate items to hold attention is a good solution. If not, a solution appropriate to your situation must be found or the appointment cannot be kept. Children should never be exposed to discussions involving adult problems, particularly where their parents are concerned. Actually, this could be construed as emotional abuse. A child may misunderstand or misinterpret. There is no excuse for inflicting this kind of trauma on a child.

It is very wonderful when churches are full of love and caring for one another. Certainly hugging is not uncommon in many churches, and we wouldn't want to discourage that either. However, the pastor should be prepared to avoid physical contact before, during, and after counseling sessions. Forethought is needed simply because it's our natural instinct to reach out and touch, hold and hug those who are hurting. This is an absolute No-No! Yes, they often do need to be held and hugged as they express their hurts and pain, but not by the counselor. Touching, holding, and hugging a counselee of the opposite sex really spells nothing but trouble. Keep your distance, pastor!

Many a sincere and well-meaning man of God has been ensnared and ruined because such behavior caused him to become physically involved. Giving thought to the potential for danger in such situations will help prepare you to sit and watch as many cry and grieve their hearts out. Of course, you are not being asked to lose your compassion. You are being shown the need to give thought to danger. Actual involvement does not even have to occur when you are dealing with hurting and mixed up people. They can jump to wrong conclusions about your expression of caring. Thoughtfulness results in you protecting yourself, them, and what you came there to do in the first place. A simple handshake when saying hello and good-bye is contact enough. Avoid any behavior that could lead to sensual or sexual involvement. Remember that your reputation is at stake, but more important than that, the witness of Christ in the community you serve is at stake.

Note taking is an area of preparation being organized takes into account before the appointment is kept. Prior to the time you will meet, you have already checked to insure pen and paper is in adequate supply, near at hand. Notes are a valuable asset when a review is needful. Many do not care to make notes while the session is going on and depend on memory to guide in summarizing the session after the client has departed. I disagree. You will forget important points and thoughts that came to you as the session progressed if you delay jotting down notes. Experience has shown most do not mind you taking notes. Perhaps because of the influence of movies, oftentimes they even expect you to. The member who trusts you will understand you are doing something for the benefit of them. It is okay to explain you will be taking notes and why.

Each member who comes to you for counseling should be assigned a folder. Here is where all data should be placed. A safe secure place to store these files is also a necessity. It must be readily at hand when you need it, but absolutely free from intrusion by anyone else. Data gathered during sessions, and all other information collected regarding the individual, is highly confidential. It must be kept under lock when it is not in your hands. Anyone who has been in government service where classified information was handled knows the rules for safeguarding privileged information. Be even more extreme than they are. It should always be for your eyes only.

Remember you are responsible and can be held legally accountable for divulging personal information. As confidential as your personal files, so is the file in your brain. Safeguard what you are told. Never, and I mean never, share what you have been told with anyone. Your future in the ministry, your very credibility as a man of God requires you keep a tight lip. Many a pastor has let slip into his sermon what was told him in the counseling chamber. It is very hard to make a new start when you lose the esteem of those you serve.

Having said all of that, I must now tell you the exceptions. Sometimes you have to tell what you know. Some instances are required by law. Others may be judgment calls where you have to face the fact you are your brother's keeper. Issues involving child abuse, homicide, and the real potential of suicide must be reported to the appropriate authorities. You cannot let anyone take another's life or destroy someone else's property. But when you report them, you must have a very high degree of certainty. Most people are seeing you to get help, not preconfess and make you an accessory to crime. So, in these circumstances, resolutions can often be found. Be careful to keep confidence, unless the situations are exceptional, as we discussed.

Preparation for counseling requires thought be given to the pastor's personal appearance. Much has been said about dressing appropriately to the expectations of the congregation that you serve, in recent times. Certainly the appearance of professionalism is not packaged in a pair of worn out jeans and dirty tennis shoes. The proper style of dress for the pastor is one that remembers he is an Ambassador for Christ. He has the appearance of such at all times, but particularly when preparing to counsel. I'm not necessarily saying the attire must be white shirt and tie. No. The pastor should be clean shaven and neatly dressed. A wife of a well-known t.v. preacher remarked years ago that the first two things she noticed about a man was whether his shoes were shined and his fingernails were clean. That assessment would be most unfair applied to a man who has spent the day working in his vegetable garden, but it is worthy of notice in a man spending his day working in God's garden, tending the branches sprouting from the True Vine, the Lord Jesus Christ. Even the, so-called, bi-vocational preacher who earns his bread at dirty labor should strive to present the best possible appearance as he ministers.

Appearance may not make an impression on all you counsel, but it certainly will some. But how will attention to this matter effect your self-image? The previous discussion implied your image in the community and to the counselee was the question, but that is only part of the picture. The secular world once held the man of God in high esteem. The local minister's social position was on a par with anyone in the community. This position was not lost because of the sins of prominent preachers who are isolated from the local scene, even though they intrude into living rooms throughout the community. It was lost by local ministers who did not set high standards for themselves and for each other. The bearing of the man can reflect the communities' view of him and his work, or it can shape the communities' view of him. If a man dresses the part, he can even form his own self-image into what it needs to be in order to be an effective minister that communicates that image to others and brings respect to his high calling. While your personal appearance may not effect your ability to counsel, poor appearance says you are not concerned about image. Let me ask you if you are giving no thought to your own image, how can you help anyone having a problem with their's?

The minister with poor self-image may very well wilt in the presence of other professionals. But, if the person has a proper outlook on his calling and realizes that the minister stands at the apex of all possible human endeavors, he can look any man into the eye without apology. It is highly likely more professional people would come to Christ if pastors and preachers magnified their office appropriately in their own estimation.

Preparation for counseling includes self-examination. To be prepared to counsel requires one to have a high degree of health in the very areas that they will tread upon in another's life. These areas are the ones we identify as spiritual, emotional, marital, mental, physical, social, and so forth. Perfection is not possible, but it is incomprehensible to think that a person might counsel in an area where his own life is falling apart. That should be obvious. Yet, many a preacher has experienced failed sermons without understanding that they are preaching in an area unapplied to their own lives and, thus, cannot be a blessing in someone else's. If we work to a high standard, it requires that we first apply the lesson to our own lives. "Physician heal thyself."

Over the years, I've seen pastors involved in counseling issues that they, themselves, were trying to deal with or needing to conquer. Again, I am not talking about itty-bitty issues, but I am talking about the issues that require a high degree of health. A pastor dealing with addictions is not capable of assisting others dealing in these matters. A pastor who is unequipped to counsel is a threat to the well-being of another, just as a surgeon going through drug withdrawal is a threat to the patient he is operating on. A pastor is a threat to the person he is counseling if he does not have the victory in the same area of his life.

If there is a lack of health in an area of your life, it will come out in counseling. You cannot teach the drug addict, sex addict, etceteras, self control if you have none. Neither can you or I teach love, affection, compassion, patience if it is obvious we are without these same qualities. Yes, counseling does demand that we stay on top of dealing with and resolving our own problems before we reach out to assist others in dealing with theirs. Really, a pastor should be doing that anyway. We've all heard the old saying, "do as I say, not as I do". That attitude does not work for the pastor or the counselor. People seeking counseling are not only looking for answers, but models, as well.

Let me conclude this discussion on taking thought about our own life's hygiene by including some personal testimony. Many years ago, after I had received the Lord Jesus Christ as my personal Savior, I persisted in continuing the sinful habit of cigarette smoking. Almost every day, a preacher friend would witness to me about the need to quit this terrible habit. Day after day, he would dog me with statements like, "You ought to be ashamed. Don't you know that doesn't look Christian?" After weeks of listening to his demands that I quit smoking, it suddenly occurred to me that he was seventy five to one hundred pounds overweight. Now, it was my turn. First, I was angry. I thought, here sits a man eating himself to death and counseling me about the need to quit cigarette smoking. I never will forget how, suddenly, I turned myself off from what he was saying. I looked him in the eye and said, "Look at you, just look! You are dying! You're killing yourself and you want to witness to me about smoking?" I watched as the blood left his face and a paleness set in. Needless to say, he backed off. Do you get the point? When I did eventually give up the habit of cigarettes, it wasn't because of this man's witness. I hope you see in this personal account how important it is that our own Christian health is up to par before we get involved in the health of others.

What are you going to do if someone approaches you in an area that you are weak in your own life? You will make a proper referral and get them help that way. You can do that because you are going to use the tools provided in this text, and you will be ready. But, you are going to give thought to your weaknesses because you love the Lord and they affect not only your service to others, but your very relationship with Him. And, that is really what counseling is truly all about, from the Christian perspective. We are to help others grow so that their lives are more closely conformed to the image of Christ than ever before.

We seriously hope that these helpful hints to the pastor's preparation to counsel will be taken to heart as you prepare to assist those who are hurting. We will be the first to admit they are, by no means, exhaustive on the subject, but do feel that if they are brought into practice they will compliment your counseling abilities and skills. Sometimes we tend to walk into situations in the dark, with no awareness of what to do. Usually, this can be traced to a lack of preparation instead of a lack of forewarning. No man goes to war without first being prepared. Preparation is of the essence in all that God sets before us to do.

Getting Started

Comfort Care Ministries, Inc.

Book Recommended:	*The Psychology of Counseling*
Authored by:	Clyde M. Narramore, Ed.D.
Published by:	Zondervan Publishing House Grand Rapids, Michigan

It has been said of Dr. Narramore's writings that he never writes anything that is not good. Scarcely could anything be produced more appropriate to supplementing our section on going forward in pastoral counseling. The section we title Getting Started is a primer of very basic information that sets the stage for pastoral counseling development. The Psychology of Counseling is the perfect continuation piece for that to occur in the dedicated minister's life.

Do not allow the title, Psychology of Counseling, to discourage you from getting into the book. It is written in an understandable manner, and divided into easily digestible chapters. The first twenty-six chapters are the reason the book is endorsed at this point in our text, however, the remaining seven chapters will be equally profitable to your ministry as well.

You should not neglect Part III of this book. We have already mentioned the value of Scripture. In Part III is a reference of Scripture to use in counseling. Also, there is an explanation of terms, and information on some books you might want to add to your library.

You will want to make notes to help you improve your counseling as you study this book and others. If you add them to the basic body of this book, it will become more personalized and useful to you.

notes: ____

____

____

____

Getting Started
Looking At People

When assisting those who are hurting, all areas of life must be examined. We define those areas in six dimensions, as do many others in counseling. These dimensions are the spiritual, emotional, mental, physical, volitional and social facets of man.

One of the challenging problems of counseling is getting to the source of the problem. Unless all areas of a person's life are examined, the pastor may fail to identify the root cause of the problem. Man must be viewed from all sides of his being if you are to see an accurate picture of the person. Too often, people and their problems are evaluated from one viewpoint. If all problems were equally distributed through the different dimensions of man, this means such a practice would have 84% probability of being wrong every time.

Referring back to our Theology of Counseling in the introduction, we discover that five counseling approaches are presented in the Scripture. This scarcely can be said to have occurred by accident. It is God-designed to meet man in the correct manner to minister to the area in which he is hurting. Presumption in evaluation not only hinders the counselors from being able to focus on the area of life that is the source of the problem, it thwarts the plan of God in ministering to His people through His servant.

A pastor can profit from understanding that people are multidimensional in other areas of work and relationship. It is essential, not only in counseling, but in everyday life that we see things from all aspects. If we do not, we may receive a wrong view of circumstances and be lead into wrong conclusions. If we understand that to be true, it is no great extension of thought to realize it must also be true in counseling. Would that all pray and practice the discipline of mind that leads to the development of understanding and wisdom.

First, let us consider a scenario where looking at the facets of a man can change how you counsel: Suppose one of your church members came to you complaining about depression. Right away it would be easy to assume they are dealing with what is essentially an emotional problem. You could spend a great deal of time digging around for a root cause in that area, or ,suspending judgment, you can look at the whole man.

Being an observant pastor, you know this once dedicated Christian has been laying out of church. Over time he became inactive, lost interest in the Bible study, prayer, and witnessing for Christ. Nothing great or cataclysmic occurred, he simply became careless in his relationship with the Lord. Now, what area does it seem the root of the problem lies? Emotions? No! The root problem can now be seen in the person's spiritual life. By examining all areas of the person's life, we discover things are not what they appear to be. The symptom complained of was centered in the emotions, but the problem lay in the spiritual realm, an area you are most equipped to counsel in. When the person returns to the right relationship with God, and the joy of their salvation is restored, depression disappears.

The importance of assessing the different dimensions before getting heavily involved in counseling cannot be over-emphasized. It would be sad to spend several sessions ministering to a person in one area of their life only to discover the root problem lies in another. After extended time counseling with no progress, you might lose the counselee. If you discover accidentally where the problem lies, and it was something entirely different from the area you were counseling in, you not only have wasted valuable time, you may also have injured the confidence the individual has placed in you.

On one occasion, a mother brought in her son for counseling. He was having difficulty with his grades at school. The child was actually failing three of his six academic subjects. During the initial interview, I noticed the child spoke with nasal tones. I asked the mother if her child had problems with his sinuses or his ears. She replied that he was taking antibiotics for ear and sinus infection. After discussing the possibility of some further problems with her, I suggested referral to an ear, nose, and throat specialist. A week later, the two returned with news that the son had been diagnosed with an 80% hearing loss in one ear and over 50% in the other. A few weeks later, surgery was performed to correct the child's problem.

The child did not have an emotional problem, unless you consider the peripheral frustration of being unable to hear and, therefore, to perform. Certainly there was a social implication to the feelings endured in being ostracized to the back of the class, because his teacher misinterpreted his frustration, but that was not the root cause of the problem, either. Without a complete assessment of the person who came to see me, apart from any preconceived notions, it would have been possible to miss the problem. You see, and perhaps this might be considered an

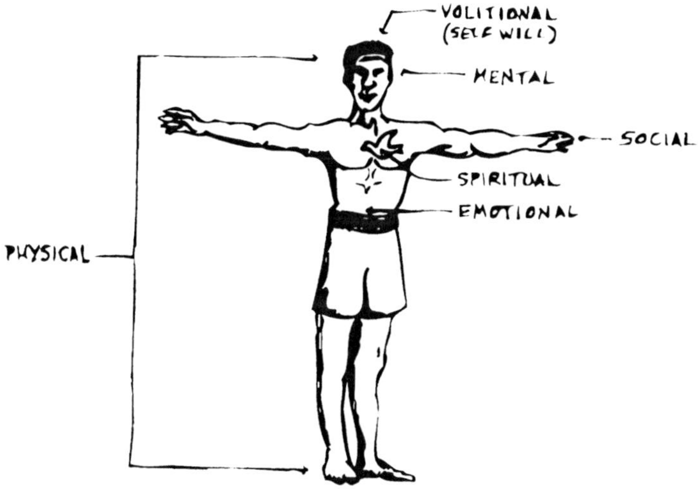

astounding thing about this story, the child had already been evaluated, by a psychologist. He had completely missed the problem. The child had no lack of mental ability to hinder the development of academic skills. He had a physical disability that could be fixed, once it was identified.

Implied in my narrative was the truth that difficulty in one dimension of a persons life effects others. Care in assessing all dimensions uncovers the real problem. If you are to be successful as a counselor, you must take great care to view each individual who comes to you from every dimension of their life. (A caution is inserted about assessing here. Do not ever presume that someone's problem is exactly like a client you had previously. Assess the individual.)

The Spiritual Dimension

The first dimension of a person's life that should be scrutinized is the spiritual dimension. An individual who has problems centered in the spiritual realm is suffering in all others as well, when the problem has matured. Herein lies the superiority of Christian Counseling over all other types and the strength of the pastor as a counselor. No other discipline dealing with the inner man is equipped to adequately assess the spiritual dimension, or to minister to it. Even the secular practitioner, who happens to be Christian, is restricted in ability to deal with the facet of man which permeates all others. Jesus Christ must be at the core of the work.

For example, a young mother suffering from anxiety and panic attacks consults with an associate on referral by Christian workers she came in contact with. In assessment, it is immediately obvious that she has had a history of alcohol and drug use. Investigating the Spiritual dimension, the counselor discovers she had made a profession of faith in Jesus Christ at an early age. Evaluation indicates that this experience of Christ was genuine, but not built upon. He introduces her to the concept of the Lordship of Jesus Christ and the security that can be ours in knowing that surrender of our lives to His control we need not fear. She seeks the Lord's forgiveness for the adultery which lies at the core of her anxiety and asks Him to take control of all areas of her recovery. The counselor introduces her into a Christ centered 12 Step Recovery Program for her drug and alcohol problem. The value of the program chosen is that it also ministers to the codependency issues common to these conditions. As she develops strength spiritually, she becomes more concerned with being the wife and mother she might be. While these issues are being resolved, she becomes aware that she has been a verbal abuse victim and has become a verbal abuser. It seems quite a full plate. And, it all did not happen overnight. But, it did happen. If the assessment had gotten stuck with the peripheries, a cycle of progress and relapse might have ensued. But when the assessment disclosed that the root cause was spiritual immaturity in not going forward with and learning to trust the Lord after salvation, a starting point was found to minister effectively. Once the issue of trust was resolved and the Lord was asked to establish His authority in her life, she never again had a panic attack so severe to cause hospitalization. In fact, strong concern was the best her fears could produce again, and they diminished as her walk in Christ (her spiritual health) grew. This woman had been in and out of secular counseling repeatedly. Her first session in Christian Counseling was when panic attacks stopped. It doesn't always happen like that, but assessing the spiritual dimension first is always a good idea.

When you find neglect of, or a break in the spiritual life, it is for sure ministering in that area is going to be essential to recovery. The assessment will determine which is impacting on which, as we shall see as we continue our discussion.

The Physical Dimension

The second dimension of an individual that calls for an assessment is the physical. Unfortunately, poor health has led many into a host of problems in other areas, not the least of which are bouts of depression and low self-esteem. And always, there is the spiritual challenge. Those who suffer physical negligence need to be educated on the ramifications of the effects of their actions. Not only that, it is high time we taught people to respect the Temple of the Holy Spirit. You will find that care paid to the physical dimension has positive effects on any disorder, no matter where the problem is centered.

Unfortunately, physical health has been minimized in considering its impact on people's lives. Ill health has the capability of causing mental and emotional conditions due to such things as hormonal imbalances, as well as other physical impacts. Poor physical well-being can be just as devastating in its ultimate effect as full blown illness. Sometimes, it can be even more so because the grinding conditions of an unrecognized and, therefore, untreated problem can be extremely long term. The impacts of poor health upon finances, family relationships and so forth can result in the whole range of potential problems in all of man's parts being realized. Pastors, particularly pastors who counsel, should realize that man is every bit as much a physical being as he is a spiritual one.

Missionaries in the third world countries have learned and relearned the value of feeding men's bellies in order to enable their minds and hearts to function and receive feeding for the soul. Unfortunately, most pastors are careless of their own health, and are not, thus, disciplined to observe the signs of physical malady revealed by members who come to them for help. It is for this reason we believe that pastors who pay attention to diet, exercise, and rest in their own lives are not only more effective in ministering in this area, but in all parts of their Christian service.

The emphasis on exercise and nutrition occurring in our first two Pastor's Plans is not repeated, but is appropriate in every section. If you are not doing things to help yourself out in the area of well-being, you certainly will not inspire anyone else.

Enough cannot be said about observation when looking for evidence of cause in the area of the physical dimension. Just as good listening and action interpretation skills can serve you in the other four dimensions of the person, the same can be said of the physical. Listening to what a person says, while analyzing skin tones, pupil dilation, twitches, etcetera, can tell you whether it is reasonable to consult a physician.

Today, not only because of the general neglect of physical health, but because of other environmental factors, more people seem to suffer from heart irregularities and other non-specific kinds of imbalances in the chemical system. Several medications, less horrific than the stuff of even a decade ago, have proven helpful in stabilizing human body systems that are irregular in these ways. Consulting with a physician who respects your value as a Christian Counselor can prove highly worthwhile in helping people recover their lives.

The physician has a very important role to play in helping hurting people. Don't be trapped by the hold-over of a yesterday when all physicians had at his disposal was medications that made some people little more than zombies. People with counseling problems do often have medical needs. As you study through this book you will gain a greater perspective of that fact. There are so many ways that you and the medical doctor need to co-operate and can work together to help people, a book could be written on that subject alone. We ask that you consider seriously the things we say in this area.

The problem is sometimes a physical one that requires you have the insight to ask the right question, and then get your client an appointment with the appropriate medical person to get the question answered. In such a case, you are not making a diagnosis, just raising a question that needs answering in order to effectively help someone. A person complaining about job stress and headaches might actually be suffering from poor vision and not from some other pressure within their person. In such a case, a successful eye exam is far more useful than unsuccessful counseling, but the counselor might be the one who recognizes the signs of the real problem.

The Mental Dimension

The third dimension of a person's life is the mental. Mental health involves our thinking processes, our belief system, awareness, comprehension, and so forth. Poor mental health is one of the primary reasons many come to counseling suffering from social dysfunctions and lack of self-will. Our focus on mental health, for the purpose of this text, will not be to expound upon the issues that involve organic and biological disturbance. These type problems are generally beyond the pastor's counseling abilities. His role when such problems are indicated is to immediately refer to specialists and follow the traditionally thought of role, giving pastoral support.

What is important for the pastor to understand is how thinking wrongly, due to false beliefs, strange concepts, etcetera, can be changed to have better mental health. Many of today's problems, especially those we see in people who come for counseling, is centered in just such deceptions. We can safely say that "stinking thinking" is at the center of a majority of other problems. The mind is a wonderful instrument. It has been called the greatest computer ever made. While we recognize that the mind is more marvelous than such comparisons imply, it does have a similarity that is recognized in Scripture. In computer terms we say, "Garbage in, garbage out".

Suppose someone comes to you for counseling complaining about depression and inability to focus on the Word of God, loss of interest in hobbies, feelings of physical exhaustion. You are looking all around the areas of the person's life for indicators, finding no problems in physical health and there is not any clear indication of problem or overt sin. As you proceed with assessing all five of the dimensions of this person's life, you discover that they have developed the habit of watching six hours of television news everyday with all its negative reports from virtually every facet of human experience. You see the member is now seeing everything with gloom and doom. They are focused on the negatives of life, and they wonder why they are feeling so bad. Do you?

Again, as with the other dimensions we have considered, a little thought begins to reveal to our eyes how this can permeate the other dimensions. This is why we proceed with care and carefully consider each area. Many a medical doctor has been faulted for successfully treating symptoms but having the patient die of the disease. The possibility in counseling is that we might unsuccessfully try to deal with symptoms without ever getting in touch with the fault on which the problem generates its tremor into the life.

Our friend who became engrossed with world events did not consider he was doing anything wrong. He probably thought of himself as a good citizen and even a good Christian by taking an interest in the world about him. It probably never occurred to him that he might be trapped as a mouse is mesmerized by a boa constrictor. He did not realize that the impact of such negatives would immobilize him. Just as many Christians anticipate the Lord's return from the standpoint of being finally delivered out of this messed up world are expressing negativism and hopelessness, so was the impact of concentration on the world's problems. It wasn't that the desire for information was wrong, anymore than anticipating the Lord's return is wrong. But the impact and result of the activity corrupted the mind, losing contact with the original purpose. This same activity, performed with a concentration on the positive, might yield a benefit to man had our subject saw an issue clearly and discovered how he could glorify the Lord by responding to it. This is what happens when a person looks for Christ's appearing for the sake of ever more just getting to be with Him. Such an attitude struggles to do the things that will be pleasing in His sight in His absence to have somewhat to present when He appears. A person with a positive outlook sees the world as a place full of opportunity for victory, instead as full of defeat. The information is no longer garbage clogging the human computer, but data to be used purposefully.

Very often, because the mind of a person is not strong in all of its hidden recesses, he has to avoid some types of mental activity all together. In the end, we do well to remember the admonition of Philippians 4: 8 concerning where the mind should dwell. It is much easier to train a mind to live in a positive dimension than it is to retrieve it from the negative once it has been surrendered.

The Social Dimension

The social dimension of man is another area that requires careful consideration in counseling. Those who come to you for counseling are often suffering from social problems. Many times this is what impels them to seek help, yet we all too often view socially oriented problems as secondary when they are not. A poor social dimension can lie at the source of more obvious problems such as depression, low self-esteem, chemical abuse and so forth. We can be trapped into focusing on these areas and exclude the socialization need. Social issues are ignored as a root cause initially in all too many cases. Many times people try to call and talk (ramble) with pastors during the day as an expression of the social lack in their lives. It is amazing that for all of our advances in communications, our ability to fulfill our social dimension's needs appear to have actually declined.

An example of the socialization dimension being expressed is contained in the following example: An individual comes in complaining about being depressed. During evaluation, you discover this person is withdrawn and has little or no interest in socializing with others. Furthermore, you discover this person has always been basically antisocial. (He may fear being rejected or be extremely shy.) It seems that they have rarely been involved with anyone socially. Failing other reasons, it seems plain that the depression is a result of a sense of alienation from other people. Feelings of aloneness are expressed in non-specific feelings of depression. Their problem is that they cannot on their own overcome this loneliness and meet their need because they did not develop necessary social skills during childhood development. This might be an extreme example, but it emphasizes that man is fundamentally designed to require and participate in fellowship with men and with God.

When the social dimension is not at the root of a disorder, it is always a vital part of recovery. This should become obvious as you go through the Pastor's Plans. Do you recall how Adam apparently felt in the Garden of Eden before Eve was created? It is strongly implied that even having the fellowship of God, he needed the interaction with another as himself. The animals could not meet his needs. The multi-million dollar pet industry in our country illustrates two things: One is that man is still trying to meet socialization needs with a system that does not work. The second part is that man still has a serious socialization problem.

The social dimension of man is a meeting point with the divine nature of God. Man was designed by God to be socializing with Him. Genesis describes how God walked and had conversation in the cool of the evening with Adam in the Garden. Evidently, God is a social God, and He created a social man. In the social nature of man the spiritual nature meets. It is of little wonder that the dysfunction will have far reaching effects on the life of a man.

From this point we cannot proceed without considering the life of prayer. Prayer is satisfying to the God shaped social need in man because it is both socializing and communicating with God. It satisfies also the spiritual dimension because it requires the comparison of ourselves with the standards and expectations that God has of us in our present spiritual position with God, and prayer contains worship.

It seems clear that man's social dimension needs both heavenly and the earthly needs met in order to be healthy. The reason secular counseling expectations must have lower standards of success is that they are by their very nature ill-equipped to function with man as he was designed by God. Understanding both the design and knowing the Designer, we can both have higher expectations and greater rates of success.

The Emotion Dimension

In the exploration of the first four dimensions, it has been apparent over and over the difficulties rooted in those areas frequently find expression in the emotions. Isn't it interesting that this is also the center with which God deals with us first. It is not our intellectual assent to His person that He wants, nor does He desire religiosity, the sacrifice of flesh, or of separation from the world. What He wants is that we should love God with all our being, a commitment that is centered in the emotions first of all.

The emotions are the barometer that warns us something is amiss in the human being so that we can seek out the cause of our discomfort. Unlike a fever which is a sign of the body fighting a malady, negative emotions are a sign that the problem has not yet been successfully dealt with. In our section on Drugs and Alcohol Addictions, we touch on how these things are often the instruments of medicating negative emotions.

When negative emotions are not tied to specific problems other than the first four dimensions, people are often in a quandary concerning the cause of the problem. Investigation must continue until the problem is solved. Erroneous focusing on a source of negative emotions can result in such things as a person being medicated by mood altering chemicals, keeping them from facing the need for Christ in their lives or other concerns that the emotions are crying out for victory over.

An associate who makes part of his practice ministering to troubled veterans has confided that he often finds clients struggling in the emotional area. Among his veterans, he has people come to him who are being medicated both legally and illegally for the purpose of subduing emotions rather than dealing with them and having victory. The key to his success in working with them has been the ability to identify with them in the area of their emotions, and to point them to the Christ who offers both forgiveness and understanding. But he will be the first to tell you that for many the struggle with emotions is often long and hard.

Emotions are complex things. What might appear on the surface is not always the case with the inner man. Therefore the emotion being demonstrated cannot always be interpreted the same way. Its nuances are such that it might mean different things at different times in the same person. My associate who works with veterans would tell you the emotions expressed and focused on war experiences often hide or reinterpret problems that actually had residence in the person prior to their entry into military service. Such are the intricate trails emotions weave through the human psyche.

The study of people and how they react is an occupation for a lifetime, but it is not impossible to understand enough to be able to help deal with their problems. Otherwise, emotions would be no good as a barometer of a person's total health beyond merely telling us something was wrong. Much of what we say about problems are defined in terms of emotions.

The Volitional Dimension

The volitional dimension is the dimension of the will. Here the doctrine of the "Free Will of Man", you no doubt studied as a seminarian or in other places, finds its expression in the field of counseling. Without man having this God-given ability to make choices it would be impossible for you to help a man to make the right decisions in his life or to turn around the wrong paths he has embarked upon, but by the same token, it is the exercise of this ability wrongly that most often gets humankind into trouble.

When we speak of the volitional dimension, we are always speaking of willful choice as opposed to the things that occur in areas where conscious decision making does not come into play. But do not be fooled, much which man does not wish to take responsibility for and would not like to admit is the exercise of the self will or volition. Thus the Scriptures that speak of man's accountability are appropriate to the area.

An example of an area where the volitional does not come into play is when a person is forced into the role of a victim as a child such as might occur in verbal or sexual abuse. Now the child has no choice in what occurs at the time, and they are the victim. But as an adult, the child who was the victim has the choice in self will whether or not they will be an abuser at any level or use their bad experiences for positive good. It is their choice whether to take what was meant to them for evil and use it for good or not.

In our introductory section we introduced you to the theology of counseling. Hopefully, you have given thought to the applications of the various types of counseling modes contained in that theology as you have studied through our discussion on the dimensions of man. It is in the area of the volitional that one particular type of model finds its strongest role. That is the nouthetic model. Some people try to use what they understand this model to be, exclusively, but many who counsel shy away from this type because they do not understand it. But, it is a Biblical model and part of the whole concept that must be used to successfully treat hurting members, and will become important to the meeting of problems that occur in the area of the will or volition.

The nouthetic method is the confrontational method in ministering to people, but if the counselor presumes that this means the counselor confronting the member exclusively, he is doomed to have a very limited practice with a low success rate. The true power of the nouthetic or confrontational method is where it is used to help the member confront the problem. Much of the time the counselor must not seem to be condemning of the person if he is to be of help. Most people do not need to hear how bad they are, neither do they need to hear how bad their problem is. But they do need to come to a point where they see the problem clearly, without rationalization or excuses and make a volitional choice that it no longer has a place of stronghold in their life.

In every problem a person has the exercise of the volitional dimension. It is either part of what got them into trouble or is at least a part of the process of getting them out of it. The volition or free will does not replace or negate God and His authority in their life. On the contrary, the will must come into cooperation with God and submission to Him and His precepts for true and lasting victory to occur in life.

Getting Started

The Initial Visit

Whenever you enter a counseling situation, never presume that you know all about the individual. You may be surprised to discover how little solid information you have about someone, even though you may have been around them all their life. Our knowledge of people is conditioned by our relationship with them. The pastoral relation often has people striving to impress you with their devotion or fervor. The friendship relation is often limited to common interests or goals. Counseling involves people unfolding feelings and thoughts they may never have shared with another soul. You may well find that the person you thought you knew is someone else entirely.

Meeting a person's need for help in a counseling relationship may well require you to do things and, therefore, to know things that are uncommon to any other situation. For instance, in deciding how to refer someone who needs outside help, you will need to know about finances and insurance. These subjects are seldom touched upon in casual discussions of church related matters. But it is no use referring to an agency, no matter how good they are, if the client does not meet the financial criteria for acceptance. So you can see just the peripherals of what you get into. Counseling changes the type, and kind, of information a person who has become a client needs to communicate with you.

The person who comes for help won't know what to tell you. You will have to ask. But very often, the person who comes to you can tell everything, perhaps even pinpoint the basic problem, if you ask the right question(s). How to begin asking those questions is really the topic of discussion here. A simple data sheet, such as the three page sheet we have provided in this section can help you get started.

If at all possible, you should have a completed data sheet in your hands from the member prior to the interview. This can help you immensely in how close you come to having a grasp on what the root problem(s) might be in the initial interview. But don't presume you have a lock on all the facts the first time you meet. The data sheet will give you an idea of where you need to go in the initial interview, as this interview will give you a toe-hold on where you need to go with counseling.

With the data sheet we have enclosed, great care has been taken to eliminate unnecessary questions, everything has a purpose that becomes more readily apparent as you read about counseling. Believe me, the reasoning behind the questions will surely become more visible as you start doing a few counseling procedures.

Before placing the data sheet in the person's hands, you have already decided that they probably have reading comprehension skills. What they put on that sheet will let you know if they actually do. You then know whether or not you can use written materials to help them. If the person who comes to you cannot fill out a simplified data sheet alone, give them help. If they need clarification about what is being asked, or the reason for the form, take time to explain. Since people come for help in distress, they might not be up to what would be considered normal functionality. Help them focus on what is going on. The time expended giving this help will not be lost. It will enable you to observe body language, tone of voice, and facial expression. You can even tell often times whether they are coming willingly to be open about the area where they are having difficulty.

One thing you should notice about our data form is that it requires a description of a person's salvation experience, but gives them no place to write it out. You decide how you want the account recorded, but the recommendation is that it be written on notebook paper. The client should be encouraged to remember and write out every detail about the event as possible. You see, Christian Counseling is anchored to the cross. The Lord Jesus Christ is the basic difference between Christian Counseling and other types of counseling.

Writing out the experience can serve two purposes:

(1) Even though you have inquired about salvation, a thoughtful written record can cement the memory of the transaction freshly into the mind at a time when being reminded of their position in Christ is essential.

(2) It can demonstrate the weakness or lack of a genuine salvation experience in the person's life. When it occurs, you know this need is the primary step to absolute victory over any problem.

The Initial Visit

Basic Evaluation- SOAP THEM OUT!

Soaping is generally easy, quick, and commonly used in hospitals and other medical settings. It also assists in a quick initial assessment.

SUBJECTIVE..........inside looking out
OBJECTIVE...........outside looking in
ASSESSMENT..........conclusion
PASTOR'S PLAN.......your plan to assist

Terms defined:
SUBJECTIVE: What the member tells you about themselves, their pain, hurt, problems, etc.
OBJECTIVE: What you see about the member that perhaps they do not see.
ASSESSMENT: Your conclusion; what the problem is.
PASTOR'S PLAN: Your plan to assist member with problem.
Example of a preplanned SOAP Sheet:

SOAP Sheet

Member's Name____

Time and Date of Visit___________________________________

Subjective ____

Objective

Assessment

Pastor's Plan

Initial Interview Information
ON THE INITIAL VISIT

Things you should accomplish with the person you are helping during the first interview:

1. Evaluate the individual's ability to comprehend (understand) what is being said.
2. Determine whether you might profit better from using tapes and videos, (perhaps either/or) instead of simply trying to talk with the person about the problems.
3. Analyze what is being presented with consideration of the possibility of referral. Do not under estimate what you can do. Do not over estimate either.

The first step is always to lead the person to Christ.

The second step is dependency on Christ to work a changed life.

(Without the Lord Jesus being central to your plan, you cannot be successful no matter how much training you have.)

4. Identify the types of problems being experienced:

mental,
emotional,
physical, classify the problem
marital,
social.

WHEN YOU EXCLUDE JESUS
YOU DON'T HAVE A COUNSELING PROGRAM

"...whosoever drinketh of the water that I shall give him shall never thirst, but the water that I shall give him shall be in him a well of water springing up into everlasting life."

The Lord Jesus Christ (John 4: 14)

DATA SHEET

Name__________________________ D.O.B.____________________
SS#____
Address ____
____
Who suggested you meet with me?____________________________
Occupation/Profession____
____
Phone: Home_____________________ Work___________________
Name of spouse or nearest relative______________________________
Address_________________________________Phone____________
Marital Status (please check) Married___ Divorced___ Single___
Widowed___
Engaged___ Separated___
# of Children___________ Ages______________________________
Level of Education: Grade School-# of years___ High School or GED Diploma?___ If NO, Years Completed___ College or Vocational Diploma?___ Years___ Major ________________________________
Family Physician ____
Phone ____
Address____
Would you want to see him/her for medical services related to your problem if a doctor was needed? (circle) YES / NO
Are you currently under a doctor's care? NO / YES
Dr. ____
If so, what are you being treated for?
____
Are you currently taking any medications? (please list)
____
____
When was your last medical exam?__________ What was the outcome?____
____
Do you have any chronic/acute illnesses, injuries, or disabilities?
NO / Yes If so, please explain_______________________________
How would you rate your health? Excellent__ Good__ Fair__ Poor__
Why are you seeking counseling? (Please check) Depression___ Alcohol/Drugs___ Suicidal Thoughts___ Communication Problems___ Self-esteem issues___ Marital Problems___ Sexual Issues___ Emotional Problems___ Stress___Parenting Issues___ Death of a loved one___ Other (explain)________________________

____
____

Please describe your primary complaint or problem.

____
____
____
____
____
____

Are parents living?____ Father only____ Mother only____
Father's Name / Age___________________________________
Mother's Name / Age___________________________________
Brothers / Sisters- Names /
Ages____
(list additional on back)

____

Do you maintain close contact with these family members? Yes / No

____
____

Any history of alcohol or drug abuse in your family? (explain)_____

____
____
____

Any history of sexual, verbal, emotional, or physical abuse in your family? (explain)

____
____
____
____

Have you ever had counseling? (explain)

____
____
____
____
____

Briefly describe yourself as a person.______________________________
____
____
____
____
____

How can we help you?
____
____
____
____

Have you ever received Christ as your personal Saviour?____________
If so, when?_____ Describe your salvation experience. (The day you made a conscious decision to invite Jesus Christ into your life.)
Do you currently attend church? YES / NO
How often?_______________
Name of church___________________Denomination____________
Do you pray daily? YES / NO Daily Bible reading? YES / NO
Briefly describe your spiritual health
____
____
____
____
____
____

Building Your Relationship On the Initial Visit

Because the member has come to you for help, whether of his own will or because he allowed someone to bring him, indicates he already has or is possibly willing to exercise a measure of confidence in you. It is yours to build on or to lose. Positive development will depend on how he sees you as your relationship progresses in this new, more personal environment. Some people may come to you from time to time because in their minds a pastor is the appropriate place to go for help. Others will come because they have no place else to turn. They very well may have been "burned" by secular counseling; are very leery, but needing help some way. In either case, the procedure is the same. You must be absolutely open to them. This does not mean you are sharing the intimacies of your life. No. You are open about your ministry; about your background. And you are open about what are the legitimate expectations the member might have, and what are not reasonable expectations.

Being open about yourself and about your ministry does not mean rambling on about what can quickly seem your favorite subject - you. They do not want an egotist, they are looking for someone who is vitally interested in them. Being open is being honest. If you are in your first pastorate, don't pretend you are overflowing with the wisdom of the ages. When the Wisdom of the Ages overflows you, realization comes quickly of your need of Him in all things. People who need help can frequently home in on a phony in a heartbeat. Don't lose before you start.

Another reason for honesty and openness with a reservation of your intimate self is protection of your person from becoming the victim of the pain of the person you are working with. It is one thing to understand what an individual is going through with a heartfelt concern, but you do not want their pain to invade your life and family relationship. Besides, confiding too much of your personal life can foster a dependency on you, which might not only lead them to assume too much about your relationship, but may be detrimental to the members emotional recovery.

The person who has come to you for counseling of types covered in this book are in a different situation than a person seeking guidance on some immediate ethical issue or other similar counseling you might do. These people are afflicted with a problem or problems that they did not get into overnight. Neither are they going to get out of them simply by coming to see you. Counseling attendance is not a magic wand. Your member needs to recognize that. Make it clear that counseling is not an event but a process; one the two of you are going to share in. You share in it, but the success of the counseling is most dependent upon the person in need. They must have a willingness to become strongly involved in their own recovery program. Without that commitment, you will find that you are either on a roller coaster (up and down), or a swing (back and forth), with the member. In either analogy, you get moved around a lot, wind up back where you started, never really have gone anywhere. You've wasted a lot of valuable time.

Help the member to understand the reason you are available to help him is that you feel called of the Lord. The time you expend with them is, therefore, Holy unto the Lord. If the person acknowledges Jesus Christ as His Savior, it is excellent to begin the session with prayer, asking His blessings and guidance upon what you are doing. With an unbeliever, prayer is still in; whether or not they respect it, you do. Be like Daniel, even when it was illegal, everyone knew he had a life of prayer. The prayer like everything else, is to be genuine, not a form to go through. Prayer is a very holy exercise, and essential to successful counseling.

In counseling with an unbeliever, make it very clear that limited or no success may be hoped for in their case without their allowing Jesus Christ into their lives. Let them know that no matter who does the counseling, it is Jesus alone who is able to transform lives.

Let any person, Christian or non-Christian, who comes for counseling understand up front the objective is not to get them to turn over a new leaf. Any leaf that is turned and not anchored to He, who is the Rock , will soon blow back over. When the leaf gets under the authority of the rock, it does not blow any more in every wind.

> *When the unclean spirit is gone out of man, he walketh through dry places, seeking rest; and finding none, he saith, I will return to my house whence I came out. And when he cometh, he findeth it swept and garnished. Then goeth he, and taketh to him seven other spirits more wicked than himself; and they enter in, and dwell there: and the last state of that man is worse than the first.*
>
> ***Luke 11:24-26***

Not intending to imply that everyone who needs counseling is beset by evil spirits, the substance of the passage is nonetheless true for the afflicted individual. This can be demonstrated by taking two common problems in our society and considering the facts concerning them. I am referring to alcohol and smoking, two of our most common addictions. The individual might be weaned from the substance; they might go a year or two (or even more) without utilizing the drug. But, without a fundamental change in themselves, they are still subject to the dependency, even though the body has been long clean of the chemical need. When they go back to it, they will shortly be, not back to where they were before they quit, but at the level they would have been had they never quit. This is why secular support programs are perpetual care. We need to leave perpetual care to cemetery programs where it belongs. Jesus Christ sets men free, and successful counseling brings a person to the point that their only dependency is on Him. So, Salvation and Lordship are central to success.

A lot of counseling philosophies treat problems by justifying them; exchanging the conduct for some other, hopefully less unacceptable form; shifting responsibility to another, and so forth. None of these are satisfactory either from the Christian perspective or in terms of practicality when dealing in human lives and relationships. Christianity recognizes the individual as accountable before God for themselves. They are not accountable for what others have done, nor are they excused by others actions. They are responsible for their actions in relationship to others as well as unto God. You are setting the stage for the individual to confront this truth when you enter the counseling process with them.

When the pastor and member enter a relationship of Counselor/Couselee, honesty of the member also becomes an issue. Some church members become hypocritical about trying to impress the pastor with themselves and/or their relationships, such as with Christ and family. Like a good cop, you must cut through the scam to get to the substance. The best way is to not let it get started to begin with, and that is no easy chore. What you can do is impress on the person:

1) The absolute necessity for honesty.

2) That absolute honesty will strengthen, not damage, your relationship.

3) Getting problems out where they can be looked at is the beginning of the recovery.

Much material is provided to you in this book to help you isolate the problem or problems. You are not really in the business of clinical diagnosis. You are in the ministry of helping people in pain and hurting, on a greater than physical level. When you give it back to the sufferer and establish a relationship of honesty, they may very well be able to tell you exactly what their problem is. If they have more than one, they can probably order them in precedence according to the severity and discomfort. They may also be keenly aware of the root cause of the condition that they are in. Honesty can short-cut a whole lot of counseling time, even order your approach to meeting their counseling need.

A person who is chronically dishonest with you will have to confront that issue early, even first in your counseling relationship, for success to be achieved. Dishonesty is a sin called lying. It must be removed. If honesty is not established, it is possible that no progress may ever be made in ministering to their needs.

The Spirit of the Lord God is upon me;
because the Lord hath anointed me to preach good tidings unto the meek; He hath sent me to bind up the broken-hearted,
to proclaim liberty to the captives,
and the opening of the prison to them that are bound.
To proclaim the acceptable year of the Lord,
and the day of vengeance of our God,
To comfort all that mourn;
...to give unto them beauty for ashes,
the oil of joy for mourning,
the garment of praise for the spirit of heaviness;
that they might be called trees of righteousness,
the planting of the Lord,
that He might be glorified.

Isaiah 61:1, 2, 3bff

During the initial visit you are striving to identify the person's problem(s), "soaping them out". It is not enough to know the problem, you must also get to know the individual. In the initial visit you begin the unfolding process. What you discover may shock you. You may feel repelled by what is shared. If you let it drive a wedge between you and the person you are there to help, you have failed.

Beloved, now are we the sons of God,
and it doth not yet appear what we shall be:
1 John 3:2a

It has been said that sin lies at the root of all disorders; if not the sin of the client, then the sin of whoever victimized them, or possibly original sin itself. Part of what brings people to seek help is often feelings of condemnation or worthlessness. Your job is not to heighten those feelings, but to focus on what causes them and help your church member deal with those problems in their lives in a way that honors the Lord and helps them to be conformed to the image of Christ.

A person who comes to you for help must feel three things:

(1) Welcomed
(2) Loved
(3) Cared for

No matter how busy or pressed you are, a person receiving your help is not someone who is "worked in" or must be endured. They are a welcome friend of great value. You see in them the infinite worth they have to Jesus and, in Christ, their tremendous value as individuals. They are loved because Christ loved them first. He loved you enough to die for you and instill His love for others in you. In experiencing your love for them, some may, for the first time, be able to appreciate or experience the love of Christ in their lives. When you give unconditional love, you are starting to express a form of God-like love. Many have no idea that such love even exists.

The person must realize that they are genuinely cared for. Genuine caring is not concern that allows you to be manipulated, nor does it condone sin in the member's life. The person who comes to you may have become a master of manipulation as a result of their disorder. Genuine caring is a lot like the surgeon's scalpel which can sever the barrier between him and the cancer, yet cut so cleanly, healing is affected because even the weakest tissue might be rejoined. Caring is being strong when the client is weak, yet sensitive to the sensibilities of the hurting member without compromising the moral and ethical demands of the Gospel. You become the first lesson in availing themselves of the reality of God's care in their lives. Realizing God's care, they can often learn to care for themselves.

Perhaps now you understand why an unsaved individual is never rejected out of hand from the Christian Counseling process. As we look into what is lacking or distorted in people's lives, we can realize many have no basis to even comprehend the possibility of such a God as we know. So acceptance of Him is out of the question. However, through seeing you in the counseling process, they might come to know Him.

Ye are the light of the world.
A city that is set on an hill cannot be hid.
Neither do men light a candle, and put it under a bushel,
but on a candlestick,
and it giveth light unto all that are in the house.
Let your light shine before men,
that they may see your good works,
and glorify your Father which is in heaven.
Matthew 5:14-16

For though I be free from all men,
yet have I made myself servant unto all,
that I might gain the more.
...I am made all things to all men,
that I might by all means save some.
And this I do for the Gospel's sake,
that I might be partaker thereof with you.
I therefore so run, not as uncertainly;
so fight I, not as one that beateth the air:
extracted from: I Corinthians 9:19, 23, 26

We need to live so we may say:
Be ye followers of me,
even as I also am of Christ.
I Corinthians 11:1

so by our actions men are pointed to Christ.

About The Pastor's Intercessory Prayer List

Success of counseling begins and ends with prayer. Contained within these pages are discussions on the lost person. You will want to read those things and have them in mind as you use the prayer list in

counseling. This is Holy endeavor. You want neither to neglect, nor allow it to be treated contemptuously in the counseling relationship.

The rest of this discussion assumes the member you are counseling with professes faith in the Lord Jesus Christ as their Savior.

Fundamental to successful counseling is the life of prayer. The prayer list is included in The Initial Visit materials for several reasons:
1. In "Soaping" out the client, you have already, by the conclusion of the initial interview, begun to identify the needs in their life.
2. You are establishing the pattern for the counseling interviews.
3. No matter what difficulty the client is experiencing, prayer is central to victory over the problem. It is part of every "Pastor's Plan".
4. Using the "member needs" section of the prayer list is an excellent tool for summarizing what you have learned and focusing on where you need to go.
5. The "member's prayer list" allows you and the client to agree on <u>specific</u> areas to be targeted for victory.
6. "Blessings to give thanks for" refocuses from the fleshly tendency of carnal man to the spiritual life of the believer living in right union with the Lord.

The intent is that The Intercessory Prayer List be developed by you and the member working together. Counseling is not you making decisions about someone's life. It is guiding the person to make the right decision(s) in their own life, based on biblical principles. Being in agreement; having arrived at a clear understanding of clearly described goals that are attainable, the member has hope. He knows that you are going to be in agreement with him when seeking God's intervention for deliverance and healing.

If you have a church copier, it is really easy to make a duplicate copy and place it in the member's hands to carry with him as a guide for his own prayers between sessions. You may find that once you have completed the defining process, it is good reinforcement to have the client hand copy his own list to take with him. Things like this you decide.

The prayer list will develop as the counseling experience develops. The recorded blessings help to reinforce in the mind of the member what has already been accomplished as you go forward. But do not force the record of blessings to be confined to just those things related to counseling material you have covered. The total outlook needs shaping into the positive mold.

When you begin to progress in an area, turn your prayers into thanksgiving for the progress made, and keep your needs focused on specifics. You will find yourself giving thanks for progress in an area while still praying on a specific need in the same area because you are "focused on specifics".

Let's get something straight. While we have been talking about the mechanics of a spiritual function with emphasis on the effects of the act, don't be fooled about our attitude toward prayer. It is really easy for someone to misunderstand and think we are insincere and merely using ritual as a manipulative tool. Don't you believe it. We really mean pray. Just because we discuss overt benefits does not mean we are content with the practice of the outward function. The overt benefit exists because the spiritual dimension of follow-through is real. As a young man I knew used to say, "Get in there and suck rug awhile." Remember when it comes right down to it, you are the repair tool of the Creator who is known as Wonderful Counselor. The tool does not function well without the Master in control.

Many pastors find prayer easy to neglect and their ministries show it. Perhaps while reading this discussion, you realized your prayer life needs a thorough workover. Maybe it is utterly lacking. Maybe you need a way to insert a shot of spiritual adrenaline into the prayer circle of your church. One thing that can help you is the 2959 plan. It stands for twenty-nine minutes and fifty-nine seconds alone with God each day. The Plan is available from Agape Ministries, 2600 Park Avenue, Titusville, Florida, 32780.

Moreover as for me,
God forbid that I should sin against the Lord in ceasing to pray for you:
but I will teach you the good and the right way:

1 Samuel 12:23

Pastor's Intercessory Prayer List

Member's Needs:

1. ____________________
2. ____________________
3. ____________________
4. ____________________
5. ____________________
6. ____________________

Member's Prayer List:

1. ____________________
2. ____________________
3. ____________________
4. ____________________
5. ____________________
6. ____________________

Blessings to give thanks for:

1. ____________________
2. ____________________
3. ____________________
4. ____________________
5. ____________________
6. ____________________
7. ____________________

The number of man is six. The number of Deity is seven.
Therefore, as we learn to count out blessings,
we see His goodness to us is always greater than our needs by at least one.

Getting Started
Establishing A Support System

Virtually every disorder of emotions is sin-related. That is not to say the person suffering committed the root causal sin. Quite often people suffer as victims of other's sin. Sometimes that sin occurred long ago. In any case, people who get counseling exhibit the classic symptoms sin produces.

Sin produces a sense of alienation and aloneness. First, people feel alienated from God, then they feel alienated from other people, particularly Christians. So, at the time they need help most dealing with their particular problem they are apt to feel most alienated. They need a support system. A support system is comprised of an individual or individuals that will aid suffering members as they recover.

A support system is wonderfully scriptural. No doubt for the sake of suffering people it was written:

Bear ye one anothers burdens,
and so fulfill the law of Christ.

Galations 6: 2

Paul spoke of Christian service in the very positive chapter, 1 Corinthians 9. He spoke of being a servant (vs 19) and identifying with persons in the area of their weakness (vs 20-22) so that he might be a Christ-sharer with us. We need people who can identify, realizing they must:

...restore such an one in the spirit of meekness;
considering thyself,
lest thou also be tempted.

Galatians 6: 1

The support system can be part of the discipling system, but it is not exactly discipleship. Discipleship can be invaluable in helping the member grow, and a person in recovery certainly has a special potential for growth. However, the function of support is providing an atmosphere of love and acceptance. As we study the need it is easy to see how the established church should be uniquely equipped to handle the role. But finding and developing the right people can be difficult. The pastor can feel imposed upon by a seemingly additional burden until he realizes that this is merely a somewhat modernized way of expressing New Testament principles. Scripture holds these principles up as goals to be attained in producing normal church functionality.

Living in a degenerating society, we need now to rediscover that church includes more than a gathering for a worship service and, perhaps, Bible study. It is the fellowship of the believer. The function of the extended family, the family of God, is the interaction of the church. Within that family is people helping people if the church is to function the way God intended. Too often we give the term "fellowship of the believer" lip service without stopping to think of all that it implies.

In discipleship, counseling occurs, but in support systems, the facilitator primarily listens. In support, the member can talk about their hurt and be heard. They can be heard and not be repeated. A person who even has the rumor about them of being loose lipped can squelch the operation of a support system. Not many can qualify to be part of this undertaking.

Saying that, in support, people primarily listen, does not mean that no counseling occurs. That is a wrong view. While the attitude may fit some world-view systems, it is inconsistent with Christianity. The support person or group serves as a sounding board. They must give the recovering person honest feed-back without being dogmatic or preachy. The best single support person is one who is well grounded in the Word of God. A good feed-back response can be, "The Word of God says...How does what you are saying relate to God's instructions to us?" An honest person who does not say what the client wants to hear, while at the same time being neither condemning or preaching, is a jewel the person he helps will never forget.

An excellent prospect for leadership of a support group is a person who has gone through their own emotional trauma. They, unlike all too many Christians, usually recognize that when a listing of sinful conditions might be read out, they could be included in the expression, "And such were some of you," (1 Corinthians 6:11a). I am thankful the Lord uses those others would discount or ignore to do His work:

For ye see your calling, brethren,
how that not many wise men after the flesh,
not many mighty, not many noble, are called:
But God hath chosen the foolish things of the world to confound the wise;
and God hath chosen the weak things of the world to confound the things which are mighty
And base things of the world,and things which are despised, hath God chosen,yea, and things which are not, to bring to nought things that are: That no flesh should glory in His Presence.

1 Corinthians 1: 26-29

It is to those who see their calling and count themselves debtors to their fellow man, like Paul, who will be most available when needed. Regardless of time, day, or occasion, they make themselves available. Some, so called professionals, speak disparagingly of those who serve counseling ministry without degrees. I suggest that until they meet the same standards of service and success, the critic is unqualified to offer opinion. Certainly Christian Counseling programs that have achieved prominence recognize the value of lay people in a successful recovery program.

When a counselee is brought into a support group that exists in the church, the individuals within the group should be mentioned to him before he is introduced to them in the new group setting. This gives an opportunity to deal with fears that may center around past relationships. In this way, no shock or dismay is experienced by walking in and seeing a particular person in the group. If a fear has arisen about participation with someone, it gives the pastor or group facilitator a chance to emphasize that everyone they will meet in a support group are on equal footing.

The pastor should be kept abreast of what is going on in the group once it begins and assist as needed. Even though the pastor will not be intimately involved with the group as it functions, he will be closely involved in guiding its outcomes and making sure that it remains headed in the right direction. When a support group is part of the church, the pastor's concerns are more complex than when it functions separately from the church.

Support groups that operate as part of a Christian Counseling organization will have trained people guiding it. However, they might still not be people who specialize in counseling. As a caring pastor you will want to monitor your referred members progress, even though autonomy has not been surrendered. This is understandable and appreciated by most. The one thing to remember when you refer to outside sources is that you had a basis of trust in making the referral to begin with. When questions arise, take them up with people guiding the program, privately. Find out what is going on. Do not communicate uncertainties to the counselee until you, without a doubt, know that the problem exists. Carelessness in such a situation can set back recovery and that is the last thing anyone wants to do. When criticism occurs in such situations confidence in you can also be damaged since you made the referral in the first place. You want to be very sure before you criticize before the client.

We have seen that support systems are only as good as the people selected to serve. They are also only as good as the literature used in support. Fundamentally, it must be like the primary program, Christ centered. Comfort Care Ministries uses and endorses the Rapha Twelve Step Programs and its literature as a primary, but not exclusive, complement to its own. How you structure and what you use must ultimately be your decision. Make it on the basis of careful, prayerful consideration.

We do recommend and use the Rapha Right Step Facilitator Training program with our own group leaders. It is a program of support and study groups designed to lead to lasting recovery for people who are suffering from various forms of addiction and codependency.

The Right Step program has a video series designed to train facilitators to lead support groups. It has a book that is referred to in the video. Reading the book, then watching the video, is a good plan for comprehension. Reading Rapha's Handbook for Group Leaders and attending a seminar using the Rapha Support Group Ministry Leader's Training Workbook helps the individual to have a pretty good grasp on the program.

You can appreciate many of the people who are active in these programs, for they share from the basis of one who has been there and has known the deliverance available in Christ.

A listing of topics available in the various resources follows:

Facilitator Training Video

Part 1 Functional and Dysfunctional Families
Part 2 The Addictive/Dysfunctional Personality
Part 3 Codependency
Part 4 Support Groups
Part 5 Leading Support Groups
Part 6 Getting Started/Follow-Up Training

Rapha's Handbook for Group Leaders

1. The Goals and Expectations of a Group
2. Organization and Selection
3. The Mechanics of a Group
4. Setting the Environment
5. The Dynamics of a Group
6. Motives for Group Involvement
7. Your Group as a Family

8. Uniqueness of Support Groups
9. Managing Difficulties
10. Questions Group Leaders Ask
11. How to Get Started

We have confidence the Holy Spirit will guide you as He does in other matters. If you review what is available, pray, and seek His guidance you will do all right.

Pastoral Counseling Checklist

1. Am I preparing for each counseling session by reviewing information about the case?
2. Am I treating the counseling sessions as a process, not a lecture time?
3. Am I arranging a sufficient number of appointments, properly spaced with each counselee?
4. Am I keeping distractions to a minimum during each counseling session?
5. Am I giving each counselee my full attention during the session?
6. Am I letting the counselees establish the pattern of information surrender as they unfold their lives before me?
7. Am I exerting leadership in guidance into problem solving, but maintaining flexibility to cope with and evaluate new revelations?
8. Am I waiting for the counselee's real problem to emerge and not grasping at the first signs and symptoms presented as all I need for understanding?
9. Am I actively encouraging the counselee to rid himself of tension and fears?
10. Am I discussing the principles of reliance on Christ, so that they are clearly understood?
11. Am I exploring the environment each person's problem exists in?
12. Am I accepting each counselee as he is?
13. Am I refusing to be prejudicially influenced because of his ideas?

14. Am I continuing to remain focused on the counselee's problem, and refusing to be distracted by similar problems I've experienced?
15. Am I continually striving to help the counselee grow in self understanding?
16. Am I helping the counselee find the basic cause of his difficulty?
17. Am I considering the possibility of physical cause when evaluating each new client?
18. Am I feeling uncomfortable during pauses in sessions or using the interlude to advantage?

Pastoral Counseling Checklist
page 2

19. Am I keeping my objectivity with the people I work with?

20. Am I determining whether decisions arrived at by the counselee have been made emotionally as well as intellectually?

21. Am I treating each problem as having more than one perspective?

22. Am I helping the counselee accept responsibility, both for the problem and the solution?

23. Am I careful in handling direct questions?

24. Am I referring when encountering problems beyond my expertise or resources?

25. Am I being successful at putting the referred counselee with the right resource?

26. Am I keeping notes on each session?

27. Am I handling unsuccessful counseling encounters healthily, realizing not every counselee and counselor can work together?

28. Am I considering all aspects of a counselee's person?

29. Am I using Scripture effectively and promoting spiritual development in every counselee?

30. Am I actively seeking God's guidance in counseling, and praying for wisdom in each counseling session?

Adapted in part from Dr. Narramore's basic guide in the Psychology of Counseling

When To Refer Checklist

1. The problem is not within your knowledge or expertise. A specialist is needed.

2. The problem should be reviewed by a medical practitioner.

3. The person is resistant; does not want your help.

4. You do not have adequate time.

5. A conflict in personalities exist between you and counselee.

6. When you become aware you are too personally involved.

7. When you are preoccupied with your own hurts, pains, and problems.

8. When you are struggling with the same or similar problems.

9. When counseling the opposite sex and feelings of attraction emerge.

10. When you find yourself becoming preoccupied and overly concerned to the point that your own life is being adversely affected.

11. When counselee (member) consistently fails to complete assigned tasks that are given to help the individual heal and recover.

Section Two

The Pastor's Plans

Pastor's Plan Index

Pastor's Plan Page

The ME Plan
Member's Evaluation

The Member's Evaluation, where they occur in the text, give responsibility and means back to the individual to let you know where and how they are hurting. Utilization of these evaluations does not provide an exhaustive method of determining the member's problem or intensity of the problems. The evaluations are merely a tool to help the pastor determine if what the member is experiencing is bothersome enough to need continued help from the pastor or other professionals. Evaluations are helpful, but they are only general common sense tools that have an effectiveness limited by client honesty. Anyone can give untruthful answers. So, to depend completely and solely upon written evaluations is not a good suggestion. Sometimes the person can best be assessed by non-verbal observations such as member's posture, voice tone, countenance, etc. The most reliable source in discovery of problematic areas in a members life is quite simply, "what the person shares". So, the personal contact and dialogue is essential.

Written evaluations, with its background data, can be a helpful tool to the pastor in understanding some of the emotions the member is experiencing, and in some cases, determining if there is a possible threat to life. In the event a life threatening problem is recognized, immediate referral is needed.

Pastor's Plan

Books to read:

Learning More About Depression by Steven W. Spotts, Psy.D.
Why Suicide by Jerry Johnston

Pastor's Plan

I. Depression

Defined:

Depression is defined in many ways, but in summary, the best description is that of experiencing negative (feelings) emotions.

Sometimes people make statements such as:

"I have the blues."
"I sure do feel down and out."
"Things seem so hopeless."

On and on we could go, but it all leads back to negative emotions. The member will most often be able to tell the pastor they are depressed. Sometimes depression is described as unhappiness associated with worry and a sense of feeling worthless.

Depression Expounded:

In the more severe cases of depression, the counselee (yes, even church members) may be entertaining thoughts of suicide or escape in the form of "just running away"; making a geographical change. What the person is seeking is relief from the pain induced by the depression. No one is immune from the depression. Some of the greatest men of God were recorded as experiencing depression. Remember Elijah (1 Kings 19) as he sat under the juniper tree and requested from God death? Then, there is King David. Do you recall his bout with depression after the death of his and Bathsheba's son? (2 Samuel 12) What about Moses and the occasions he suffered depression during the Exodus? You see, it is simple; no one is immune even if they are spiritually fit. From time to time everyone experiences depression. Depression has no bounds. Regardless of gender, finances, popularity, abilities, talents, whatever, we are all susceptible to depression. This fact alone makes it all important that the pastor be prepared to counsel the depressed person. By the way, the only embarrassment or sin in depression is refusal to seek help.

Ninety to ninety-five percent of all those suffering from depression can be treated and often cured. Every pastor should encourage the members of his congregation to seek help when experiencing depression. Many church members refuse to share their depression because of the fear that others will think they are not spiritually mature. The devil would not have it any other way. The devil knows if he can prevent the depressed person from getting help, he can rob believers of their joy in Christ. It can hamper their service and worship. Depression is and has always been one of his most used instruments against God's people. Remember pastor, depression is in most cases curable, so do not let the problem overwhelm you.

Blessed be the Lord, that hath given rest unto His people...
there hath not failed one word of all His good promise...
1 Kings 8:57

For the eyes of the Lord are over the righteous,
and His ears are open unto their prayers:
1 Peter 3:12a

Peace I leave with you,
My peace I give unto you:
Not as the world giveth, give I unto you.
Let not your heart be troubled, neither let it be afraid.
John 14:27

Blessed is the people that know the joyful sound:
They shall walk, O lord, in the light of thy countenance.
In Thy Name shall they rejoice all the day:
And in Thy righteousness shall they be exalted.
For thou art the glory of their strength:
Psalm 89: 15-17a.

Pastor's Plan

I. Depression

Signs and Symptoms

Quick Look Sheet

1. Feelings of worthlessness (no value, low self -esteem)
2. Thoughts of escape (running away)
3. Feelings of guilt and shame (past or present circumstances)
4. Irritability (over sensitive)
5. Isolation from friends and family (withdrawal)
6. Feelings of hopelessness (no way out)
7. Chronic fatigue (feeling tired)
8. Decrease in sexual desire (loss of interest)
9. Changes in appearance (poor hygiene, unkempt)
10. General unhappiness (sad)
11. Inability to sleep or over sleeping
12. Loss of appetite or Increase in appetite
13. Indecisiveness (inability to make decisions)
14. Anger (turned inward to self or outward to others)
15. Crying
16. Mood swings (happy one day , sad the next)
17. Inability to focus (concentrate)
18. Lack of motivation (doesn't want to do anything: work, hobbies, etc.)

Pastor's Plan

I. Depression:

Signs and Symptoms

Discussion

There are many signs and symptoms of depression. No one has all the indicators, and no exhaustive list is truly possible. However, we do need to know what these signs and symptoms are for. They are our body's indicators to let us know that something is not right. A sign is something a pastor will be able to see, such as: crying, anxiousness, outburst(s) of anger, and so forth. A symptom is something a depressed person experiences that may not be noticeable, visually, to the pastor, such as: inability to sleep, constant worrying, self pity, feelings of guilt and hopelessness, etc.

Referring to the Members Evaluation on Depression should help the pastor confirm the presence of signs and symptoms in the member seeking counseling. Although the evaluation is not exhaustive, it is a good basis to begin exploration about the individual's status. The most reliable thing the pastor will have is what the person says about their condition.

Again, the depressed individual will almost always be able to tell you they are depressed. Pastors are encouraged to use the listed signs and symptoms and review them with the person seeking counseling. Remember they need not have all of the symptoms to be suffering from the problem. Signs and symptoms of depression will vary according to the degree of depression.

Depression often causes a person's physical health, attitude, and environment to change. You have to be sensitive to the indicators. Depression can cause alterations in a person's physical health. So, you have physical problems, mind induced. Doctors may have been spending time treating symptoms with no basic cause identifiable. Changes in attitude may have been observed by you if the association related to the duration of the condition has been sufficient. However, this can be deduced from statements made by the spouse, children, or friends. Or, the information might be unwittingly provided by the member. Change of environment can be a big indicator, but again you have to be looking for the clues.

The Signs and Symptoms can be thought of as a different kind of language that you have to be able to read in order to understand the problem. The various pages are filled with what a person says and given meaning by the accompanying signs and symptoms. One client put heavy covers over all windows in her house. What she was saying was very plain once you knew where to read on the page.

Pastor's Plan

1. Depression

Causes

Quick Look Sheet

1. Anger turned inward
2. Career changes
3. Failure of some type (examples are: failing; academically, business, etc.)
4. Financial problems
5. Geographical changes (such as moving to a new home)
6. Grief (death of a loved one)
7. Guilt
8. Health problems (examples: infections, cancer, diabetes, heart condition)
9. Hormonal imbalance (caused by: menopause, PMS, glandular disorders, etc.)
10. Known sin (wrong behavior) Unknown sin
11. Loss of job
12. Low self-esteem
13. Medications
14. Mid-life crisis (aging)
15. Negative thinking

16. Poor nutritional habits (not eating properly/overeating)

17. Rejection (example: turned down for employment, etc.)

18. Self-pity (feeling sorry for ones self)

19. Separation/Divorce

Pastor's Plan

1. Depression

Causes:

The causes of depression are many:

20. Death of a loved one

21. Separation and Divorce

22. Loss of job

23. Poor health

24. Financial difficulties

24. Burn-out

25. Stress

26. Negative thinking

27. Physical Exhaustion

28. Mid-life crisis

29. Hormonal imbalance*

30. Post-menstrual syndrome

31. Sin

32. Career or business failure

The causes of depression are virtually endless. What may promote depression in one individual may not affect another person at all, but regardless, depression is never to be minimized or ignored. Depression is the body's way of sending a message that something is not right and needs investigating. The last thing a church member needs is a pastor's refusal to assist in helping discover the cause. In most cases the member is able to tell what is actually causing the depression, but sometimes they genuinely cannot. Sometimes medication may cause the depression and is the reason the depressed person cannot pinpoint the cause. Poor nutritional habits can be another hidden cause. Other causes often obvious to the pastor, but hidden from the church member, are:

Self pity (feeling sorry for oneself)

Moving to a new location

Past sins

Feelings of failure

Whether the pastor can readily identify the source or not, the goal is the same, "Discovery of the Cause" by the member. When investigating the cause or causes of depression the pastor should be prepared to invest some time. Discovering the cause is not always an easy task. Also, failure to identify the cause of depression diminishes the lasting effects of counseling. Pastor, get to the root cause. Be willing to get involved!

It also goes without saying that some causes of depression are justified. For example, if a church member loses a loved, one their depression may be the result of grieving over their loss. In this case, depression is simply a response to what is happening or has happened in the individual's life. When they are helped through the grief process the symptoms go away.

Bear ye one another's burdens,
and so fulfill the law of Christ.
Galations 6:2

Looking diligently lest any man fail of the grace of God;
lest any root of bitterness springing up trouble you,
and thereby many be defiled.
Hebrews 12:15

And let us not be weary in well doing:
for in due season we shall reap, if we faint not.
Galations 6:9

Pastor's Plan

1. Depression

Assessment:

Non-verbal communications:

Read the body language for depression indicators:

Sad look:
- head down
- slumping in chair
- poor eye contact
- crying

Obvious anger:
- clinched fist
- angry facial expression
- tight face and/or lips

False signals:
- smiling at wrong times
- constant smile
- smiles only with lips, not with eye muscles

Helpless attitude:
- hands in lap (particularly palms upward)

Pastor's Plan

I. Depression

ME Evaluation

Members Evaluation on Depression

I am depressed. Y___ N___ I feel sad. Y___ N___
I am sometimes depressed. Y___ N___ I sometimes feel sad. Y___ N___
I am frequently depressed. Y___ N___ I frequently feel sad. Y___ N___
I am always depressed. Y___ N___ I am always sad. Y___ N ___

I have been having feelings of depression since...(how long; can you pinpoint a specific incident where depression began?)

____

____

My feelings of depression usually last for...(how long; hours, days, weeks)

____

____

After my feelings of depression past, I feel good ___, just return to normal which for me is: things are okay ____; just getting by ___; other ____

As I see it, I feel depressed because ______________________

____

____

check or circle what describes you.
I am not really depressed so much as I just feel sad. I really don't know why I feel sad ______________________________

I feel sad because ______________________________

____

I have problems sleeping. Y ___ N ___
Sometimes/often I have problems sleeping.

I usually get ___ hours of sleep nightly.

I get irritable often. Y ___ N ____. I seldom feel irritable ___.

I express my irritability ___. I cover up/hide my feelings ___.

I get angry. Y ___N ___. I express my anger ___.
I cover up my anger ___.

I do not know why I feel anger ___. I feel angry because __________
____
____

Sometimes I just start crying. Y ___ N ___

Sometimes I cry because ______________________________
____
____

This happens when? (Daily/weekly/) and last for
____

I am not spending any time with my family ___ friends ___ now.

I have not spent time with my family for ____________________.
(How long?)

I have not spent time with my friends for ____________________.
(How long?)

I feel separated from them because ______________________.

I feel that my situation is hopeless. Y ___ N ___
I really doubt that anything can be done to help me. Y ___ N ___
I am experiencing new hope that I can see these things change in my life. Y ___N ___
I never feel like eating anymore. Y ___ N ___

I can't get enough to eat anymore. Y___ N___
I can/cannot eat when I feel depressed.

I am taking prescription drugs. Y ___N ___ named
______________________________.

I am using some non-prescription drugs. Y ___ N ___ named
____ .

(Please indicate quantity and frequency of use)__________________
____

I have been using drugs (prescribed and non-prescribed) for _______
____
____. (How long/purpose)

I am/am not having sexual relations on a regular basis.
I am/am not enjoying sexual relations,

I want to have sex _____ do not care about sex _____do not think about sex ___ think about , but do not desire sex ___.

I attribute my feelings about sex to
____
____.

My hobbies are:
____
____
____

I work on my hobbies when
____
____
____

that was (approximate date)
____.

I enjoy/do not enjoy my job. To me my job is
____
____
____
____

I used to work but do not do so now ___. This has effected my life by
____
____

My other activities besides hobby and job are ________________
____
____.

Sometimes I feel like running away _____. I never feel like running away _____.

If I could go away, I would travel to
____

because
____
____.

I feel tired sometimes ____, occasionally ___, often ___, frequently ___, all the time ___.

I feel guilty ___ I feel guilty , but don't know why ___.

I feel guilty about
____.

I feel ashamed ___. I feel ashamed, but don't know why ___.

I am ashamed about
____
____
____
____

I feel worthless ___. I feel worthless, but don't know why ____.

I feel worthless because
____
____
____
____

I have been treated/counseled for depression in the past. (Circle if appropriate)

I would/would not see a medical doctor for depression.

I would see a doctor if he was not

____

____

If you have been treated/counseled for depression in the past, please tell about it in your own words.

____

____

____

____

____

I would like to tell you about:

____

____

____

____

____

____

____

____

Pastor's Plan

I. Depression

Building Relationships

In dealing with depression you should always seek to eliminate, or at least diminish, the depressed person's pain and hurt. In order for the pastor to be able to help the depressed person, he will first have to establish a relationship. Hopefully, this has already begun in the initial interview stage(s) of counseling. You can build on what has occurred by showing concern for the person's difficulty. Concern is best shown by being a good listener. A good listener will not be thinking about what he is going to say after the counselee (church member) finishes speaking. Listening involves hearing what is being said and not focusing on the solution before having heard the problem. Listening also has no place for interruptions. Just listen! Most pastors are not good listeners because they perceive their business for God as talking, and talking they can do! Now, though, it is time to listen! Quite often listening to a person who is hurting will give them immediate relief. So, let them talk and you listen. As a matter of fact, encourage the depressed person to talk about their hurts and pain. Let them know it is okay. Help them to understand you are there to listen. When we listen we are sending a clear message. That message is that they are important; we are concerned; we are there for them and we want to help them in any way we can.

Another suggestion in building the relationship in the counseling setting is to refrain from ever being critical or judgmental. The last thing a depressed person needs is someone to criticize or judge them. Even in cases of willful sin, the pastor is to direct criticism and judgment to the sin and not to the individual. (Hating the sin and not the sinner). Ministering to a depressed person has no place for a "better than thou attitude". Depressed people do not need to be pushed down, but to be pulled up. If sin is at the root of the individual's depression, show them, through God's Word, the way out. Our successes in ministering to the depressed effectively will be few if we have critical and judgmental attitudes. It will also result in a poor, if any, pastor-church member relationship. It's difficult and often an impossibility to minister to individuals until the relationship is established,

Probably the most important and essential elements in building a good pastor-counselee relationship are those of love and trust. If a depressed individual does not feel loved and unconditionally accepted, it is not likely a relationship will ever be built. It is so simple, no love, no relationship; no relationship, no likelihood of success in counseling. To love a person means to care about that person, and not only that person, but their problems as well. The by-products of love , to list a few, are: concern, encouragement, acceptance, kindness, patience, understanding, and willingness to help. The by-products of love alone will assist in helping the pastor build the type of relationship with the church member that is essential to helping the person overcome depression.

In the area of trust it should be stressed that the depressed church member will not respond effectively to counseling if he or she cannot trust you. Trust involves confidentiality. When a person shares with you, the pastor, their most intimate self, they must have the assurance you can be trusted. Trust will often take some time to build. Be Patient. The depressed person may want to share with you some things that they must trust you will never share with anyone, not even your spouse. The last thing a depressed person needs to fear is that their problem(s) have the possibility of being broadcast to fellow church members. When a depressed person comes to you they are, or at least should be, coming in confidence of the freedom to say what needs to be said and in the full assurance that it will never be repeated to anyone. It may be helpful for you, the pastor, to tell the individual that what is said is and will always be between you, them, and God. But you have been building your reputation for being circumspect since the day you entered the pastorate. There are occasions when confidentiality should be broken. These are in cases that involve threat to life or destruction of property. Even in these instances though, great care should be taken. Do not jump to conclusions. Be sure you and your counselee have a clear understanding about confidentiality.

Establishing a pastor-counselee relationship is not always an easy task. Often it takes hard work and time. The pastor must be willing to go the length. Don't start something you are not prepared to finish.

As the hurting person opens up to you, evaluation of the intensity of their depression should be going on. This can be done by utilizing your written questionnaire. You gauge the responses to questions and compare that to their non-verbal evaluation. Once your evaluation has been completed, you must decide whether you can continue to work with the person alone or if you need to make a referral and move into a support role. Referral always has to have the member's approval. Indicators that a referral is in order are: threat to life; signs of biological irregularity; finding yourself unable to assist in the particular case in question.

Remember that referral does not mean, usually, that you are excluded from the recovery of the individual. It simply means you are bringing other fields of expertise into partnership in ministering to the need, perhaps making them for a time the central focus of the recovery process. But after each referral plays their part, the member is ultimately coming back to you. You are the pastor. And the member who achieves victory loves you for being their enabler.

Pastor's Plan

I. Depression

Exercise

The pastor should encourage the depressed to get involved in some type of exercise program. Depression tends to cause a decrease in an individual's energy level, which in turn intensifies the depressed condition. In this discussion, we make some very definite recommendations with the understanding that each person must be viewed as a whole, so physical liabilities must be taken into consideration when guiding a person into an exercise regimen. Your initial evaluation form can give you some insight into what is the current state of the member's health. But we can say that virtually everyone, even people suffering from disabling conditions, can find beneficial exercises they can employ in their recovery from depression. It may be necessary to enlist the help of the doctor treating the member, or even to consult a physical therapy specialist in extreme cases, but exercise is important for people suffering from depression.

Walking is probably one of the best exercises to recommend in normal cases. Walking has proven to increase the energy level, not only of those suffering from depression, but anyone who is suffering from a low energy level not the result of disease. Walking is, however, an ideal exercise to help control high blood pressure, increase lung capacity, lower high blood sugar in diabetics, and so forth.

There are also many other benefits to walking. Walking done out of doors refocuses people's attention on the world about them. It provides an opportunity to see neighbors out and about, and if nothing more occurs than a smile and a wave, it provides a positive friendly interaction. On several occasions, I have known of people who observed a neighbor building a shed or a garage, or even a housing addition, who so caught the walker's interest that they daily had to go by and see the progress. The only bad result from a healthy walking regimen that I have heard of was the guy in Florida who discovered a family of skunks had moved into an abandoned car while he was out walking. So, if you warn the client not to get too interested in skunk families moving into their neighborhood, they should do well.

As I have already indicated, a benefit of exercise for depression is that it will give the individual something to focus on besides their pain. People can get caught up in the daily increases of performance in specific exercises and this is beneficial. People who need to refocus often go full bore into some special exercise challenge like tending their yards or gardens, and have been known to be so involved that they mark the changes in their various plants on a daily basis. This refocusing is important because this enables the normal healing processes of the mind room to work. When people are focused negatively on what is causing their unhappiness, it becomes like a sore that is constantly having the scab torn away and being scratched. It just keeps getting deeper and deeper.

While riding a bike, stationary or street, is another good exercise for people suffering depression, we recognize any type of aerobic exercise is going to have its benefit. Individuals involved in exercise tend to be more responsive to counseling. When a person feels better physically, they feel better emotionally. I not only suggest exercise for the depressed counselee, but for the pastor as well. When the pastor exercises he becomes, in this as he should be in all other areas, a living example of what he has been talking about. Good health makes happier people. People who are in exercise rarely get into severe depression. This is not to say they are immune, but even when they do succumb, recovery occurs more quickly.

Senior citizen/nutrition centers now have walking machines and stationary bicycles as part of their normal equipment. (Even pool playing is good for seniors as it promotes stretching in a social environment.) Many times I have observed senior adults exercising side by side and carrying on animated conversations at the same time, oblivious of the fact they were actually out performing what many much younger people are not capable of doing. The drawback of these centers is that many of the people who once had their lives gravitating about the church are now spending their time at the center.

Almost every church has a Fellowship Hall. Some even have gyms and other large recreational areas. Few churches are devoid of some area that might be pressed into service ostensibly for their Golden Age Group, but also to serve the needs of the depressed. In seeking to be a part of the lives of people in one ministry, vitality could be breathed into two groups of people. After all, our older church members are sometimes the most neglected and are among those who suffer chronic depression. It is a shame we do not help them with exercise to raise their energy levels and occupations to restore feelings of usefulness.

We could go on and on, but in summary, suffice it to say, you cannot go wrong with a common sense exercise program. For individuals who are taking medication, have heart disease, are under a doctor's care, are over weight, over forty, or have not had a check up in over a year, you may want to recommend a doctor's visit before starting them on a program.

The pastor should encourage them to start out slowly and work their way up into a more involved program of exercise. Be sure to have the counselee use good common sense. They will do better in counseling and recover much more quickly.

Pastor's Plan

I. Depression

Nutrition

Proper nutrition is essential in the program of recovery from depression and virtually every other problem that effects mankind mentally, emotionally, and physically. Good nutrition should never be overlooked when ministering to the suffering individual. This section on nutrition is applicable to every counseling subject covered in this Pastor's Plan. It is placed in the depression section because virtually every other problem is accompanied, at least from time to time, by depression of some degree.

As a matter of fact, poor nutrition can be a cause of depression, but during bouts of depression an individual is also likely to experience suppression of appetite. Some neglect eating altogether. Strangely enough, having problems seems to encourage neglect of this very key element to recovery. People with problems tend to stick the wrong things in their mouths, when they do eat. It's just one more detrimental part of whatever vicious cycle is afflicting the human being. You don't have to be a nutritional expert to understand when the human biological system is working against you in helping the member, making success farther away.

Failure of regular and healthy eating can rob the body of much needed nutrients, in the best of circumstances, causing emotional health to suffer. Stress puts pressures on the body that intensifies the negative effects of poor nutrition. It is very possible for poor nutritional habits to take a person so far down that resulting body rebellion can disguise emotional problems that contributed to physical downfall. In short, you must make a concerted effort to raise the awareness of anyone you counsel to the fact they have a need not to neglect themselves in this area. You will probably find that one out of a hundred will readily consider nutrition when you first tell them about it, and that one will be better, quicker. The others you tell again.

The Pastor's Plan should always include a planned program of good and balanced dietary intake. Emphasize the value of eating raw fruits and vegetables. They are loaded with needed nutrients and particularly beneficial to good health when consumed uncooked or at least not overcooked. Meats place a burden on the body's digestive system that is not needed by someone who already has a stressed out system. Red meats should be particularly discouraged for a person going through any type of stressful experience. Even competition weight lifters lay off the red meats to reduce stress on their system prior to a big competition, because it means the difference between winning and losing.

When a person gets interested in their nutrition, they sometimes discover a new hobby that is really excellent for the individual who suffers emotionally. That hobby is gardening. Almost anyone can grow something, and for many watching and inspecting their plants progress daily provides as much a stress reliever as anything that can be named. It can be, for many, the means of escape from temptation to slide backwards in their recovery. People have been known to grow little gardens in window planters, and almost any small yard might accommodate a small patch of vegetables. There is even a book out called Square Foot Gardening, but several tell the interested client how to make the best use of their space. In any case, when people become interested in their physical health, they lose many of the negatives that hinder progress in the other facets of their lives.

You are not expected to play nutritionist with the member, but sounding a clear warning to them about the negative effects of junk foods is a very loving thing for you to do. You don't have to be an expert, scarcely any periodical of consequence that is read by those in a "people" profession has failed to mention the effects junk foods have on mood swings. Today fundamental nutritional information is common knowledge, not specialized knowledge. But you will discover those that you try to help will regard the whole business as a brand new revelation.

If you come to consider the nutritional aspect of the person's recovery to be significant enough, and they have not shown any interest in working on that area, you might have them read a little book called, "Why Christians Get Sick," written by Rev. George H. Malkmus and published by Hallelujah Acres Publishing, Eidson, Tennessee. While we do not necessarily agree with everything in the book, it certainly should serve to raise both the member's and your awareness of the issue.

Nutritionists, medical doctors, and pharmacists can all be useful from time to time in helping people with their nutritional needs. We also like health food stores that are manned by conscientious capable people, but they have to be carefully sought out and might not be available in your area. For that matter, even with medical people, you have to exercise discretion because the negative results of jealousy over who has domain in health care issues tend to cause some to give poor counsel in this area. People who can help you have had to overcome much misleading information floating around the health care industry. For instance, you don't want a doctor advising a client on what vitamin is good for them if he does not believe in taking vitamins.

You really might want to get a person on vitamins or encourage them to actively be replacing enzymes that promote digestion. Normally the human body can take in through good food choices all it needs in terms of nutrition. But we are talking about people who are hurting, and this places their system under stress that often depletes their important nutrients abnormally fast. Also, stress kills the very things that aid digestion in the human system. Replacing them through supplements is often a very wise move. However, some people react adversely to some vitamins. Natural vitamins and ingredients found at a health food store are best, but just like anything else you put into your body, too much of a good thing can be bad for you. Let your member talk to people who have knowledge about what is good or bad. Let them make the decisions about what they will ultimately put in their mouths in the way of supplements. After all, you're not the expert, you're a very loving pastor. Point them in the right direction, and as in everything else, make them responsible for their own decisions and acts.

In summation, lack of good nutrition robs the client of energy and strength needed to recover. The lack of good nutrition can actually prevent recovery or increase the problem. God designed the human body to use the nutrients found in food to make our bodies function properly. When we neglect to supply our bodies with the proper fuel, we get in trouble. Hurting people need the vitamins and minerals found in fruit and vegetables. They do not need things going into them that the body finds both hard to process and impossible to get nourishment from.

And God said,
Behold, I have given you every herb bearing seed,
which is upon the face of all the earth,
and every tree, in the which is the fruit of a tree yielding seed;
to you it shall be for meat.

Genesis 1:29

Pastor's Plan

I. Depression

Rest and Relaxation (R&R) For Recovery

Rest and relaxation are essential to recovery from depression. As mentioned earlier, lack of rest can in itself be a cause of depression. Therefore, R&R has to be seen as an important part of the Pastor's Plan for recovering from or overcoming depression.

The two words, rest and relaxation, mean a lot of things to different people. Some define R&R as lying in bed and perhaps napping. Others see it as a good game of golf, tennis, fishing, etc. Both types of definitions are good, I suppose, since the goal is the same. The goal is to take the mind off preoccupation with troubles and cares.

Soldiers take R&R from war fronts. When they do take such R&R, it is often filled with sports activity. The more fortunate soldier's Rest and Relaxation retreats have included being reunited with that special loved one, and so forth. Inevitably, a soldier begins R&R by getting cleaned up and crashing, getting some sleep, without having to stay partly alert while he rests. A soldier's R&R takes him away from the troubles and cares of war. Similarly, this is what we want for the client.

This touches on the problem of activity as an idea of rest and relaxation. We are not talking about a soldier's break from battle, despite similarities. We are talking about everyday people who either have depression from lack of rest, or, are losing rest due to depression. The situation we deal with is a daily need to stop and let the world go by without notice, while the body system gets a needed relief. Golf, fishing, and tennis, for example, require physical exertion. What starts out to be a relaxing game can turn into competitive sport that has the potential to create frustration and anxiety. Substituting activity for rest can intensify already existing depression.

Our society is filled with everyday stress and tension. Also, there is only so much we can do, even though there might be much more we want to do. Even a couch potato can be bombarded with a myriad selection of sensory inputs called television, twenty-four hours a day.

People suffer from lack of rest. Then they wonder why they are depressed. Now days we have to discipline ourselves even to get proper rest. Pastors should encourage their people to take time out. Remember, our Lord frequently went off to rest and be restored.

For our purposes, R&R, in overcoming depression, should be used in the context of eliminating any and all exertion. The body needs rest as does the mind. So, the goal is to get the client to cease all activity when investing in R&R.

Everyone should have a thirty to forty-five minute block of time each day to lay down their load for a while. Finding a quiet and peaceful place to sit, better yet, lie down and rest, is the desired activity for this time. If the individual naps, okay. If not, that is okay, too. The main goal is just to rest and relax. People can be encouraged to do this by being informed of the many who have achieved renown that made this rest & relaxation practice a normal, daily part of their lives.

At first, R&R may feel awkward and require some adjusting. Be persistent. It can be enjoyed. The result has been demonstrated in many lives that discovered such a time actually increased their daily productivity. The fact is that most people in our society have lost the art of resting and relaxing, and for that loss, society is paying a heavy price. When Christ practiced the art of Rest and Relaxation, the time of physical recovery was coupled with the spiritual communication with the Father. Laying life's burdens down in the throne room of God, the Father; resting in His peace; then, going on rested with our loads left behind to God's attentive care, makes for a happier more carefree life, under any circumstances.

We talk about needing rest from the aspect of the lack of rest overloading the body and contributing to depression. However, depression alone does put a physical demand on the body. This makes it very important that the Pastor's Plan include R&R. At the very least, going long periods without R&R will intensify any emotional condition even as it caused physical deterioration. Being overcome and lingering in such a negative state is just not honoring to the Lord no matter how you look at it. It demonstrates a basic mistrust of God's care for the person, and a lack of belief in the promises made in His Word.

The vicious downward spiral of depression is usually already in full swing by the time you are consulted as a counselor. Body and mind are under considerable strain that can give rise to additional physical and emotional maladies. So, you have no time to waste in assisting your counselee in learning the art of R&R. Help him to discover and set aside the block of time each day to get the needed period of quiet and recover. You may find it needful to intercede with an employer on your member's behalf. Once an employer sees the improvement worked in the individual's life, he might require all of his employees to start taking a break.

While this discussion has not dwelt on the need of the human body for a full eight hours sleep in most people (it varies a little with age), the need is a forgone conclusion. People who are susceptible to stressful inputs should turn off the television early, even eliminate the highly charged news program. Get cleaned up and go to bed early. If the body wakes too early, as it might do especially to start with, stay in bed. If you are only a couple of hours ahead on your day, it may be that you will discover a productive Bible study and prayer time. Many books deal with techniques to deal with night time loss of sleep. This need must be met even as you must take the daytime retreat from the world's cares.

It may be wise to eliminate anything that might be going into the body that might rob rest. Caffeine is a big thief to many people. It often takes away the ability to shut down physically and mentally. Coffee, tea, soda, hot chocolate are just loaded with caffeine. Custom does not make a thing good. Drinking soda and coffee in the evenings pushes the nervous system into high gear late into the night. For some, R&R requires changing whole chunks of lifestyle around. Be patient. Patience is promoted by good R&R.

By the way, pastor, you may want to try getting into R&R yourself. It is essential to maintaining all facets of health. Dr. Eleazer Benenhaley, the great South Carolina pastor, used to counsel young preachers about the dangers of burn-out in the ministry. To say you'd rather burn-out than rust-out may sound good, but it's bad stewardship of God's possession—-you! It is also a bad example to the flock when you fall. It discourages others from heeding God's call in their lives. If it is the practice in your own life, when someone comes to you needing R&R in their lives, you can say, "I want you to try something I do in my life...."

Pastor's Plan

I. Depression

Spiritual

Spiritual health should never, under any condition, be overlooked. Sometimes depression is the direct result of sin. When known sin is present, the pastor should assist the church member in immediately dealing with it appropriately and expediently. Even when sin has not arisen as an issue, it is still worthy of the pastor's attention. As long as unconfessed sin remains present, whether it is large or small sin by human standards, the depressed individual's condition is not likely to be satisfactorily resolved. Humanist techniques merely mask such problems, setting up a time-bomb in people's lives.

Salvation is not a matter to be overlooked, even in the lives of regular church attendees. Until a person truly trusts Christ, their depression cannot be eradicated. Without the power of Christ working in us and through us, no true healing of depression takes place. Let me make this point clear. It is only through the power of Christ that the healing of any disorder of the human being occurs. The lost person is without power, and salvation is a must! I cannot emphasize enough, salvation is a matter that should be taken care of at the outset of counseling!

I do assume the subject of salvation was raised in some phase of the initial interview because you followed your outline in that section and naturally have a pastor's heart. However, people lie to God, to you, and even to themselves. If it becomes likely that you are dealing with a lost person, by all means explore the issue. Their condition with God is, of course, not yours to determine, but it is legitimate to question when evidence for His grace in their lives is lacking or reasonable belief to the contrary is present. Make salvation certain, if at all possible.

Teach the depressed how to draw strength from the work of God. Even those who are depressed because of biological causes can profit during episodes of depression, no resource exists better than the work of God. Pastors should direct those church members who are struggling hard with depression to appropriate victory verses. Several good "Precious Promises" type books are on the market which provide quick reference to appropriate passages.* They are inexpensive. Many pastors equip their lay workers with them, and you may even want to give them to certain members who come for counsel. But whatever the method used, teach the individual to claim the marvelous promises of God.

This brings us to the most overlooked tool available to the depressed. That tool is prayer. Pastors should guide the depressed to seek the Lord Jesus Christ for deliverance. He is, by the way, the Great Counselor.

And His name shall be called Wonderful,
Counselor,
The Mighty God,
The Everlasting Father,
The Prince of Peace.

Isaiah 9:6(b)

Not only should you lead the depressed person to pray, but following the example of the Lord, you the counselor, should do so, too. Your own Intercessory Prayer Plan is essential. Your prayer life will greatly effect your success in this ministry:

And the prayer of faith shall save the sick,
and the Lord shall raise him up; *

James 5:15a

When you pray together about the issues affecting the hurting member, let your own utterances focus on praising God for the blessings the hurting member has received from the Lord. You want to teach the individual to concentrate on blessings as a tool for effectively dealing with depression.

You can benefit the client and your understanding of his situation by asking pointed questions and using these as a teaching tool. You will notice that in the following list of basic questions are some you will already know, or at least have a good inkling of before they are posed. Your knowledge is not the issue in many counseling questions, but rather the questions become the vehicle of bringing the issues to the counselee's attention. In this technique you are imitating Jesus Christ's example as He ministered upon this earth.

Basic Questions Assessing Spiritual Health

(1) Do you spend time in prayer? How much?

Get down to specifics about what happens in the prayer closet.

Very often you find that time is either not actually spent in prayer or that prayer is actually a very superficial event in their lives.

(2) Questions about church attendance. You may ask, "Do you attend church regularly?"

Regular attendance should be redefined for the member who thinks that it is showing up on Sunday morning.

(3) Do you tithe and give to the cause of Christ?

Remember the widow's mite. Participation with the right spirit is a very strong indicator and an essential function in a victorious person's life.

(4) Do you read the Bible daily?

The altering of habits in prayer and Bible study in a Christian who has been strong in faith in times past and is now depressed is a strong sign of a sin having become a stronghold.

(5) Do you tell others about Jesus?

Many people define telling others about Jesus as inviting people to church or living a good life in front of people. Nail it down. Christ sharing is done either through joy or obligation. Depression is contrary to joy.*

(6) Do you spend seasons in thanksgiving?**

These are just a few questions that illustrate how inquiring about the depressed individual's spiritual health may assist in uncovering the root cause of depression. When a person is unhealthy spiritually, he will be unhealthy emotionally, mentally, physically, and perhaps in even other areas. Each issue can be dealt with individually and appropriately.

At the beginning of the section on depression you were told that experiencing depression is not sin. You have seen that depression can occur as a result of sin. Then, it is a symptom that says something needs to be corrected. Continued depression can lead to sinful conditions existing in a person's life which range from not trusting God to overt acts of a sinful nature.

Depression can also be a direct result of satanic attack. It is the desire of Satan to oppress and depress God's children. In cases where satanic attack is suspected, the first area of concern should be confessing and forsaking any known sin. Afterwards, much prayer should be continued and sought from other brothers and sisters in Christ who are involved in intercessory prayer.

Name giving to prayer partners is not essential to effect in agreeing in prayer. What is needed to be known is that the problem exists and they can pray about the person the pastor knows of. Just get prayer busy. Confidentiality remains unbroken in such cases. In every counseling situation we encourage the pastor to pray a hedge of protection about his counselees. We live in depressing and oppressing times and many, if not most, people's problems are influenced in some degree by satanic forces.*

It should go without saying that pastors should be spiritually healthy, too, if they are going to be of use to God and help those who are hurting. Pastors should keep a check on and maintain their own spiritual health.

Our first order of business for depressed individuals must be God's business.

**Depression either separates from,
or is caused by separation from
the life in Christ.**

Pastor's Plan

I. Depression

Social Relationships

Social interaction is of the essence in recovering from depression. Pastors who are counseling a depressed individual, whether the depression is a primary or secondary symptom, should encourage the socialization of the member.

Quite often depression produces isolation. Isolation is sometimes voluntary because the depressed withdraws. Sometimes it is social ostracism because people respond to the fact the depressed are depressing. In either case, isolation from family and friends has a tendency to compound the depressed individual's condition.

During depression, the last thing needed is separation from people who are dear and willing to be accepting of us. Friends and family who love us are often God's method of comforting us. Depressed people need interaction with others. However, it is important that these individuals be "upbeat people".* Misery welcomes company. So when the depressed are seeking out friends and family to socialize with, they need to be happy people or at least people who can give a boost.

If the depressed argues he does not "feel up to" interacting with others, the pastor should strongly encourage him to do so anyway.** Get them to go through the motions. God put in all of us a need to be with others, especially during times of hurting and pain. Social activities going on at the church and in the community could be pointed out to the member. Social events generally carry a lot of laughter and if anything is needed in a depressed person's life it is laughter.

Depressed individuals need to stay active socially. Isolation welcomes self-pity and focus on depression.

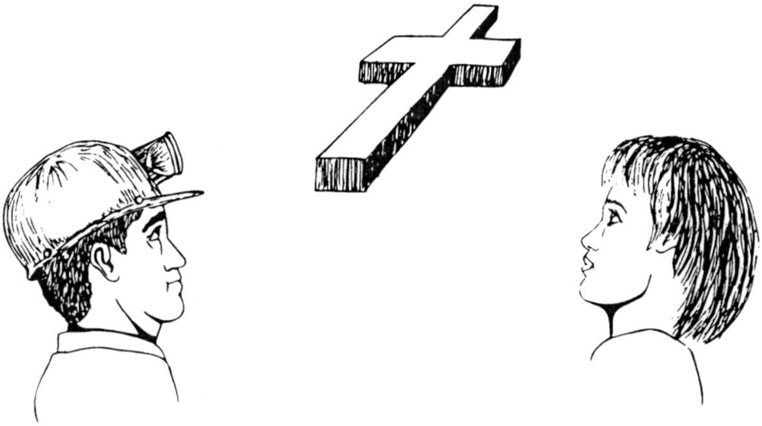

Pastor's Plan

I. Depression

Mental Health

Mental Health is always of concern. Pastors should encourage positive thinking. This is not positive thinking in terms of a worldly context, but that which is firmly founded on and rooted in the Word of God.

Depressed people do tend to focus on and almost seem to try to harbor negative thoughts. Negative thinking is detrimental to well-being and recovery of the depressed.

Pastors are encouraged to direct the depressed individual to the Word of God. There is not a book available that has as much positive thoughts for thinking than God's Word. They have the additional advantage that they reflect the mind of God rather than the mind of man. Choosing uplifting verses and having the member memorize them is a counter process to the negative thoughts they are being bombarded by in their depressed condition. In times of depression, the verses once memorized, can be recalled by the Holy Spirit into the person's mind to counter the negative that tries to arise. Having the Word beginning to dwell in the member's mind, richly, is a key to helping the individual take control of their thoughts in a Biblical, positive manner. Wrong thinking leads to wrong behavior; it is not the other way around. Simply put; depressing thoughts lead to depressive behavior or intensifies existing depression.

You see now how the pastor should encourage the counselee to make a conscious effort to dispel negative thoughts and habitual thinking in exchange for the Biblical positive mode. It takes time and effort to train the mind to respond to our commands, but with practice it is possible. Negative thinking people are not happy people, just as a positive thinking person is not sad.

Pastor's Plan

I. Depression

Encouragement

Always encourage. Depressed individuals need a huge dose. It's amazing what words of encouragement can do for those who are "down and out" going through a "bout of depression".

Encouragement can come by helping the member understand that God loves them and is concerned with their situation. Sometimes the person you are working with cannot understand that God loves them and is concerned with them, but tell them anyway even if they can't visualize such a love as God has for them; tell them.

Help them to see their value. Help them to understand by focusing on the fact God loved them so much, He gave His only Son for their benefit. They must see there is hope for their situation. It is not hopeless. All the resources of heaven are available to help them have victory.

Hopelessness is the devil's way of destroying. Help them see this. Appropriate passages on Spiritual Warfare can let them know of the conflict as well as the certainty of victory to those who "strive lawfully".

Hope is one of the most important things you communicate. Help them to see that "there is light at the end of the tunnel". Just because the client, or even you, do not see how it will all come to pass does not mean it is not there. There are many ways of encouraging the discouraged, and it costs nothing but a little time filled with positive input.

Pastor's Plan

I. Depression

Love, Acceptance, and Self Worth

Love, Acceptance, and Self-worth; key ingredients in counseling the depressed.

Often depressed individuals feel unloved. Whether imaginary or not, it is their feelings. Alienation from the reality of the love of God exists in the depressed, and this problem needs to be resolved in their lives. Enough cannot be said about directing people to the Word of God, but added to that is the need for the person you are helping to see that you love them and care about their situation. Emphasis has already been placed on telling them you love them and are there for them to help in any way you can, but the way they will find most noticeable is the manner in which you demonstrate pastoral concern for the individual's well being.

Acceptance is another issue of consideration. It is usual for the depressed to experience feelings of rejection. Here, the demonstration of concern is conveyed by the demonstration of acceptance of the individual. The person is accepted regardless of what may be occurring in their life. The demonstration of acceptance must follow the model set by the Lord Jesus. People need to/must come to the Lord Jesus as they are. Pastors should practice this behavior. As you, Pastor, receive people from where they are in life, you must as counselor do the same. No matter what the present conditions or circumstances in their lives, the Lord stands with open arms to accept and restore. All the person has to do is come. The pastor's voice tone, approach, patience, kindness, and understanding will convey that they are accepted.

The abnormality of low self-worth is the usual situation for a depressed person. It can itself be the cause of the depression, but if not the cause, it will, more often than not, be present. If individuals cannot find anything good about themselves, it is highly unlikely they will find anything good about anything or anyone else. A sense of self-worth is a fundamental part of the hierarchy of needs we all have and must be met for a person to become stable emotionally. Usually, people arrive at the counselor's door with a very poor self-image. This sense of poor self-worth is part of satan's plan of destruction. Satan knows that if he can instill in a person such a sense of worthlessness, he will not only be rendered ineffective but possibly even detrimental to the work of Christ. Even though it has been said before, I repeat, it is urgent that the member is taught, using the Word of God, how much God values them. Emphasize that self-worth is based on a relationship with Christ.*

For God so loved the world,
that He gave His only begotten Son,
that whosoever believeth in Him should not perish,
but have everlasting life.
John 3:16

Help the person you counsel for depression come to understand John 3:16. This one verse alone puts a high price tag on mankind, the depressed person included. No one is a special case, an exception to the rule.

Self-worth is a need the pastor can help the counselee fill in a Biblical manner.

Pastor's Plan

I. Depression

Eliminating The Cause

Causes of depression must be eliminated, if at all possible. Depression causes will be of two types:

Identified
Unidentified

Unidentified causes of depression should become identified after a little investigation, but what if the root does not reveal itself in a reasonable period? It is necessary to consider referral. If you have suspected the cause could possibly have been medical in origin, a referral to a cooperative medical practitioner should have been an early option with counseling continuing from what the referral revealed. When medical causes are not early indicated, it might yet be worthwhile to check out the possibility, depending on what you observe as you go along.

Identified causes of depression also have two general types:

Causes that can be eliminated
Causes that cannot be eliminated

You desire to eliminate the cause, but if it is not eliminateable, then the client must learn to accept and deal with it. For instance, sin is a cause of depression that can be eliminated by repentance, confession, and receiving forgiveness. Death is a cause of depression that cannot be so simply eliminated, but will pass in time as the normal grief process takes place in the human life, unless it is complicated by guilt. Normal death depression only needs Christian support for the believer, but when something like guilt is associated, then that issue must be resolved before the healing process can become complete. An ongoing medical problem or even an untreatable illness may also cause recurring or ongoing depression. These would not necessarily be eliminateable, but these are certainly conditions within which the believer might find victory.

Today, a primary root cause of depression is substance abuse. By that, I mean alcohol and drugs. We usually think of illegal substances in this category, but always remember prescribed medications may also be abused and not always by the volition of the person you are counseling.* When you identify abuse, mind altering chemicals should be removed. In substance abuse cases, whether the source is legal or illegal, you will probably need to do some referral because of the strongholds of dependency that is established in the body.

Helping the depressed person is often a tiring, as well as, a trying task, so do not give up. Follow the pastor's plan and acquaint yourself with ways to help eliminate what is revealed when the causes are identified. Deal with each facet according to the type of symptom it is.

After several sessions be sure to re-evaluate the counselee, as well as, what you have done with them. If the counselee has made no progress, explore for reasons why, and make proper corrections.*

If there is evidence of resistance to counseling, maybe more encouragement is needed. Perhaps the individual is unwilling to reveal to you the really hard-core issues that are troubling him and hoped to get some magic release out of Christian Counseling, without uncovering the most uncomfortable parts of their persons. The issue of relationship and confidentiality may have to be returned to. Eliminating the cause sometimes means removing the blockage. In that case, the cause of the hindrance has to be identified. Other areas of counseling may not require that all be ferreted out, but when depression is the root and not the symptom, this is simply not the case.

Make sure your depressed member understands you, your instructions, and the information you ask for and impart, as well. This is sometimes one of those barriers to progress. Some people have poor reading and comprehension skills. Some of them get pretty skillful at covering up these types of problems, but they are folks who need special attention. Clear instructions are a must for those who have lower level abilities. If the client is able to deal with the openness, suggest that the counselee solicit help from family and friends understanding materials. Having on hand audio and visual aids dealing with counseling issues can resolve a lot of difficulties.

It is a must that once begun, the pastor make every effort possible to help the hurting church member. If all of your efforts fail and no progress is made, you make the ultimate referral bringing into the equation a professional trained Christian Counselor whose theology of counseling you have determined to be in conformance with the Work of God. But, as long as progress is being made, stick with it brother! It may be going slow, but if your counseling 'ain't broke, don't fix it'! These things take time.

A closing note about eliminating the cause of depression within overweight people. This problem can be eliminated by diet and exercise regimen in most cases, coupled with specialized counseling designed to eliminate attitudes toward food that often must overcome certain triggers that occur in the brain. Your role in encouragement is indispensable, but the issue of weight control is a subject that medicine is still learning about. New discoveries have revolutionized some previous concepts and much is yet to be learned.

Something you can count on is that depressed, obese people have suffered many remarks by those who do not have any basis for identification with what they go through. If you want to be successful in helping these people you must understand this. They even hurt one another at times by careless comments, even as they try to support and assist. Such is the tenderness of emotion experienced in the condition. Probably this problem is one of those very difficult ones for most pastors.

Some people cannot keep from being overweight because that is how they see themselves. Eliminating the cause in these cases means helping the person to become comfortable with whom they are. For some, this will then mean that they are able to lose the weight, for others it will mean weight loss no longer matters one way or another unless health becomes an issue.

One thing people do not accept readily is that overweight conditions do not necessarily mean people are involved in the sin of gluttony. If sin is not present, and physical health is not an issue, it is better to help an individual live a productive, happy life that might be statistically shortened by weight, than force them into a life that is unhappily filled with guilt and frustration which impedes them doing things that enable them to feel good about themselves and be in harmony with their Lord.

Since dieting to lose weight has been shown to be a roller coaster ride, up and down the scales for the majority of people, and since dieting is accompanied by both physical and mental complications, the change in attitude toward food that must be co-existant with a dieting regimen must be in place as the actual weight loss process occurs. Most dieters must accept that they will have to be under nutritional control for the rest of their lives. And that control generally means they must not only eat less than they do now, but will probably eat less than others about them. They must eliminate the anger that they might feel that a life similar to others may not be practical.*

Pastor's Plan

I. Depression

When to Refer

In the event a cause of depression cannot be identified, the pastor will do well in making a referral. A referral is not to be made until it has been discussed with the counselee. A referral is also needful when there is evidence of suicide, homicide, or destruction of property. Counselors have a responsibility to protect life and property. A pastor is also wise to make a referral when there is lack of progress. For example, after four to six sessions you note there is no improvement in the depressed person's condition; consider referral.

We have already touched on the necessity of making referrals in cases where you suspect biological or medical causes are primary factors. Pastors are not to delay in getting help for individuals who are experiencing problems that require a specialist. Hopefully, you will already have identified the most likely rescue for that referral, so the member can be guided smoothly in the right direction.

Other situations that call for a referral are:

1. Cases where the depressed individual is resistant to help.
2. Cases where severe personality conflict is a hindrance.
3. Cases where the pastor may feel sensually drawn to the counselee of the opposite sex.
4. Cases where the pastor feels he in incompetent. Many find that is particularly true in areas involving children or childhood disorders.
5. Cases where the pastor is too closely involved, such as those involving a family member or close friend, etc.

The bottom line is this, in any case the pastor feels he cannot be of help to the client, or needs the input of a specialist, he should make a referral.

Referral does not, or should not be construed as a lack of ability to help the hurting. When you make a good referral, the counselee is going to recognize you are a top performer, and you should, too.

Pastor's Plan

I. Depression

Member's Monitoring List of Things To Do

The following Member's Monitoring List of Things To Do is a tool that should be reproduced at the appropriate time in your counseling program and given to the depressed member. Sit down and go over the items contained in the list with the member. Discuss with them the reasons behind these very obvious things they need to do for themselves.

When the member suffering from chronic depression takes the list home and posts the List in a prominent spot, it becomes their tool to remind them daily of things they need to do in helping themselves overcome depression. Since you have gone over the list in detail with the member, emphasizing those items of special consideration for them, it becomes the daily prompter for what they need to do.

Too much emphasis cannot be given to the choice of location for the List, or for the need to use it as a daily reference. You might point out that people do things by routine. They brush their teeth at certain times, take medicine, eat meals, take vitamins, and so forth. The member needs to set specific times to review the List and remember what their objectives are. Some might want to use locations like a refrigerator or memo board for the List, but others might find these spots too prominent. The point in choosing a location for the List is that it be one that will not lend itself to causing the list to be ignored.

People have to take responsibility for their own lives before they can completely recover from any emotional or mental disorder. This is true whether we are talking about people in their relationships with other people and the world about them or with the Lord, Himself. You can point people in the right direction, but they have to do the walking. For instance, the List calls for reading God's Word and directs the member to choose encouraging Scripture verses. You have been feeding the member Scripture as you've progressed in the counseling relationship. But now, regarding them following the list, it is okay to point them toward the latter half of the Psalms, but let them search for appropriate verses on their own. It's not only Scriptural, but it allows them to take charge. Your roll can move into the support mode as recovery progresses.

Pastor's Plan

1. Depression

Member's Monitoring List

Things To Do

Rest and Relax

Socialize - Avoid isolation from friends and family.

Think Positive - Take control of your thought life.

Eat Regularly - Take vitamins; avoid junk food.

Exercise - Do some form of aerobics daily; focus on good health.

Express Yourself - Practice doing this both with others and to God.

Pray and Surrender - Both yourself and your problems to God.

Read God's Word - Select encouraging Scripture verses.

Find an Unopinionated Friend - One who will take time to listen.

Get Involved in Christian Support Groups

Determine to Overcome Depression - Make a personal decision.

Get Involved in Hobbies and Sports - Make time to enjoy recreation.

Read Recommended Materials - You must "learn" to overcome depression.

Seek Counseling - Having begun, do not withdraw before you and counselor concur it is time.

Avoid Thoughts of Escape - Purposely decide to resolve conflicts.

Avoid Alcohol and/or Drugs - These are depressants. Use can cause guilt and, therefore, depression.

Learn to Accept Things You Cannot Change - This does not mean condoning what is wrong.

Eliminate and Avoid Sinful Behavior - The challenge of Life in Christ.

Go Through Motions Of Everyday Living - Even if you do not "feel" like it.

Attend Church Regularly - Be involved in worship, don't just be there.

Associate Yourself With Positive Thinking People - People who think negatively drain your energy.

Remove Yourself From Threatening and Abusive Situations - Nobody has a "right" to mistreat you; You belong to Jesus.

Seek Medical Care and Evaluation When Needed - Take care of yourself.

Seek Discernment - Learn what God is teaching you through depression and problems.

Make Necessary Changes - Eliminate causes of depression.

Encourage Yourself In the Lord. Don't depend on somebody else to remind you the Lord is good to you.

Pastor's Plan

I. Depression

Resources

Books to Read

Booklet Recommended:	*Learning More About Depression*
Authored by:	Steven W. Spotts, Psy. D.
Published by:	Rapha Publishing/Word Inc. Houston & Dallas, Texas

Useful in helping the depressed person understand the causes of depression. Helpful in assisting the depressed Christian to lose additional depression related to guilt about being depressed.

Excellent primer for the pastor who has little or no experience dealing with counseling the depressed.

A possible application in a church pursuing a continuing program of teacher/Christian worker development using the book as an educational tool for promoting a Biblical model of caring ministry within the church.

Contents:
What is Depression?

Christian Attitudes

Who Gets Depressed?

What causes Depression?

What Does Depression Look Like?

Typical Responses To Depression

What Types of Help Are Available for Depression?
Note: Read the appendix.

Minister's Notes:

Books To Read:

Learning More About Chemical Dependency by Robert D. McGee

God is For the Alcoholic by Jerry Dunn

Book To Use:

Rapha's Twelve Step Program For Overcoming Chemical Dependency

Pastor's Plan

II. Alcohol and Drug Use

Foreword on Intervention

Intervention should always be approached with a clear understanding that it may not be accepted or welcomed. Believe it or not, there are many chemically addicted people who do not want help. Pastors will on occasion have spouses and other family members approach them asking that they intervene in a loved one's life to rescue them from addiction. Many believe the preacher can "fix" the problem. It is no more so that the addict will respond to the wisdom of the pastor in this issue than that they will when he presents the Gospel message. Most addicts refuse intervention, especially when it is done in an inappropriate manner. Intervention is seldom received even when it is done properly. The number of chemically addicted people in the world compared to the number of drug and alcohol intervention programs is proof in itself of the poor response of addicts. Pastor, if you understand nothing else on the subject, understand this; a person does not and will not become chemical free until they decide to. Never forget that you cannot help those who do not want help. Preaching to a drunk about the sin and destruction of booze and dope will not do any good. An addict who is high on alcohol or dope cannot hear, is not interested, and does not care.

It is clear you should never attempt intervention while the addict is under the influence. Convey to the spouse or other requesting family member that you will be glad to talk with the person once they are sober. Also, make it plain that an appointment will be made and approved with the addicted individual. Suggest that the place be neutral,* such as the church office or other such place that you can mutually agree on.

When you keep that appointment, have as few people there as possible. Make it plain with the family that they are not invited to sit in. Too many individuals trying to pursuade an addict to get help can cause the person to feel pressured and pushed. It also can create a sense of threat and confusion for them. The addict should be approached in a peaceful environment, in a calm and loving attitude. The message that he needs to hear is that he is loved, is valuable, needs help, and help is available. Never in your demeanor ever convey, even momentarily,a sense of hopelessness about their situation.

Be prepared prior to the meeting with a course of action. Know before hand if the addict accepts intervention, the what's, where's, and how's of your assistance. If you have a weakness in your personal Referral Resource System, resolve it prior to the meeting. Be prepared! We plow in expectation!

Intervention does save lives and lessens the destruction, but intervention must be done properly or not at all.

Do not be discouraged if you are not always accepted in your willingness to reach out in this matter. You know very well that the majority you share Christ with will reject the Gospel message. It is not you that is rejected; it is the Lord Jesus. You are the instrument of His desire to establish His Lordship in every human life in intervention as in every other facet of Pastoral Ministry. Many choose the slavery of sin to the freedom of Christ. But, just as we go forth sharing Salvation, and proclaiming His Lordship, we go forth in our service of aiding in setting the captives free from specific sin. If you go out with the expectation of failure, you most assuredly will fail.

The abundance to be found in the life transformed and the benefits in those lives touched by that transformation makes the sacrifices and rejections experienced in this part of ministry a small matter over time. It is conceivable that no matter where you are, the benefits of your faithfulness will spread out even across the world within a decade or so. You might say that this is the testimony portion of our contemplation of intervention. In helping others to experience life, and life more abundantly, we find that we also are sharers in that abundant life.

Jesus Said:
The thief cometh not, but for to steal,
and to kill,
and to destroy:
I am come that they might have life,
and that they might have it more abundantly.
John 10:10

Paul asked us:

How then shall they call on Him in whom they have not believed?
And how shall they believe in Him of whom they have not heard?
And how shall they hear without a preacher?

Romans 10:14

Paul told us:

How beautiful are the feet of them that preach the Gospel of Peace,
and bring glad tidings of good things!

Romans 10:15b

He continued:

But I say, Have they not heard?
Yes verily, their sound went into all the earth,
and their words unto the ends of the world.

Romans 10:18

The highest calling is to be God's Minister of the Gospel of Peace who brings glad tidings of good things, proclaiming that He, the Lord Jesus Christ, sets the captives free, and gives life, and that more abundantly.

Pastor's Plan

II. Alcohol and Drug Use

Addiction Defined

Addiction is often defined as the giving up to a habit. In the case of mind altering chemicals, it is generally the giving up to the habit of alcohol and/or drugs. Alcohol and drug addiction usually begin with an occasional drink or drug to "knock the edge off" or just to "get high". In many cases addiction to a chemical begins as a way to medicate some type of emotional pain such as depression, low self-esteem, grief, anger, frustration, etc. At first, the chemicals seem to produce the user's desired effect. They get high (euphoric) and the pain seems to subside, at least temporarily. As time goes on and usage continues, the body builds up a tolerance and the quantity demand to produce the same effect increases. The user suddenly finds that the demand is not an option, but a need; he is hooked.

There's a fine line between abuse and addiction, but the results are the same..."trouble". Addiction is the result of chemical abuse, and as time passes, abuse is the result of having an addiction. Hand in hand they go. For the addict, "one drink or one fix is too many, and a thousand are not enough." What starts out as an occasional drink or fix to boost self-esteem, medicate pain, or just have a good time ends in disaster.

Addiction to alcohol and/or drugs is also defined by the American Medical Association as a disease. Something genetic is supposed to influence a greater likelihood of addiction, so they say. God's Word calls addiction sin, and sin it is. As a recovered alcoholic and drug user, I personally believe the AMA and other organizations have misdefined addiction to alcohol and drugs.* Defining alcohol and drug addiction as a disease removes man's responsibility for this immoral behavior and contradicts the fact man is a free agent according to God's Word. When a person uses, abuses, or allows themselves to become addicted it is a clear transgression against God's Word.

Regardless of the definition, all can agree, chemical addiction is heart breaking and every pastor should be prepared to minister to those who are suffering from its evils. It is really not like a person sits around and one day decides to become an alcoholic or drug addict. No! It is the subtle work of satan! It starts as behavior with no harm intended. Isn't that the way the devil works? He starts you out small and works you up to something big. Before long, instead of the person controlling the chemical, the chemical is controlling him; that's addiction. The chemical has at this point become the addicts "lord and master". The addict has to use. At one point and time the addict "lived to use," but after addiction he "uses to live".

In addiction, chemicals are now a must. Dispel the illusion that the addict is only the continual user from your thinking. The weekend user can also be an addict. When it is a pattern, a pattern that must be satisfied, it is addiction. The addict's life is consumed with using. Even if it were to cost him his job, family, career, or very life, his habit and craving must be satisfied. Using drugs is now a way of life for the addict. When we allow anything to control us such as alcohol or drugs, we are allowing something to take over that removes us from the control of God. Addiction, use and abuse, is not the Will of God.

Wine is a mocker, strong drink is raging:
and whosoever is deceived thereby is not wise.
Proverbs 20:1

And be not drunk with wine,
wherein is excess;
but be filled with the Spirit;
Ephesians 5:18

In the Scriptures, use of mind-altering drugs is likened to the sin of witchcraft. The specific Scripture is not quoted because in the King James text it is not clear. The Greek text uses the same word from which we take the word pharmacist; translated into the KJV as witchcraft because of its use in occultic ritual.

Pastor's Plan

II. Alcohol & Drug Use

Signs and Symptoms

Quick Look Sheet

1. Is the client drinking or using drugs with increased frequency?
2. Is the client's speech slurred (not clear)?
3. Is there an increase in consumption?
4. Has there been any traffic citations? Other encounters with the law?
5. Is the client defensive when approached about usage?
6. Does the client lie about his usage? (Hiding)
7. Is the client wallowing in self-pity?
8. Is the client demonstrating signs of depression?
9. Does the client exhibit mood swings?
10. Is the client showing increased anger (lacks control)?
11. Is there a pattern of lost work time?
12. Have poor work performance complaints been made?
13. Is the client having difficulty focusing or exhibiting other signs of mental confusion?
14. Is the client spending more and more time sleeping?
15. Is the client exhibiting insomnia or sleep disturbance?

16. Do you see physical signs such as glassy, blood shot eyes, or dilated pupils?

17. Is the client suffering digestive system complaints?

18. Has there been weight loss? Have you been told he has poor appetite?

19. Is the client isolating himself more and more from friends and family?

20. Has a negative change in hygiene habits occurred?

21. Is the client complaining of feeling tired a lot?

22. Has the client exhibited irritability without obvious reason?

23. Has the client exhibited interest in A & D use environments such as parties, bars, etc.?

24. Does the client exhibit judgmental/critical attitude?
    (Negative conduct must be personality shift from previous character)

25. Has alcohol/drug paraphernalia been discovered that belongs to client?

26. Is there denial or responsibility for acts?

27. Is there denial of responsibility for usage (blaming others)?

28. Has the client been caught/suspected of stealing?

29. Is the client abusing family members?

30. Are hangover symptoms present (withdrawals; shaking, nervousness)?

Pastor's Plan

II. Alcohol & Drug Use

Signs and Symptoms

Youth Extra
Quick Look Sheet

Note: Signs and Symptoms on the adult sheet may also apply to youth.

1. Has there been a loss of interest in sports, hobbies, or other normal extra-curricular activities?

2. Has he been laying out of school?

3. Has school grades dropped?

4. Has there been an increase in rebelliousness?

5. Does he exhibit a dislike for authority?

6. Has there been a change in the peer group he associates with?

7. Has there been a change in dress or habits? (Music, family time, etc.)

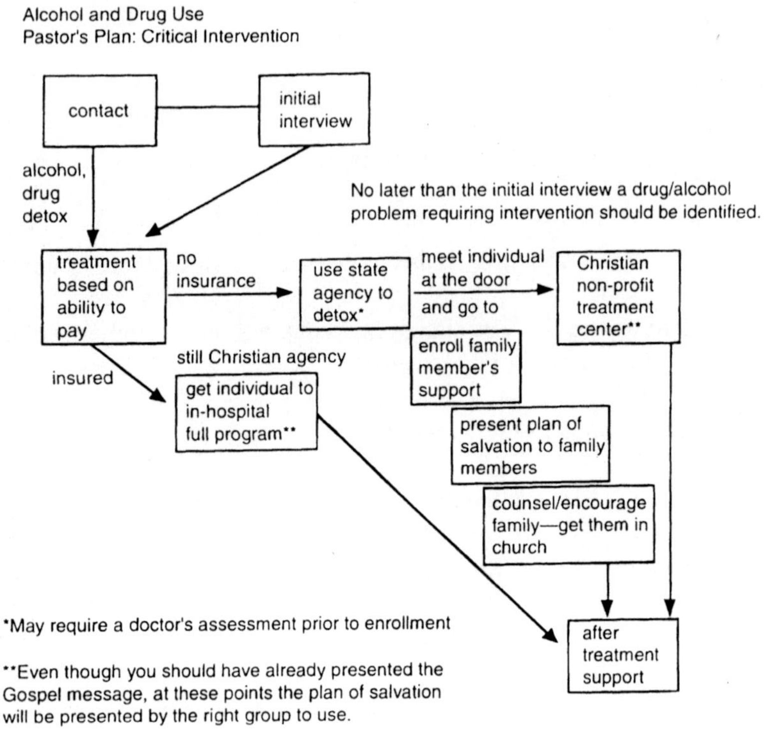

Critical Intervention Diagram

Pastor's Plan

II. Alcohol and Drug Use

Causes

Ultimately, the cause of addiction to chemical substances, alcohol and drugs is choice. The other causes are: choice, choice, choice, and choice. Alcohol and drug abuse takes a lot of effort. Anything that takes effort, takes thought. Anything that takes effort and thought usually results in action. A person abuses and uses chemical substances because they make a choice. No matter how it is turned and looked at, the cause of addiction is the same; a choice to use and abuse. It is only when one reaches addiction that choice has finally been removed.

It is at the addictive state that chemical substances are in control. Addiction brings the addict to a place of helplessness to the cravings of use. What happens then to the person's freedom of choice, you might ask? Quite simply, he has been robbed. It is at the addicted state where he is no longer in control, but under control. The "drug of choice" is now "calling the shots". All the will power a person can muster after crossing the line from abuse to addiction cannot compete with the power of chemical dependency. Why would anyone allow themselves to get to this stage? The answer again is choice. Anyone who plays with fire will get burned.

Some believe traumatic childhoods cause people to be addicted to chemical substances. If this is true we must be able to explain why so many others are raised in the same type of traumatic childhood environments and never use or become addicted to alcohol or drugs. How did they escape the claws of addiction? Because they made a choice.

Others believe it is emotional pain that causes addiction. If this were so, everyone ever born would, at one time or another in their lifetime, become addicted. The difference between an addict who medicates his emotional pain and the person who chooses other, healthier ways to deal with emotional pain, is choice.

Man's causes of addiction are innumerable. God's cause is one. Choice! By the way, whatever happened to man's responsibility? It wasn't Eve who made Adam sin, nor was it the serpent who made Eve sin. Read the story; they made a choice. Want to know why people use, abuse, and become addicted? Wrong choices!

Having established that substance abuse is ultimately by choice, precipitating factors can be discussed. The underlying elements that make some more prone than others are real, but not excuses. Hold on to the knowledge that excuses make performance excusable, but no excuse exists for willful acts.

Individuals who are products of childhood environments that were infected with chemical use, see the consumption of these things as a learned behavior. Many develop dependent behaviors because they were taught, directly or indirectly, that this is the way to deal with life. The American Indian, initially, was unexposed to the debilitating effects of "firewater". Subsequently, addiction plagued the tribes, not because Indians can't hold their liquor, but because alcohol used as a coping device became learned behavior. If alcoholism was genetic, every Indian should become an alcoholic. This illustration best presents the two precipitating factors, environment and lack of coping skills, in action. Unfortunate for the red man, those who learn to cope with conflict in a healthy and mature way (make the right choices), are not the people who get the publicity. They are the ones who live happier lives, though.

There are those who use these things to medicate some type of pain, whether it be emotional, mental, or physical. Pain resulting from the frustrations of life involving marital conflict, financial crisis, and death of a loved one are all situations and circumstances that cause pain of some type. Individuals who find themselves caught up in chronic, never-ending, painful situations look for relief. Precipitating factors need exploration, explanation, and resolution. But the reason for that is not to remove the excuse for actions, but to bring the user to see the real truth of their addiction. Otherwise, when faced with a new uncomfortable challenge, the pattern of wrong choice is repeated again. The myth of the incurable alcoholic lives on, when in truth it is the pattern of wrong choice that is alive and well.

Innumerable excuses for alcohol and drug addiction exist. The excuses are as endless as time. Never has there been a sin that has found so many excuses for man's involvement. Some excuses man gives for his addiction have a legitimacy within themselves, but make no mistake, they still leave him unexcused. The only ones who get victory are those who come to the "knowledge of truth", that it is a choice, and Jesus is the answer to the wrong choice.

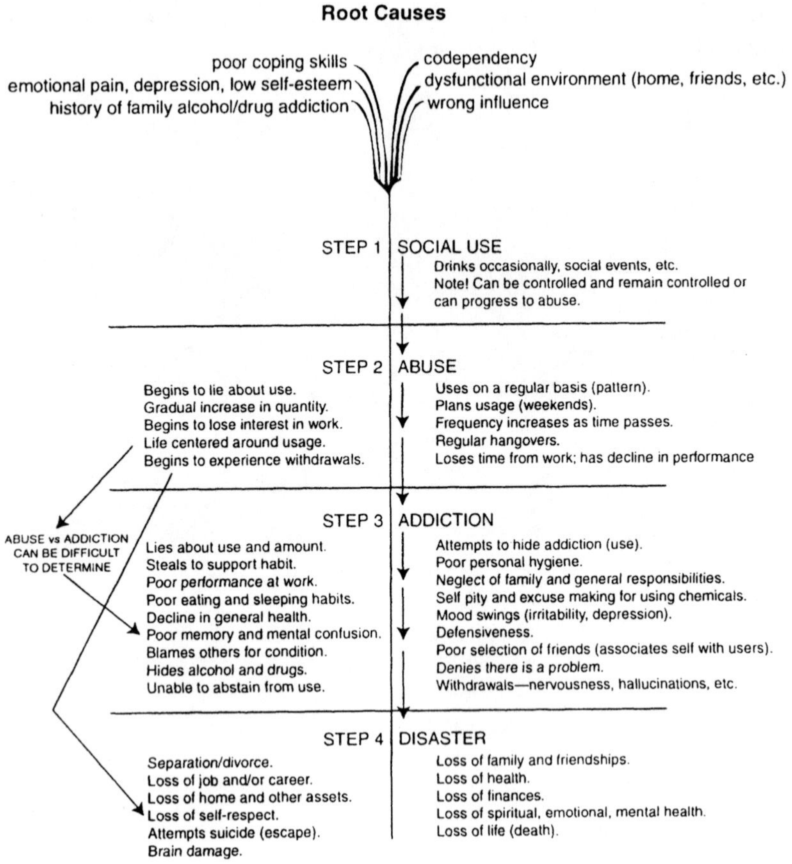

Root Cause Diagram

Pastor's Plan

II. Alcohol and Drug Use

ME Evaluation

Member's Evaluation on Alcohol/Drug Usage

I am going to be absolutely honest with myself and with my counselor. I know he is a friend the Lord Jesus Christ has sent to help me. He will treat my confidences as a sacred trust and seek my well-being. In return, I will give him honesty so he can help me.

Signed ____

I began drinking/using drugs in (place and /or time)

____

The way I began was __________________________________

____

____

(check or circle) I now drink/use drugs socially ___ when alone ___ both ___.

What I use now is (name what you use)

____

I use some amount every day ___ every other day ___ other ___.

My usage has increased from __________ to ___________.

Explain if necessary: _________________________________

____

____

I start using: in the morning ____ and/or early afternoon hours ____

My usage habit is: ___________________________________

____

____

<u>On the following write Y if the statement is true, X if it is false</u>

I have lied to others about my use of alcohol/drugs.___
I often lie about my abuse/addiction problem. ___
I find it necessary to hide my activities from others.___
I often hide usage from family and/or friends.___
I am ashamed of myself, but feel powerless to deal with the problem.___
I feel worthless. ___
I feel trapped, and I want out. ___
I have tried to get help before. ___
I feel guilty about what I am doing. ___
I think people do not understand what I am going through. ___
I have done things I am ashamed of when I was under the influence.___
I have done things I am ashamed of to get more. ___
I have stolen to support my habit. ___
I do things that make me feel ashamed more and more often. ___
I am losing more and more time from work. ___
I have lost a job because of this.___
I am having financial problems because of this. ___
Sometimes I am happy and sometimes I am very sad. ___
The only time I am happy is when I am using. ___
I get angry ___ feel angry ___ when asked about my use. Y/N___
I get angry ___ when

____

Sometimes when I get angry it seems that I am not in control of myself. ___
I often find myself arguing about small matters. ___
I have acted violently toward other people. ___
I have regular hangovers.___ I must have more to get over hangovers.___
Sometimes it seems my mind just will not work. ___
I can't remember what I say or do when using.___
I am forgetting simple things. ___
What happened yesterday escapes me frequently. ___
Sometimes I can't remember what I've done or where I've been.___
I am feeling tired often.___
I have sleeping problems. ___Too much. ___ Too little.___
When I sleep more, I do not seem to rest. ___
I often have stomach problems. ___ Check:Diarrhea ___
Cramping ___
Vomiting ___

narrative:

____

____

____

My hands shake when I get up in the morning. ___

I am nervous when I get up in the morning.___

My eyes are bloodshot ___, dry ___ , and irritated a lot ___.

I seem to be losing weight. ___ Write down how much weight you have lost over how long a period:________________lbs. Over ______

I have lost interest in family and friends ___

It seems like nearly everyone ___, has deserted me.___

I am having conflicts with my family ___, some of my closest friends ___.

They are acting very unreasonably towards me.___

I really do not have a real problem; I could quit anytime I get serious enough to do it.___

I am willing to get help to get better.___

Complete these statements:

I drink/use drugs
because:____

____

____

I would quit using alcohol/drugs if

____

were to occur.

I believe my use of alcohol/drugs is the fault of
______________________________because

they

____

____.

Pastor's Plan

II. Alcohol and Drug Use

Caring for the Addicted

Treatment and care for alcohol and drug abuse, like all addictions, begins just like use - "choice". The pastor cannot give care and assistance to those who are addicted unless a choice has been made to receive help. So the pastor must first determine a choice has been made before becoming involved in assisting the client in his quest for freedom. Many will seek out help with no genuine intentions of recovering. Why? Quite simply, it is the playing out of the insanity surrounding addiction. Sometimes the motivation is the need to manipulate people who are putting pressure on the user. Many want to be set free from the power of the addiction over them, but at the same time hold onto use. This is an impossibility and certainly not the will of God, which brings me to this thought. God requires a genuine choice and choice is in the crises life is made of. Choices involving salvation, servitude, worship, etcetera must be made all along the way. So why should it be so unreasonable to require choice from those seeking help from chemical abuse and addiction? The answer is, it isn't!

How do we know or measure a person's genuineness and sincerity when they come to us for help? That is more often than not a very difficult question to answer. Are they willing to do whatever is required to become chemical free? If not, they are probably not yet ready for help. If yes, then there is more than likely a sincere desire to be released from bondage. Making deals and spending hours prodding a person to do something he or she does not want to do is likely to be a waste of time, and falling into that trap can set up unhealthy patterns in your own life. Explain clearly that you are willing to help. Tell them what must be done, and how to receive your assistance. But, do not get involved unless you have reason to believe they are willing to go the distance! Otherwise you will expend a good deal of time for nothing!

Choice is a must. Remember the rich young ruler who sought out Jesus for eternal life? The Lord Jesus explained clearly what must be done to inherit eternal life and left the young man to make a choice. Sadly, a choice for eternal life was rejected. Did Jesus beg, plead, or even run this young fellow down? No, Jesus knew you could not make a person choose. They must do that themselves. I cannot over-emphasize that the pastor's plan for recovery cannot be initiated until a choice has been made. Hold the line– no choice, no involvement.

A phrase was developed a few years ago, perhaps by Dr. James Dobson, called "tough love". Well, that is what helping people with chemical addictions requires. It is not love that is lacking but love that is hard headed enough to hang in; durable enough to stay the course while failing to give in; determined enough to hold to a standard; successful enough to outlast the critics... Get the picture? I could give you more, but you will write your own with your experience of helping users achieve victory.

Likewise reckon ye also yourselves to be dead indeed unto sin,
but alive unto God through Jesus Christ our Lord.
Let not sin therefore reign in your mortal body,
That ye should obey it in the lusts thereof.
Neither yield ye your members as instruments of unrighteousness unto sin:
but yield yourselves unto God,
as those that are alive from the dead...
Romans 6:11-13a

Once the commitment has been made to accept help, the pastor must, next, decide if the addict needs in-patient or out-patient detoxification. Withdrawal from alcohol or drugs can be devastating, even very dangerous, to the addict. The pastor should note signs and symptoms of withdrawal such as:

Nervousness

Shaking and Trembling

Seizures

Depression

Mental Confusion

Violent Behavior

Profuse Vomiting

Diarrhea

Stomach Cramping

Hallucinations (Immediate medical help should be sought)

In general, any complaints should necessitate medical evaluation.

Medical evaluation is always a good idea to pursue when dealing with addicts who are withdrawing or desiring to withdraw from chemical abuse and/or addiction. Anyone who has been using chemical substances over a period of time cannot go wrong in being checked out medically. It is always better for the pastor to be safe than sorry. Counseling is best given and received after the completion of detoxification. Until a safe withdrawal has been completed or a medical doctor has given the greenlight to proceed with counseling, it is best to limit the pastor's plan to that of getting the addict through the physical part of recovery.

After detoxification and/or medical clearance, the pastor should direct the addict to a Christian alcohol or drug support group. Depending on what you observe, the first support group might be one that takes him completely out of his current environment and temptations where mind and body both get reconditioned for real living. It might be that the individual can come directly into a local support group. In either case, support groups are essential to good alcohol and drug addiction recovery.

Involvement in Christian support groups will expedite recovery and lessen the chances of the addict having a relapse or set-back. It is also here that the addict can identify and share with others the common problem. It is a discipling process where the addict is exposed to the wisdom of experience, learning how to live and maintain a chemical free life. With a solid Christian support group the member can receive much needed encouragement, acceptance and love. People in the group can identify with his situation "as touching". It is here, too, that the addict can be well educated about addiction, its destruction, and how to recover.

The pastor should now integrate the member into counseling. It is here that specific issues other than addiction can be dealt with. Issues such as financial problems, marital conflicts, parenting difficulties, job and career problems, all come along with the recovering member into this process. Actually, you may discover even more issues, each of which must be faced up to, and faced responsibly. Now you are monitoring the members recovery on a more personal basis. You provide needed encouragement and help the member work on self-esteem and co-dependent problems. Help is available to you on those issues in sections III and V.

Remaining chemical free is not an easy task for someone who has been a user for a long period of time. Sobriety can be a rude awakening. Quite often the recovering member has poor coping skills and will require much assistance from the pastor in overcoming the obstacles of daily living while these are being learned. Life isn't easy, especially if you've never been taught how to deal with it.

The pastor will do well to teach the recovering member that God does care about their recovery, and faith must be placed in the Lord Jesus for their present and continual deliverance from addiction. Directing the counselee to selected Scripture for hope and encouragement is always beneficial. As the recovering individual gleans from God's word, much needed strength to stay free will be obtained. It is essential that anyone who is recovering from chemical addiction get involved in their Spiritual health. Prayer, Bible study, church attendance and service are a must. Only through the power of Christ will sobriety be obtained and maintained.

Another area requiring the pastor to focus is the recovering addicts physical health. (Read Section I, Exercise and Nutrition segments) Over long periods of chemical use physical deterioration comes. The pastor should encourage the member to get involved in a moderate exercise program such as walking, jogging, etc. You might ask the medical doctor to assess his physical state and propose exercise limitations as part of his medical clearance after detoxification. (You can see why it is so important to have a medical doctor who will work co-operatively). A former addict's body is generally in need of an overhaul.

Muscles and organs that have been damaged by prolonged use of chemicals can be greatly helped to repair themselves by simple exercise. The program will also benefit by raising the energy level and helping to ward off depression.

Enough cannot be said about mental health in maintaining sobriety. "Stinkin-Thinkin" sends many back to booze and drugs. The pastor must help the recovering member reprogram their thinking processes. (Phillipians 4:8 mentality would bless the lives of all church members.) Wrong thinking results in wrong behavior. Wrong thinking is what has led many down the destructive path of addiction. The recovering addict must be taught how to recognize wrong thinking, how to dispel wrong thoughts and to be in control of what they allow or disallow themselves to think.

Over the years of self-abuse, some mental damage can be expected. You work with what the individual is when they begin the journey into right living. Their mental faculties were sufficient to say "No more" to addiction. They are sufficient to take them all the way. Right thinking can be ingrained into the damaged brain. It is a matter of choice by the individual. Good mental health can best be obtained by a good mind washing. The best place to wash the mind is through the Word, God's Word.

....Christ also loved the church, and gave Himself for it;
That He might sanctify and cleanse it with the washing of water by the word,
That He might present it to Himself...
Ephesians 5:25b - 27a

And be not conformed to this world:
but be ye transformed by the renewing of your mind,
that ye may prove what is that good,
and acceptable,
and perfect will of God.
Romans 12:2

Praying the Word

Create in me a clean heart, o God:
and renew a right spirit within me.
Psalm 51:10

I will sing a new song unto thee, o God... Psalm 144:9a
Great and marvelous are thy works, Lord God Almighty;
just and true are thy ways,
thou King of Saints.
Revelation 15:3b

We now understand that the counselee must take control (exercise discipline) over what they allow themselves to think. And we know it is the pastor who is going to help them learn to do this. The battleground for the addict is the mind. Whoever controls the mind, controls the heart and therefore rules behavior.

The thoughts of the wicked are an abomination unto the Lord:
but the words of the pure are pleasant words.
Proverbs 15:26

Because the carnal mind is enmity against God:
for it is not subject to the law of God,
neither indeed can be.
Romans 8:7

This I say therefore, and testify in the Lord,
that ye henceforth walk not as other Gentiles walk,
in the vanity of their mind. Ephesians 4:17
And you, that were sometimes alienated and enemies
in your mind by wicked works,
yet now hath He reconciled in the body of His flesh through death,
to present you holy and unblameable and unreproveable in His sight.
Colossians 1:21 - 22

The devil will persist in trying to gain back lost ground even after some days of sobriety. This is spiritual warfare. Do not allow the devil this pleasure.

Submit yourselves therefore to God.
Resist the devil,
and he will flee from you.
James 4:7

Teach the member to submit to God and to give their mind and thinking process over to Him. It is very hard for the recovering addict, but not impossible. Remind them that they walk a road others have walked successfully before them.

I thought on my ways,
and turned my feet unto thy testimonies.

Psalm 119:59

The thoughts of the righteous are right:
but the counsels of the wicked are deceit.

Proverbs 12:5

You must grasp the importance of helping the member deal with the mind. As a pastor, you have been able to observe the truth about sin being conceived in the mind before it is entered into by the act.

But every man is tempted,
when he is drawn away of his own lust, and enticed.
Then when lust hath conceived, it bringeth forth sin:
and sin, when it is finished, bringeth forth death.

James 1: 14-15

The first presentation of this important insight is the account of the fall of man. Before Satan could accomplish his goal in the garden, he first had to get control of their thinking. When he did that, they ceased to pay attention to God's precepts. It does not matter how much a person knows about how bad drug or alcohol abuse is if they surrender in the battle for the mind.

Pastor's Plan

II. Alcohol and Drug Use

Discipleship

Discipleship is an essential response from within the church in the battle for the mind of an individual recovering from chemical slavery. Discipleship is important to any believer who is spiritually young in the faith, but for the person coming back from chemical bondage, it should be thought of as an essential. Sunday School classes are fine. Church programs are good. But the personal involvement of someone, strong in the faith, has far greater impact than either.

A discipler or mentor is a person who is seen by the disciple as worthy of respect and response. Discipleship is a personal interaction by a mature believer within the life of a weaker, that is developed out of a loving concern and belief in the worth of the person. Both disciple and discipler have to enter into the association willingly.

One thing discipleship is not directly concerned with is the substance abuse issues of the disciple's life. That is the province of the Counselor/Pastor and the support group. This is not to say those issues do not come up or may not be discussed. It is simply not the focus of the discipling relationship.

Discipleship is directly concerned with the need of every believer to be conformed to Christ. It focuses on spiritual growth. It follows then that the relationship centers around three spiritual activities in life. These three are prayer, scripture study, and scripture application to daily life. This highly personal relationship is one of inclusion. The young believer is included in the life of the elder. The discipler does not formally preach, and teaching is done informally. Much of the discipling instruction is done by example as the disciple is included in the normal activity of the mentor. It is the personal involvement that encourages a novice to bathe in the Scriptures. He aspires to first be more like his mentor; then, he desires to be more like the Christ he sees in the mentor.

This relationship is so close that once it is formed, it will usually continue for the remainder of the people's lives. However, it will mature and change if it is successful. In the segment we call Playmates and Playgrounds we talk about former associations. These associations were important to the old life and provide a pull back to that life by the illusion of personal relationships they present. A discipler provides the reality of a one on one genuine relationship. A person who has entered into the personal relationship with a genuine discipler will find the world's illusion inadequate, henceforth. The depth of the discipling relationship is illustrated in the fact that whenever the death of a discipler occurs during the developmental period of a disciples life, (Having occurred after the bond is established) the intense mourning demonstrated by a disciple may be greater than for a family member. The great depth of this unfeigned relationship has absolutely nothing contrived about it.

The effect loss of a mentor has is so profound it serves to show the value such a person has in a life. A way of thinking about the impact of the mentor on a man's life during the developmental period can be related to the human body. A man is designed with two legs. If we think about counseling and the support group as one leg of the recovering individual, discipleship and church relationship can be thought of as the other. Lose the major muscle out of the leg and the leg collapses. A man can learn to stand and walk again, but never so well as with two solid legs. The loss of a mentor in the early stages of recovery can virtually guarantee a relapse into the addictive life. However, even then, a mentor leaves something to build on.

People in recovery need a whole lot of Jesus. This is the value of the discipler. Without the Lord Jesus, full and complete recovery is not likely. The discipler, by his very character of life helps to define what Jesus is like, as well as, guide the growth of the person who is trudging forward. While a person can fall into substance abuse like any other sin, they did not get into the involvement because they were on fire for God and responsive to the influence of the Holy Spirit on their lives. Both the fire and the influence in their lives came from somewhere else! The whole goal of Christian Counseling regarding any problem is transformation, not reformation. It just cannot be done unless the power of Christ is activated and growing in the individual. No better way to accomplish this than discipleship.

It is wise to realize that a discipler cannot be assigned. It is a mutually accepting relationship. However, a wise pastor can identify those mature men and women who have the capacity for discipleship. They can become the "Minister of Introduction", then stand back and let the Lord do His work. Developing insight into, identifying, and arranging occasion to present the two people to each other can be one of the best things you do in assisting recovery. The discipling relationship is the field where the battle for the mind is frequently won. When the mind is renewed toward God by the response of a caring person who directs in paths that center the whole man on God's Will, the whole church benefits.

Pastor's Plan

II. Alcohol and Drug Use

Encouragement

Encouragement has already been mentioned in the text. But we must face the need for encouragement as an issue. Recovering addicts need lots of encouragement. Pastors should be ready to provide this commodity to the member in their quest to remain chemical free. There will be times the member will feel hopeless, alone, forsaken, and unable to get on with a new life. It is such times as these that the pastor must encourage the member to continue on. Pastors should help the recovering addict to see, most of all, that there is hope and that they are not all alone. Most particularly, an awareness of the abiding presence of Jesus, that He is with them every step of the way of their struggle to have and maintain a life of sobriety.

Remember the theology of counseling presented at the beginning of this book. Do not mistake the need for encouragement to indicate you should be tolerant of all things. Times will come when you must be stern and firm, but even this can be an encouraging time if criticism in the form of personalization is avoided. Let the Holy Spirit do the convicting, and without sounding dogmatic, you point the way.

Often encouragement will be the determining factor whether the addict will return to his or her Proverbs 26:11 condition or choose to go forward to a chemical free life. You may be counseling with a person who is not only trying to stay free from the substance, but is at the same time coping with the loss of a wife, family, job, home, career, children, and every other thing that was once held dear. You most assuredly will be working with someone who has at least some other problems besides substance abuse in their lives. That is the nature of the problem. Discouragement, heartbrokenness, and inability to see hope of a better life can almost seem somewhat justified given the circumstances. But don't fall into the trap that attitude hides. Encouragement is good medicine. It is free. There is an unending supply in the relationship with the Lord. So give all you got.

Teach the recovering addict to encourage themselves in the Lord even as King David did. Guide the member to uplifting and encouraging Scripture verses. There is no greater encouragement to mankind than that of God's Word. Introduce your member to the praise Psalms. Help them to tap into support systems of men and women who will encourage and comfort during their discouraging times. We thank God such resources are available.

Pastor's Plan

II. Alcohol and Drug Use

Family

The user is not the only person who needs ministering to, but all those that have been directly and/or indirectly affected by the addict's conduct. Too often in recovery, the family is overlooked. Many times it is the pain of spouse, children, parents, and friends that goes unresolved. Not to include those who have been injured by the addiction is to decrease the likelihood of successful recovery. So you have a two-fold problem. You must involve the people close to the user in their recovery, while helping them recover, as well. They will be part of the solution or part of the continuing problem.

Quite often communications within the family of the addict has to be re-established. Apologies, restitution, and so forth must be made. Doing these things in a right manner cannot only heal others but help the former addict recover his self respect. Anger, bitterness, and resentment toward the user must be resolved. The unsettled conflicts are detrimental to everyone's recovery and the establishment of a healthy, wholesome family.

Recovery progress will be blocked or hindered as long as these internal conflicts are allowed to exist. The family should be encouraged to become totally committed to working as a team to establish a Christ honoring household. If possible, getting the family involved in 12 Step Support Groups is a good idea. There are a variety of such groups, and you have the tools to identify them in your Pastor's Referral Resource System.

Broken trust will only be reestablished through time and patience. Too often the person who has used chemicals has also lied and lied and lied, till truth cannot even be imagined as being part of the person's life. The family should be encouraged not to cast doubt upon the sincerity of the expressed desire to stay free. They can be the catalyst that causes relapse. It is entirely possible they were participants in triggering the abuse cycle before. So, a whole pattern of relationship must be corrected. The family must learn to express and to feel trust.

Skepticism must not be allowed to become a stumbling-block to God's accomplishment of His purpose in these lives.

It is not easy for the family to establish these patterns. Old memories must be dealt with and resolved. But forgiveness is essential to establishing trust. By the way, it is God's will that we forgive, but don't be over optimistic about how quickly this will happen. If we have a miracle, thank God, but be prepared to help the family work these things through.

Establishing the Spiritual life of the family should come early in the healing process. Encourage them to join together, with the now former abuser, in prayer, Bible study, and church attendance. Mutual involvement, as a team, in these spiritual activities will aid in mending the family. There is no damage God can't fix. Coming to the Lord with all that lies in the past should be constantly promoted. Children might be drawn to look upon the quest for relationship as a kind of challenge. Identifying what hurts in their lives, and seeing how God works, can become a king of epic adventure. This experience could build their faith and relationship with God for the rest of their lives.

Before the discussion can continue you must be introduced to two terms, Care-taker and Care-giver. For the purpose of our discussion they are as follows:
Caretaker - A person who assumes responsibilities for another. They might attempt to rescue, fix, or otherwise undertake responsibility for another person's life, problems, etc.
Caregiver - A person who might assist another to accomplish their responsibility, but who remains detached, not assuming responsibility for the other person's actions, success, failure, etc.

During the time of the using individual's addiction, the various family members very likely operated in variations of the Caretaker role. This must stop. Sobriety is ultimately the choice of the individual, so the family must realize they cannot "fix" his life. They must focus on their own lives and responsibilities. The person who used must also assume his rightful responsibilities. He cannot do this if others are doing it for him, neither can he regain self-respect necessary for recovery. Sometimes this adjustment is not easy, for the patterns of conduct have become ingrained. Being a Caregiver should be the activity of everyone within the household toward all others within the family. It will take time to re-establish roles, and you can be a stabilizing influence during this critical period.

The pastor may want to suggest or assign Christian reading material on Codependency to each family member. Several useful books are suggested in that section of the Pastor's Plan. The family must learn how to detach with love and break the habit of care-taking.

Your objective observations and guidance will be invaluable while these things are taking place in the family circle. Keep you objectivity and don't be drawn into the Caretaker role yourself.

As has already been implied, the pastor should make himself available to counsel with family members either separately or as a unit. You have to determine what is required according to the situation. Quite often the family simply needs someone they can share their pain with. They are looking for the person they can trust and confide in who has the additional quality of caring about them. You have to make yourself available, not simply be available. Minds numbed with emotional pain, just like physical pain, do not recognize what others think should be obvious. Communicate availability.

Issues arise for the family in recovery that necessitates a "listening ear" and a place to go just to be heard. People need a place to cry, to be angry, and to be sad, where a person is available they can turn to and express fears, frustrations, and disappointments. Pastor, you are the best person for the job. If the Lord is willing to hear the cries of His people, shouldn't His servant also have a willing ear and a sympathetic heart? Lock on the expression "a place to go to". Depending on your preference and the need, two good places to meet are your home and the church office. Whatever the setting selected as most appropriate to the persons, a location away from the members home represents a temporary escape in itself.

Throughout this text, we refer to instruction in maintaining a positive attitude. You should instruct the family in principles of developing and maintaining a positive attitude as lifestyle. It is not enough to say, "Well, you need to have a more positive attitude." They don't know how to have that positive attitude and such statements will kill what you are trying to do. Instead, teach them about biblical attitudes of mindset, and discuss the ramifications of those attitudes and how to apply them to life. The individual will have to work to bring them into application in their lives. They will only be as successful as the effort they put into dealing with their problems in a right direction. But, there is no place for negative attitudes in recovery. At the risk of sounding like a broken record, I can't emphasize enough the value of getting them to ingest God's Word.

Hereby perceive we the love of God,
because He laid down His life for us:
and we ought to lay down our lives for the brethren.
1 John 3:16

Pastor's Plan

II. Alcohol and Drug Use

Education

We have already said the recovering addict needs to be educated about the destructiveness of their condition and how to recover. The Twelve Step Program and your personal attention are the vehicles of accomplishing that education. Likewise, the battle for the mind has already been touched on in its spiritual dimension, and we have surveyed your role from that perspective. Both the physical and spiritual dangers of returning to abuse need to be brought out as part of educating to increase chances of success and lessen chances of setbacks and failures.

The pastor should always have on hand Christian oriented books and other materials that can be given, or at the very least, know where such materials can be purchased. Another suggestion is to use Christian video and audio material. It is an investment that pays in this day of declining readers. Also, videos stimulate both the ears and the eyes, as well. Good visual presentations are always particularly good at improving retention of content.

A plethora of materials exist on virtually every subject related to the human condition. Alcohol and drug dependency is no less blessed, or cursed, depending on your point of view and what book you pick up.

In this book we don't want to be redundant by repeatedly saying do not recommend what you haven't read. And we don't want you to think merely having read the text and finding it gave a nod to Christianity is sufficient grounds to justify endorsement. Selection of materials may require as much wisdom as anything else you have to do in counseling. Of course, you see in our recommendations certain preferences of materials. These are based on experience. What you might not apprehend is that within these books are sections more appropriate for one person than another. Some portions of materials may have little or no value for some people. Familiarity with materials and the counselee enable you to skip portions of materials that are not useful or not useful at the time. Lack of familiarity will directly effect how you carry out your Pastor's Plan.

Other books and videos that we do not recommend here may be good. Many will not be. Common sense and discernment with a spiritual vision can weed out many bad or poor books. Be selective. People are depending on you.

Education is not aimed merely at the recovering addict. You have possibly already surmised the family has need of education, too. It could be that you have not really thought of what you are doing in terms of it being education, but it is. The great Commission is centered around teaching, and great pastors teach the people God gives to them.

> *And He gave some, apostles; and some, prophets; and some, evangelists; and some, pastors and teachers;**
> *for the perfecting of the saints,*
> *for the work of the ministry,*
> *for the edifying of the body of Christ:*
> ***Ephesians 4: 11-12***

Within this text we have touched on some of the issues that might be needful to cover in counseling. Each person is an individual, however, and you must minister to each according to his or her need. This is another reason you should study these various books we recommend as a minimum. The knowledge you gain will help you to identify a need when it is being displayed.

Sometimes the process of education can be carried on in groups. It is possible that information on addiction and recovery can be presented to the family of a person seeking recovery at the same time he is being exposed to it. The use of audio and video tapes then becomes a tool to involve the family as a unit and bring them together. The right kind of family involvement can be a key to success. The medium of education has become nearly as important in such a case as the content.

In the above situation we can also see the importance of controlling the people environment, as well. In the case of group involvement, particularly with family members, condemning speeches and 'you' statements are banned beforehand. Family or other types of group discussion of the information can help bring people together.

When you went to school, homework was not unheard of. It exists in the educational portion of counseling, too. Don't be afraid to assign homework and hold people accountable for its completion. They are already responsible for practicing what they discover in counseling sessions. Have them report what they learn using the educational materials you assign.

One individual with a long history of DUIs and failures, after many alcohol programs, revealed that a key problem in his life was anger. One area anger was expressed several times related to a childhood experience where adult responsibility and conduct was expected. It became clear that the child had been responsible for the good conduct of the other children in his very dysfunctional family. Now an intelligent, middle-aged man, he was given an assignment to write about his childhood and put on paper an account of the very unpleasant events that continued to plague him. His "homework" was the basis of viewing the childhood experiences with a clear perspective. He needed to say, "I am not a black sheep who failed as a child! I am not going to be the victim of guilt over failing my family, nor will I be a victim of my anger at the unfairness of the standard my parents imposed on me anymore!" Everybody knows a black sheep can't help but fail. Losing the black sheep mentality was for him a step (one step, but a big step) to deliverance from recurring alcohol abuse.

Pastor's Plan

II. Alcohol and Drug Use

Set-backs and Relapses

Unfortunately, set-backs and relapses can and do occur. This happens in the lives of people who do ultimately gain the victory, and pastors should be aware that this does happen. It may occur with the person you are working with. A set-back or relapse, alone, should never be a reason to give up on the person; it is often part of the recovery process. When it happens, it does not mean they are not trying to stay sober and chemical free.

If you have anticipated that this might occur, (without actually encouraging it) you will not be overwhelmed when it occurs and can turn the occasion into an opportunity to explore and identify triggers that may have led to the episode. While we know that God would rather we did not falter, it is certainly His Will that we learn from our mistakes.

It is very easy to be critical and judgmental in response to the member's failure at the time of a relapse or set-back. However, it is no time to do so. The pastor can set the example for the family and the church by encouraging them to grow closer to God and each other. Learn from the experience. This stage is a lot like when a child is learning to walk. If we were to measure the child's progress by the number of times they fell, we would see the problem as hopeless and end up giving up on the child.

When we fail as ministers or in anything else, we do not, cannot, just give up. We pick ourselves up, brush ourselves off, and try again. What do we do when others fall? We encourage them to try again. Just because this is a particularly unpleasant condition does not mean that, here, we should do any less. God provides people a means of escape from sinful actions. You are very likely a part of that means of escape.

In the section on alcohol and drugs, the term "triggers" has been used several times. It is important that you understand the term because you need to be able to recognize them when they occur. We define triggers as things that provoke us to such a degree that we take action. The action response to a trigger can be either healthy or unhealthy depending on the situation and the response. In relation to the addict, a trigger confronts him again with his need to choose whether to respond in the old pattern of surrender to his thorn in the flesh or not. Some of the most common triggers are the same sort of things commonly found in depressed people's environments. Surrendered to, they lead to set-backs and relapses. Frequently, someone close to the member knows just exactly what will trigger them. They may be experiencing in their own lives an anxiety of anticipation, expecting a relapse. Consciously or not they engage the trigger and relieve the tension they are experiencing momentarily. That momentary release of anticipatory tension is a relapse for the addicted. Identifying the trigger and making the appropriate corrections often means not only educating the person in recovery, but several others close to him. Be prepared, people who are exercising triggers harmful to someone they love, when confronted, will often be very vehement in their denial. Be patient in explaining the issue and understand that it may take more than one session for the truth to sink in.

You are familiar with triggers, but you may not recognize it by that term. Often an unregenerate man with a church going wife of aggressive spirit finds himself confronted when the pastor comes to visit. These kinds of wives usually like to get the new pastor early on. When the man of God arrives, the woman might say something like, "You tell him pastor! I've tried to, but he just won't listen to me!" Every pastor with experience knows that at this point he might as well pack up and leave as far as the man of the house is concerned. The husband just got triggered into being as closed minded to the preacher as he is to his wife. It is now time to acquaint the woman in that situation with 1 Peter 3:1 through 6. That is what you have to do when confronted with triggers in other situations. Acquaint people with the facts. But do it in love.

In summary, assisting and ministering in recovery is not an easy task. Pastors who do so must take steps to eliminate any factors that threaten victory for the lives affected. It requires patience, patience, patience. So don't give up with the little set-backs and relapses. Hang in there and try again.

Pastor's Plan

II. Alcohol and Drug Use

Playmates and Playgrounds

Avoiding wrong influences is a must to recovery. The story is told of Saint Augustine, after his conversion, he was confronted by one of his former female partners in the previous licentious lifestyle he lived. She called out to him on the street. He began walking in the opposite direction. She followed him calling out several more times, all the while having to increase pace not to lose him. Finally she said, "Augustine; it is I!" He then, while breaking into a dead run shouted back, "Yes, but it is not I." The pastor, working with people in recovery must teach their client to have the attitude of an Augustine. They are not, do not want to be again, the person they were.

Helping the individual to understand the old drinking and drug using buddies have a vested interest in his failure to go all the way is a must. If he views these old associations correctly, then he will comprehend his chemical free state is an indictment of their lives. If he fails then that justifies their continuing to be failures in their own lives. Especially during the first months of recovery, the former addict is particularly vulnerable. For some, this period of vulnerability can be very long.

> *Wherefore let him that thinketh he standeth take heed lest he fall.*
>
> ***1Corinthians 10:12***

While not wanting to create someone who is dependent on you or lacking in self-confidence, you must discourage over-confidence in the ability to resist temptation. People are often duped into believing they can still enjoy old associations and succeed. Next, they start to think they can indulge once for "old times sake" or "have one for the road". Church covenants which speak against any use were already ignored by the abusing member, and might be completely unknown to a person saved while a user. If you can help the individual to see his former cronies as tools of the devil, and their friendship as lacking in the basic essential of true friendship, the Lord Jesus Christ, you go a long way toward helping them avoid pitfalls along the way to recovery.

Foster an understanding in the member's mind that it was one drink, one pill, one joint that got them into trouble in the first place. They must realize they can never use any chemical at all with impunity. And, the closest of old associations are the most dangerous to his new life. Encourage the former addict to be direct in telling his old friends he must avoid associating with them until they have ceased their own self-abusive activities and get into a recovery program. This is not an issue they should debate with old relationships, but just make plain.

Help the member always remember that misery loves company, and he is the only one with any good news. Have them restate aloud and often, "A true friend would never invite their friend to become involved in the sin of chemical use." This will help them prepare to say the same words when they are approached as was Augustine. They will be!

Encourage the development of a new set of friends. Probably they were not close with people in the church, if they were church members before entering into recovery. New friends should be people who have met Jesus in the free pardon of sin, and who are living a chemical free life.

Now that we understand that a person in recovery needs to change playmates, it is not hard to go the next step and understand the importance of changing playgrounds. Returning to the drug and alcohol infested environment is what a sow does after she is cleaned up and allowed to get back in the sty. She lays down in the mud and filth and wallows.

> *Beloved,*
> *follow not that which is evil,*
> *but that which is good.3 John 1:11*
> *Abhor that which is evil;*
> *cleave to that which is good.*
> ***Romans 12:9***

People, when converted, need to be taught that no one who claims the name of Christ should be "hanging out" in places that do not bring honor and glory to the Lord. Changing both playgrounds and playmates is not unique to abusers, it is just more visibly needful for them. If they can stay keenly aware of the folly of setting themselves up for a fall, the need to hang-out can be satisfied in an active church's activities and a Christian twelve-step group. In these places, new relationships can be formed among people who have a common bond, gratitude to the Lord who delivered them from the bondage of sin. These people now share a common goal, glorifying the Lord in the conduct of their lives, which for your client means a life of sobriety.

The pastor should never minimize in his own mind the necessity of monitoring the member's associations and environments (playmates and playgrounds). The member should understand the right of the pastor to question his activities in the counseling environment. It is merely an extension of the right he has by virtue of being pastor in the first place. This may not be a popular subject in today's church filled with so much distaste for authority. But that does not change its rightness or scriptural foundation.

> *Obey them that have the rule over you,*
> *and submit yourselves;*
> *for they watch for your souls, as they that must give account,*
> *that they may do it with joy, and not with grief:*
> *for that is unprofitable for you.*
> **Hebrews 13:17**

The individual who has come to you for help and gone this far into the recovery process now resenting your inquiries into his lifestyle probably is reacting guiltily because something is wrong and they don't want you to know it. Having established that accountability early in the recovery process makes it easier to maintain all the way to a successful conclusion.

Pastor's Plan

II. Alcohol and Drug Use

When Enough is Enough

Up to now you have been encouraged to continue working with an individual in spite of setbacks. Do not make the mistake of seeing this segment as contradictory to what has gone on before, but we have to acknowledge that sometimes the pastor has to postpone further assistance.

As long as genuine effort is going into recovery by the individual the pastor, once committed, must continue to minister to the person. But, when strong evidence plainly demonstrates the commitment to recovery does not exist, the individual must be confronted and clearly informed that help has been withdrawn until he shows you a reason to invest your time.

Does what we say sound harsh? It is not at all unkind. In this treatise we have emphasized how peculiarly obvious choice is in this type of affliction. You have been told the individual must be held responsible for his actions. This responsibility, we have seen, must be required of him, both by you and his family. If someone in his family circle was deliberately interfering with his progress, you would confront them and hold them accountable for their actions. To do less with the user when he is demonstrably insincere and uncommitted, is to agree with the mindset that he is incapable or unable to achieve victory. You actually do damage to any hopes he has of future recovery.

Pastors have a tendency to feel guilty about detaching themselves from a situation. They should not. A very true old-time expression was; "There are some folks you just can't help." And there are some who can't be helped, yet. So often the individual has to see himself at rock bottom before he can get serious. It is not enough to know the need of dealing with a problem for the commitment to action to take place.

The mentality of delaying until the crisis comes is part of the human condition. Everyone knows a homeowner who delayed replacing an aging roof till water leaks ruined his ceiling, I suppose. The same attitude causes people to delay receiving Christ till it's too late, and it causes people to delay dealing with problems in their lives. Pastor, you are too busy ministering to souls than to waste your time standing by, losing time, while one is toying with the idea of getting serious.

The individual who has come to you complete with participating family has not been completely abandoned when you detach yourself from his recovery. You will be continuing to be involved in the family's progress. They must understand, and it will probably be very obvious, the reason for your action. Sometimes the family needs to detach, too. Don't misunderstand, divorce is not in our proposal. But physical and emotional well-being can demand separation. Sadly, help from government agencies to the family might depend on such detachment taking place. If the family ever reaches such a decision, it must be their own. But if they do, they will need you more than ever.

How do you know it is time to bail-out? We have already discussed the fact that a recovering user may experience a set-back. Perhaps they will go through more than one. There is no cause for alarm at this point. You encourage the individual to return to his program of recovery recognizing it is not at all uncommon for a person in recovery to attempt to use again. That is information you do not share with the individual because you are not in the business of providing excuses. Even in the pulpit you seldom find it expedient to tell all you know. Two, even three set-backs may occur, but when they become a pattern and you have eliminated triggers, no way!

Another point about knowing when it is time to bail out is when the individual continually and willfully returns to associations that lead to setbacks when no need whatever exists for them to do so. Especially where a profession of faith in Christ is concerned, such a pattern is contradictory to desire or genuine intent to be an overcomer.

> *But it is happened unto them according to the true proverb,*
> *The dog is turned to his own vomit again;*
> *and the sow that was washed to her wallowing in the mire.*
> ***2 Peter 2:22***

> *As a dog returneth to his vomit,*
> *so a fool returneth to his folly.*
> ***Proverbs 26:11***

When a person falters, who has made a profession of faith in the Lord Jesus Christ, they need to be introduced to the concept of the authority the Lord has over their situation. They need to know that a way always exists. You might even discuss possible ways out of failure situations (ways of escape).

There hath no temptation taken you
but such as is common to man:
but God is faithful,
who will not suffer you to be tempted
above that ye are able;
but will with the temptation
also make a way to escape,
that ye may be able to bear it.
1 Corinthians 10:13

When they continually go back after receiving the truth, the only answer can be is that they want to. It's a matter of choice. Ezekiel clearly outlined the necessity and limitation of warning in chapter 3. Warn the person who has a setback of their three choices:

1. They can continue to sin and die.
2. They can continue to sin and live miserably till they die.
3. They can quit the sin and live a chemical free, productive life.

The cycle of re-detoxification (or less sever drying out), going on to pick up the pieces, restarting assistance, and discovering what else is new in the equation from the last fall can become a game the user puts you through. If the pattern develops or if the person insists on having things their way in the recovery program, (rejecting accountability) it is likely that they are not serious. The client is responsible for his actions, not you. Don't play games with him. Nobody has ever succeeded in overcoming addiction, whether drugs or alcohol, without facing up to their responsibility and accountability. They must make the choice, not you.

Behold we count them happy which endure.
James 5:11a

Let him know,
that he which converteth the sinner from the error of his way
shall save a soul from death,
and shall hide a multitude of sins.
James 5:20

Pastor's Plan

II. Alcohol and Drug Use

Drug & Alcohol Recovery

Things To Do List

1. Exercise - (Moderate) After medical clearance.
2. Involvement in Support Group (At least 2-3 meetings weekly)
3. Proper rest and relaxation.
4. Regular and nutritional eating habits.
5. Regular church attendance.
6. Daily Bible Reading and Study (Select encouraging scripture and record)
7. Stay in counseling (Christian only)
8. Involvement in hobbies and/or sports. (Choose what you like)
9. Education - Reading material on addiction.
10. Refrain from associating with former abusing friends.
11. Refrain from going where alcohol/drugs are served (parties, etc.)
12. Maintain a positive attitude/Avoid hanging with negative people.
13. Make amends - Go to people wronged. Apologize/make restitution.
14. Work on codependency and self esteem issues, coming out of counseling.
15. Establish an accountability friendship with one or two persons.
16. Express-Establish accountability relationship for expression.
17. Socialize-Do not isolate yourself.
18. Assume total responsibility for your sobriety and daily living.

Pastor's Plan

II. Alcohol and Drug Use

Resources:

Booklet Recommended: *Learning More About Chemical Dependency*

Authored by:Robert D. McGee

Published by:Word Publishing
Dallas

This booklet is the primer for anyone wishing to have a grasp on what Alcohol & Drug problems are really all about. We would recommend reading this booklet as a key to understanding the basis for guidance we provide the counseling pastor on the issue.

We use this booklet, also, as a teaching tool for those entering into recovery, people whose lives are impacted by the substance usage of friends and family, and for equipping workers in prison ministry.

The value of the booklet is demonstrated in the titles of its seven short chapters:
Why Does A Person Abuse Alcohol and/or Drugs
Stages of Addiction
Symptoms of Chemical Dependency
Experiencing Recovery
Trusting In Christ
Your Role
Stages of Acceptance

The material in the booklet will provide the basis for understanding how broad the impact of chemical dependency is on people. It will encourage you to exercise the patience necessary to guide people through the recovery process.

Pastor, in preparing to help others you would do well to take the Fear of Rejection or Failure Test on pages 6 & 7. Have your wife also take the test. Then the two of you swap roles and answer the test as if you were taking it for your mate. Now score the results of all the tests. Compare your answers about yourself with those of your mate answering for you. Read the score key. On a separate sheet of paper analyze what you have learned about yourself.

An additional use of the Fear of Rejection and Failure Test can be realized in teaching a class on standing up as a Christian. When dealing with worldly influence and pressures to compromise, the test yields the student a better understanding of their own susceptibility to being pressured into conformance with the group.

Minister's Notes:

Workbook Recommended: *Rapha's 12 Step Program For Overcoming Chemical Dependency*

Authored by:Robert S. McGee, Pat Springle, Susan Joiner

Published by:Rapha Publishing
Dallas

Every person in recovery, with little exception, should be encouraged to work through this workbook as part of their program for success.

The comparison of the alcoholics Anonymous Twelve Step on page vii with the Rapha on ix and x quickly reveals why any pastor should choose the Rapha over the AA. The Twelve Steps of the Rapha program are the chapters of the book. The last step may be called the Great Commission of the Chemical Overcomer. It is the call to carry the Good News of God's deliverance to those still in chemical bondage.

Reviewing this material as the recovering member goes through it can be an integral part of the counseling process. It will open up issues that need to be addressed in the person's life. It will also give you an understanding of whether a person is genuinely participating in their recovery or playing at it.

An example of insights that might be gained about the counselee from reviewing his workbook that can be used to help them consists of taking the chart responses on attitudes toward God, father, and mother and comparing them on one chart. The counselee can see how much of a role parenting played in his attitudinal development. You will be amazed how much that they tell you in counseling will correlate with what shows up on a combined chart.

The combined chart can also reveal where the individual might have already developed some strengths that can be capitalized upon. Religious instruction or discipleship may have benefited, separating the relationship between God and parental attitudes that exist in a negative frame of thought.

You may also find strengths in the family relationship that are covered up by bitterness or anger in the client. Since the client needs to develop a positive and rational response to these people as part of recovery, this information can give you a basis for building. This one facet of the workbook makes it worthwhile, but it will provide much, much more.

Minister's Notes:

Book Recommended:	*God Is For The Alcoholic*
Authored by:	Jerry Dunn
Published by:	Moody Press Chicago

The book is a gold mine of insight into the alcoholic's problem, written by someone who has been there and has come back. It is very descriptive with case histories and personal testimony. It is not a goody-goody account in the sense of happy endings abounding in unbelievable progression. The book is full of the pathos of destroyed human lives. These losses are given purpose because they demonstrate and help us to understand why these tragedies took place. The book also recounts success and how it is achieved, beginning with Salvation in Christ.

In part one the discussion on alcohol's effect on the human bodies' basic structure lends insight into why alcohol is so insidious. The reader will understand from then on why a twenty year abstainer must not think he can indulge in so much as a single beer. Realizing that God designed the human physiognomy; the apparent contradiction between God's deliverance and continuing susceptibility that perplexes so many Christians is resolved.

This book not only deals with the situations experienced by the alcoholic, but it touches on the lives of family, particularly spouses, and the roles they play in success and failure. The counselor's attitude in the relationship is also not neglected. The emphasis on long term commitment and patience is emphasized.

The pastor will come to appreciate the need and value of support groups in aiding him to enjoy success in helping people who hurt escape from the scourge of alcohol.

Minister's Notes: ____

____

____

____

Pastor's Plan

III. Codependency

Learning More About Codependency by Pat Springle
Close Enough to Care by Pat Springle
Codependency by Pat Springle

Pastor's Plan

III. Codependency

Defined

Codependency has become more popular and more talked about than the common cold. Seems like everybody's got it, too. Truth is, most do. Codependency has caught up with America and is now taking its toll. The condition was basically unrecognized for years, and generation after generation of codependents have been raised. The problem is now lying at our door. What is this codependency stuff anyway, you may ask? Well....that's another problem.

Not only do most Americans have it. Everybody has a different definition for it. For example: Some define codependency as a need to control others. Others emphasize a need to be controlled. People pleasing; feeling responsible to make others happy; the need to control the behavior of others are all within the scope of codependent definitions. But the definition I like best is an "adult child". This term is used or incorporated into the definitions used by many counselors. It is my personal preference because it is the best all around description of a codependent and one we will give special attention to.

Codependents are the individuals who often feel responsible for everyone's life but their own. They are the ones who seek to make everybody happy, control everybody's life, take on other's responsibility, and the story goes on and on. Sounds like an adult child, doesn't it? With all this said, it is still hard to nail down just what a codependent is. For the purpose of condensing and clarity, we will further define codependency as "emotional immaturity".

The truth is, all the negative behavior we have alluded to is the direct result of emotional immaturity. That's why we say codependents are adult children. It has often been remarked that codependents are people who live in big people's bodies, drive big peoples cars, and live in big people's houses, but who have not become big people emotionally. Have we given you two definitions? Maybe. But one thing is absolutely certain. The type of behavior we have been discussing is not the way God wants us to live.

Brethren, be not children in understanding:
Howbeit in malice be ye children,
but in understanding be men.
1 Corinthians 14: 20

Why, you may ask, would anyone put themselves in a position to be codependent? The truth of the matter is, people are sometimes born into environments that predispose them toward codependent behavior. Others acquire the behavior out of a need to be loved and affirmed as worthwhile. The unhealthy involvement in various types of manipulative behavior is the direct result of unfulfilled needs in their lives. The behavior they indulge in gives them a sense of worth for a time. That's why they do it. Every human needs these basic needs met, but going about getting it in the wrong way never quite satisfies. The codependent returns again and again to their private feelings of being unloved and worthless.

The acts of allowing others to depend on them is how they prove they are lovable and how they, too, have value. The need leads to the compulsion. People pleasing is a term that has been around for years. A codependent can often be very well described as a people pleaser. People pleasing in the codependent can result in the loss of identity to the point the person is no longer sure who they really are. They are whoever or whatever everyone else wants them to be. They are dependent on other people's acceptance and approval for the sense of value they place on themselves. It only stands to reason that anyone who continually sacrifices themselves to be what other persons want them to be will ultimately lose their identity. They would have to. People pleasing comes with a very high price tag.

As you can see, such a person has a very unhealthy view of responsibility. Being involved so deeply in caring for other people's lives, they neglect their own. Eventually pastor, they knock on your door! Usually the pain, frustration, guilt, anger, etc. becomes such a burden they can no longer bear the load. At this point, they can see what they are doing does not and will not work. They can't stand the self-delusion that it will one day meet their needs no longer. They need help! They need the acceptance and approval of Jesus in their lives, and pastor, they need you!

When the codependent person comes to you for help for this problem, whatever they were doing to meet their needs is not working any longer at all. They do not know what the problem is usually, but they do know that whatever it is, it needs attention. Codependency does not only cause pain, it is pain. The codependent is tired. They are exhausted from expending so much energy trying to feel all right about themselves.

While codependents have been busy trying to control others and very often being controlled by others, they have been under the control of their codependent problem. Do you see now how appropriate the terms adult child and emotional immaturity are to describe what is taking place in the person's life? Immaturity is not alleviated by simply telling a person to grow up. People grow up emotionally by learning how to be adult in thoughts and actions. Those are learned behaviors the codependent must acquire in a growing process:

Casting down imaginations,
and every high thing that exalteth itself against the knowledge of God,
and bringing into captivity every thought to the obedience of Christ;

2 Corinthians 10:5

If so be that ye have heard Him,
and have been taught by Him,
as the truth is in Jesus:
That ye put off concerning the former conversation the old man,
which is corrupt according to the deceitful lusts;
And be renewed in the spirit of your mind;
And that ye put on the new man,
which after God is created in righteousness
and true holiness.

Ephesians 4:21-24

He that passeth by,
and meddleth with strife belonging not to him,
is like one that taketh a dog by the ears.
As a madman who casteth firebrands, arrows, and death.

Proverbs 26:17&18

Pastor's Plan

III. Codependency

Signs & Symptoms

Quick Look Sheet*

1. Does the member exhibit poor self-image?

2. Does the member express feelings of inferiority?

3. Are there indications of addictions? Drugs/alcohol/sex/food/etc.

4. Is the member always in need of approval from others? Spouse/parent/etc.

5. Does the member express feelings of guilt when forced to say no?

6. Is the member oversensitive to what people say or do?

7. Is the member unable to maintain healthy relationships?(Often avoids intimacy)

8. Does the member believe love, acceptance, affirmation must be earned?

9. Does the member have an inability to identify feelings?

10. Is the member unable to express feelings such as anger, fear, happiness, etc.?

11. Does the member have an inability or a problem in expressing self?

12. Does the member feel unloved, rejected?

13. Has the member a fear of being abandoned?(By God and others)

14. Does the member suffer from illogical guilt or shame?

15. Is there a lack of objectivity?

16. Does the member exhibit perfectionist tendencies?

17. Does the member see everything as good or bad? (Black & White Syndrome?)

18. Has the member expressed a sense of responsibility for other people's behavior?

19. Does the member demonstrate a compulsion to be needed?

20. Does the member exhibit difficulty in decision making?

21. Does the member have an extreme fear of failure?

22. Does the member display constant attempts to rescue or fix other's problems?

23. Has the member a need to be controlled or to be controlling? (Control of behavior or emotions of someone else)

24. Is there a lack of identity?

25. Has the member a fear of others? (Uncomfortable out of his area)

26. Is there a fear of conflict with others?

27. Does he express feelings of unproductivity? (Not getting things done even with effort)

28. Does the member express the belief that self worth hinges on what he has or who he is?

29. Is the member self-centered?

30. Does the member need to be the center of attention?

31. Does the member have feelings of loneliness?

32. Does the member express depression?

33. Does the member express /display grandiosity? (Wildly unrealistic dreams of success or recognition)

34. Is the member unable to accept constructive criticism without attaching strong feeling?

35. Does the member exhibit signs of compulsive behavior? (Not listed above)

37. Does the member display manipulative behavior to get needs met? (Pouting, self-pity, anger to get control of others)

38. Does the member exhibit responsibility for things clearly the responsibility of others?

39. Does the member display attitude that his happiness must come from others or that theirs is dependent on him?

**We regret signs and symptoms must be fairly long for a quick check, but the need for thoroughness requires this minimum list. You will note many facets of Codependent Behavior border on Personality Disorder.*

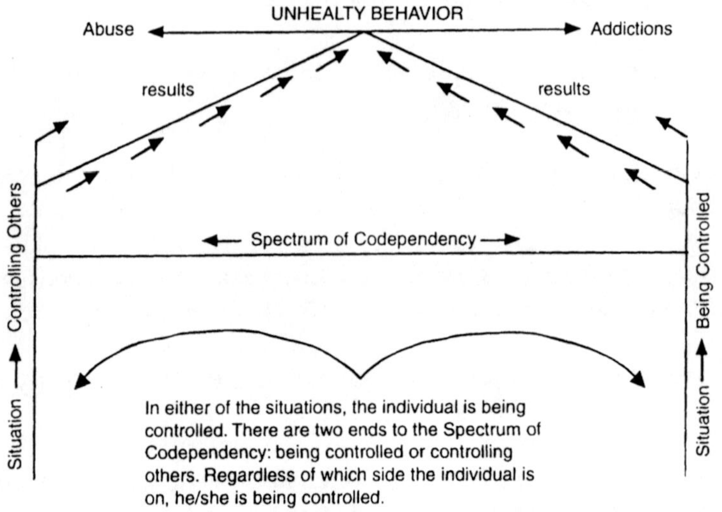

SPECTRUM OF CODEPENDENCY

Pastor's Plan

III. Codependency

Causes

The primary causes of codependency are well demonstrated in the codependency illustration. Studying it will give you insight into what codependency is and how it reveals itself. As can be seen, the condition is primarily a direct result of the dysfunctional home. However, to stop with that assertion would be unfair and certainly incorrect. It is better to say that codependency is contributed to by a dysfunctional environment. This encompasses not only the home, but other environments, as well. Educational settings, work places, various kinds of peer groups, and associations can produce codependency. It goes without saying though, that it is the home where an individual spends the majority of his or her time. It is here the bondage of codependency (emotional immaturity) generally gets its initial grip. It is for this reason we will focus on the home environment and its contribution to codependency in this discussion.

Focusing on the home by no means excludes other sources which contribute in the development of codependency, but it offers the best practical approach. The dysfunctional home does not contribute properly to growth and development for the growing child, therefore the end product is the emotionally under-developed adult. It stands to reason if you place a newborn child in a pasture with cows for sensory input, over a period of time it would learn to eat grass and moo. On the other hand, a child placed in a pen with dogs would over time learn to bark and growl. I said that to emphasize how much we are the product of our environment. If the environment is healthy, the likelihood of a healthy adult is almost assured. On the other hand, an unhealthy environment would more likely produce an unhealthy adult.

What is the dysfunctional home? We might say a home is dysfunctional when it does not provide the basic essentials needed to grow emotionally mature adults. The essentials needed for such growth are love, communication, acceptance, affirmation, positive self-concept, honesty, and understanding. Other things might be added to the list, but they would only further refine the point that people need to feel valued as much as they need to eat in order to live. When a person develops the traits of codependency it is certain that at least some of the needed essentials are absent.

When codependent symptoms show up, more often than not there are also addictions present. This does not mean just alcohol and drug addictions either. You may also find some kind of abuse and or general neglect and abandonment. That is just the kinds of things that also help produce the codependent in the first place. It is virtually impossible for an individual to develop properly in such an environment. The person growing up in a dysfunctional environment is more concerned in his inmost processes with survival than he should have to be as a child, leaving insufficient energy for emotional growth and development. God's Word makes it clear that we become like what we are exposed to:

We have sinned with our fathers,
We have committed iniquity,
We have done wickedly.

Psalm 106:6

It is very difficult for anyone to break the bondage of habit and thought patterns formed in the early developmental stages of life. That is why it is not enough for a home to merely be "Christian". It must live out the dynamics of the principles of God's Word daily in order to raise well-adjusted human beings who are capable of living to the Praise of His Glory. There is an old joke about the pastor's kids being so mean because they play with the deacon's kids. Too often, spiritual leaders are so busy taking care of God's business that they forget their first business for God is taking care of their own house. And, if it is so hard to be successful in an established Christian home, what is the situation for those who are not raised in the faith?

The above scripture reminds me of the numbers of young men suffering from alcoholism who have confessed they began their lives of drink with their fathers. These extreme situations, so common, illustrate a very important point. While the dysfunctional home can be said to provide the elements that produce an unhealthy codependent individual, the greater the degree of dysfunctionality in the home, the more intensely codependent its product is likely to be. A home missing ten basic elements needed for proper growth and development is compared to a home missing only three. Of the two which environment is likely to be least congenial to a good self-image? It's not hard to figure out which environment will produce the greater degree of codependency.

All human beings have a need to be raised in a loving, caring, affirming, sharing, trusting, communicating, understanding environment. Anything less produces an under-developed product. A codependent individual. People grow up feeling unloved, abandoned, guilty, shameful, and worthless because what they needed to affirm them in those areas was missing. They are without the everyday skills to handle life in general in a healthy manner. Varying as to extremes, they are today's depressed, alcoholics, drug users, abusers, overeaters, divorcees, workaholics, emotional wrecks, and mentally stressed. They are today's adult children.

It is amazing, but true, that the codependent living in a haze of self-abasement also lives with the pain of feeling responsible for everybody's problems. They do not know why they are unlovable and unaccepted, but if they can just fix someone else's problem, or measure up to someone else's standard then....they feel like a misfit. In success the hidden thought is, "If those around me really knew how I really am....."they feel unproductive. They feel as if they never quite fit in. They are without identity. It got lost somewhere in all the confusion. If you want to discover why an individual is what he is, look where he came from.

We are ready to further refine our pinpointing of cause now. It is not exactly fair to say the dysfunctional environment causes codependency. It merely fails to provide the needed essentials for growth and development. So, the individual is left to seek other ways of getting their needs met. Methods used to meet basic needs are often people pleasing, manipulating, performance for recognition, controlling other people's lives, etc. It is through these and other unhealthy means the dysfunctional individual seeks basic types of realization necessary to survival.

Over a period of time, unhealthy methods of meeting basic needs become so ingrained that they become a way of life. The sad thing is these methods are not only unhealthy, but short-lived. They may work sometimes, but not all the time. They may bring temporary relief, but not permanent relief. Over and over again the individual goes through the cycle of striving for fulfillment only to end up empty-handed and still codependent.

One reason for the emergence of codependency as a big problem in this generation may be connected with what has happened with the family itself in the past two generations. The industrial revolution began the process of damage to the family structure. But the redirection of the American dream toward material affluence began after World War II, when women stayed in the work place instead of returning to the less-exalted status of homemaker. Gone was the affirmation of feelings, self-worth and belonging, fostered by former relationships with grandparents, mother, father, and other relations, so integral a part of the traditional family. Relations were often separated by many miles and types of work. Family intimacy lost its former focus as a new term, "latch-key kid", was coined. Mom was no longer at home to bond with her children. Dad might be commuting several hours a day, in addition to working long hours. He did not feel like fooling with the kids when he got home. Male and female roles began being blurred, causing further loss of identity. To this mix, external influences like the educational system deciding its purpose was to be a medium of social change, instead of education, really boiled the pot.

In this context of turmoil, problems within various family social hierarchies found a fertile ground to become more pronounced in their impact. A father who had been raised roughly in past years had the ameliorating influence of social interaction with his dad on the farm and at family and church functions. This was gone. Now the rough dad did not interact in any other way except discipline because his hours were spent away from home or in activities that isolated him from children. No chance for affirmation existed, only times of criticism and punishment. The rough dad's son became the abusing father. Dysfunctional himself, an even more codependent child has been produced. Some come for help.

The above is only one example of how the scenario is played out even unto the third and fourth generations, but suffice it to say, the problem is more the norm than the exception, today.

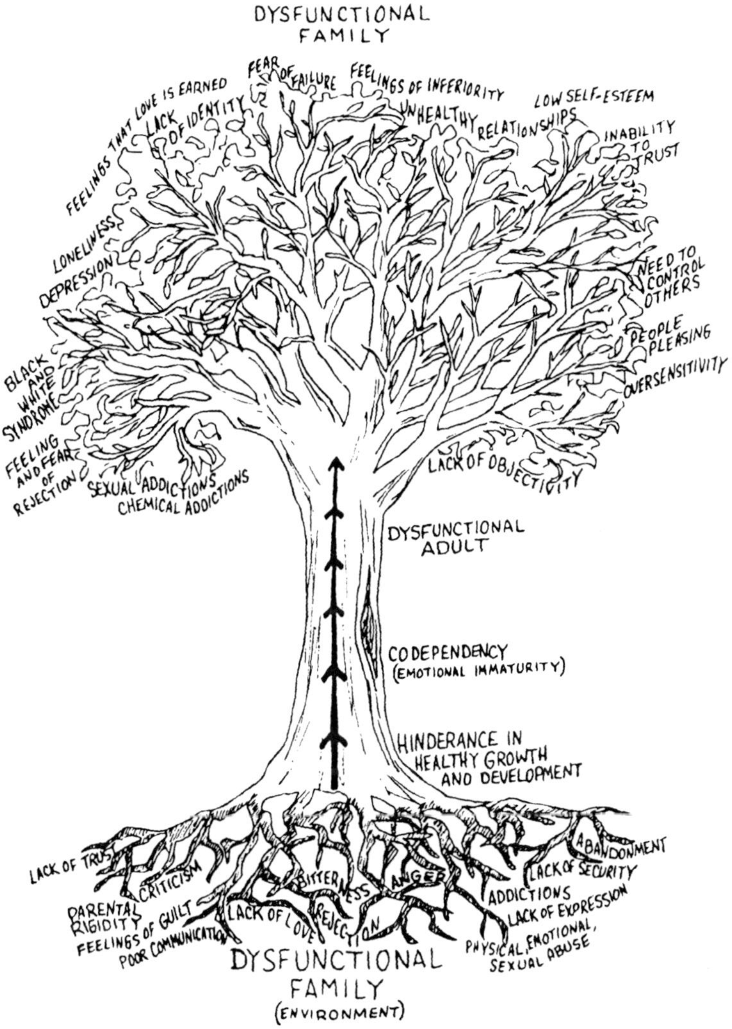

DYSFUNCTIONAL FAMILY TREE

Pastor's Plan

III. Codependency

Fundamental of Recovery

Salvation and Surrender

Codependency does not just go away. As a matter of fact, it is progressive. Unless help is sought and solutions implemented in lives, the problem is likely to worsen. Sadly, there are no quick cures and fast solutions. Overcoming codependency takes time, patience, and a lot of work. The longer a person practices codependent behavior, the greater the intensity of problem it causes and, consequently, the corresponding need for care. The first and foremost need of every person suffering from codependency is Jesus. Without the power of Christ in their lives, their situation is absolutely hopeless. Codependency issues might be called foundational to virtually every other emotional problem. Christ and Christ alone delivers from the slavery of codependency. Directing people to Jesus, even those who proclaim their salvation, is the first step for obtaining freedom from this bondage. Lordship must be established. With accountability and responsibility in life focused solely on Jesus, new freedom is discovered from all the false holds that had laid claim upon the hurting member's life.

Superficial remedies do not work. Just like putting a band-aid on a fracture, attempts to solve codependency problems outside of a proper relationship with Christ will result only in fresh hurt and disillusionment. This is not easy for the codependent. In spite of what might seem to be, the codependent has become such a self-sufficient character, trying to meet his own innermost needs as a person, it is very difficult for him to leave and let go from these patterns. Actually, a codependent finds changing roles within codependent models easier than accepting that his worth and his deliverance is not dependent on them, but upon what God has already done for them through Jesus Christ, His Son.

The codependent, who is genuinely a born again believer, who comes into your office, is not fighting for victory but from victory. The failure of recognizing the right of Jesus to be Lord is one of the great failings in Christendom today. It is only under the Lordship of Christ, not under some other person's authority, not even his own, that the codependent can find true freedom from the bond of dependency. So, what do you do with a person where codependency is the issue? Lead him to Jesus. Saved or lost, when they come through the door, lead them to Jesus.

With the Lord Jesus in view, the pastor should assist the codependent to focus on his own life and problems instead of everybody else's. This is not an easy exercise. Peter, present with the resurrected Lord, and just having received His forgiveness for the sin of denial, exhibited codependent behavior in regard to John. Jesus told Peter how he would die, but Peter was concerned with John's future (John 21:20-21).

> *Then Peter, turning about,*
> *seeth the disciple whom Jesus loved following...saith to Jesus,*
> *"Lord, and what shall this man do?"*

The Lord quickly put things into perspective for Peter when He said:

> *If I will that he tarry till I come, what is that to thee?*
> *Follow thou me.*
>
> ***(John 21:22)***

Of course, everyone around focused on the prophetic aspect of what the Lord said, but Peter got the point aimed at him you can bet. It was not Peter's job to assume responsibility for others. The Lord Jesus had given him a personal command to follow Him. He had not made Peter responsible to insure what others would do.

In other words, let others care for themselves is the message you have for the codependent. Is this selfish? The user taking advantage of codependency might label it such, but it is actually healthy. Real love, acceptance, affirmation, demonstrates worth that does not come by what we do. It is dependent only on the finished work at Calvary. We should focus on the fact that God commended His love toward us, while we were yet in a fallen state, not because of what we were. We did not have to earn the commitment of His love. Anyone who does not accept you on the same basis, does not measure up to God's standards of acceptance. Therefore, acceptance tied to performance must be rejected. The rub is, simply rejecting those who have made demands on the codependent, is just exchanging one codependent type for another in response to the ongoing demand. Unless the actions of your client are founded in Christ's precepts of acceptance and value, that is what moves toward independence are apt to be.

Nothing can substitute for realizing how greatly loved and valued we are by our Lord. When we get a true picture of that position, it is not an ego trip. Some call the realization greatly humbling. Whatever else it is, there is no doubt that it is infinitely reassuring. Pastor, do you have that wonderful reassurance of your value alive in your life? If not, how can you hope to convey it to another? Please read those special passages in God's Word. Read of your worth and pray for peace to be realized in your life before you go forth to serve.

Pastor's Plan

III. Codependency

Fundamental Recovery

Scripture

No other Scripture expresses any more clearly how greatly loved and valued we are than John 3:16:

For God so loved the world (that is you and me)
that He gave His only begotten Son,
that whosoever believeth in Him (the Son) should not perish,
but have everlasting life.

Certainly, we should not ignore the complementary statement in *Romans 5:8:*

But God commendeth (present tense, continuous action)
His love toward us,
in that, while we were yet sinners,
Christ died for us,

Our importance can be demonstrated in that while we are being formed in the womb, the process is under God's supervision (Psalm 139). The Hebrew expression of our formation could be literally described from the Psalm as "fine stitchery". That same Psalm proclaims this caring God never loses sight of where we are. But it was the Lord who proclaimed the present benefit intended in this care:

...I am come that they might have life,
and that they might have it more abundantly.
John 10:10b

There are many verses that remind us that we are loved. Some scripture will speak to a heart with more power than another. You discover what has the most impact in a person's life as you "wash" them in the Word. Selective readings from Psalms is ointment for many struggling and suffering people. Perhaps some other person, seeing the Lord ever making intercession, guaranteeing our acceptance in spite of circumstance in Hebrews, will be spurred to accept themselves and find victory in life. Whatever the scripture that brings light into darkness, you will introduce the struggling soul to it.

It is the Scripture that will also lead to victory concerning the peripheral issues that have fed and fostered codependent behavior. What is needed is genuine repentance and subsequent receiving of God's forgiveness, or the forgiveness of others coupled with abandonment of bitterness. Perhaps the need is for recognition that some things that held the person in bondage (to guilt) were not their fault and not their burden to bear to begin with. Whatever the need is, the Word of God offers the definite and final statement on the subject. You cannot leave the Word of God out of the formula. This is why every reading recommended to complement this section is filled with God's Word. The things put forward in those recommended books are supported by the Word.

Summarizing what has been presented as the Fundamental of Recovery from Codependency are the three S's. These are salvation, surrender, and scripture. The three are indivisible and comprise the only permanent solution to the problem. Your advantage over secular counseling is profound. They theorize about man's make-up and how to help him. The answer to his need, however, is your stock-in-trade. It is incumbent on you that you be adept in presenting it. Just as in preaching, you must first apply the sermon to your own life to be effective in preaching it to others, so these things must first find root in your own life. Do not, having ministered unto others in these matters, suddenly find your own self cast-away upon the treacherous shoals of codependency.

Pastor's Plan Reproducible

III. Codependency

Handout

Member's Things to Remember

1. Avoid people pleasing - approval seeking.
2. Stop & Think - Before reacting and getting involved in situations, etc.
3. Avoid controlling and manipulating other people's lives.
4. Avoid being controlled and manipulated by others.
5. Get involved in <u>church, prayer, Bible study</u>.
6. Let God have control of your and other people's lives.
7. Enlist yourself in a Christian 12-Step Support Group for overcoming codependency & stay committed to victory.
8. Do not assume responsibility for resolving other's problems.
9. Remember you are loved and accepted of God. You do not have to <u>win</u> His approval!
10. A Support System has emotionally healthy people in it. Unhealthy associations drag you backwards, delaying recovery.
11. Remember you do have value. You are of great worth to God!
12. Stay with Christian Counseling. Avoid worldly value-systems.
13. Keep educating yourself through reading & studying about codependency.
14. Always remember you are not alone!
15. Be dependent on God to deliver you from the bondage of codependency.
16. Enlist someone who is able to assist you in seeing things objectively.
17. Be patient-Overcoming codependency takes time.
18. Learn to detach.
19. Learn to say no to involvement in codependent behavior.
20. Avoid seeking out others to "fix" your codependent problem(s).
21. You do not have to be dependent on others for your happiness.
22. Remember to maintain healthy eating & sleeping habits. Proper rest and nutrition is essential.

Pastor's Plan

III. Codependency

Support Groups

Codependent behavior people find support groups of great benefit to them when they function properly. You will want to direct people you are working with on codependency issues to a Christian 12 Step Support Group. Care must be exercised in your selection because not every group that identifies themselves as Christian automatically gets a pass for operating according to genuine Christian principles. As Comfort Care Ministries' influence has stretched overseas, we have found that having groups operating with philosophies incompatible to their labeling is not confined to this country. You will want to know what your member is being exposed to.

Twelve Step groups generally have on hand books, tapes, and videos that can be purchased or borrowed to enhance and expedite recovery. One advantage to having any support program within the church you pastor is that this gives you more ability to monitor and control the group's material. When that happy situation does not exist, you still want to examine any material your member selects. Having on hand your own books for lending also helps you to control input. The book that we recommend on codependency, by Pat Springle, is my personal favorite. Having utilized this book in counseling, repeatedly, I can attest to its effectiveness. It is the best.

The Christian 12 Step Program used in group therapy has an advantage because it provides a variety of people the member may be able to enlist as a support-system. Those recovering from codependency need much encouragement and support. Support does not mean fixing a person's problems. Indeed, that cannot be done. Support means giving encouragement and help in facing, understanding, and ultimately dealing with problems. When you understand what support really is, then you can see why support other than that with a Christian perspective is unacceptable and probably ineffective. It is all too common an experience to encounter in counseling those people who have already been through the secular mill. Sometimes, they have been through it two or three times, each time being told something different about how to consider, face, or resolve their problems.

In Getting Started is included a little section on setting up a support system or group. It cannot be emphasized enough that the members selected to lead in such a group must be now spiritually healthy, full of honesty, and have personal experience in matters concerning codependency. Persons who are still codependent and looking for others to fix their problems are the stuff many counseling horror stories are made of.

People who can help are also people who are available. Availability does not mean they are not busy. It means that helping others through the support group has a priority in their lives that makes them willing to take time in times of need. People who can help are also people that exude an aura we can call "the comfort factor". Having the comfort factor means that people find being around you and associating with you, easy. It is very difficult for anyone who makes people uneasy or whom people find difficult to talk to, do anything positive for a troubled person. They are only thinking of escape from the unsettling individual.

Support systems often take time and patience to establish. Be prepared, knowing it is not likely to fall together overnight, and don't be discouraged. Discouragement is a great enemy of pastors. It is why so many move on every few years instead of pastoring the same church for twenty or even thirty years. Discouragement puts limitations on your ministry. And it will put limitations on the effectiveness of your counseling ministry, just like any other part of your work in the Lord.

Sometimes, it seems hard to believe it when you minister to people, but there are people who are emotionally, spiritually, and mentally healthy. Some of them walked a difficult road to get that way. Others made conscious decisions at some point in their lives to not cave in to unhealthy attitudes. Others were raised in healthy affirming environments and unconsciously have developed into positive adults. Of those who are now healthy in those three aspects of their lives, two-thirds are excellent candidates for helping you in your work. They can identify with the need. They know recovery should not be done alone. They recognize that God's Word makes it clear that we need each other. Don't be afraid to establish a support system. The reason the Lord equated our work with fishing is that fishing, too, requires patience.

Pastor's Plan

III. Codependency

Church Attendance

The pastor has a unique advantage in ministering to people with codependency problems within his church family. Encouraging the codependent to be regular in church attendance and active in participation within the church should be a given when the three S's of the Fundamentals of Recovery are considered, but the value is worthy of elaboration.

Let us hold fast the profession of our faith
without wavering;
(for He is faithful that promised;)
And let us consider one another
to provoke unto love and to good works:
Not forsaking the assembling of ourselves together,
as the manner of some is;
but exhorting one another:
and so much the more, as ye see the day approaching.
Hebrews 10:23-25

Comment has already been made about the value of expository preaching in the general commentary of this book. Genuine expository preaching ministers to the human condition. The pastor who wishes to grow strong churches and develop strong Christians concentrates on that type of preaching. Expository preaching makes a lasting reinforcement to what has gone on in the counseling environment. But the preaching itself is not the end of the benefit of church attendance. The recovering codependent, like every other person dealing with issues in their lives, will do well to be in church every time the doors are opened.

Churches that are healthy provide an environment of love, encouragement, acceptance, affirmation. This is the environment where a person can grow spiritually. It is also where the codependent can cease to be an "adult child". Spiritual growth is an absolute must to overcoming codependency. The church was designed by God to be a place where the hurting find help.

If the person who has come to you for help does not attend your fellowship, it is inappropriate to attempt to woo him away from another. Of course, if a person is tied into a cultic group (and they do feed on codependent people) you would want to rescue them. But, if the person is in a church that gives him satisfaction, do not try to bring them into your congregation, even though you might have denominational differences. His pastor just might say something that could have a positive input on the life of the one overcoming codependency. Respect the other pastor's ministry and calling in the Lord, and do not be trapped by denominationalism into doing something that might not be beneficial to the client. It is the same Holy Spirit that works and inspires every man of God and every congregation where there are those who love the Lord.

The client's love and appreciation for the one who helps him through counseling is not a proper motive for either changing churches or denominations. Trust the Holy Spirit to inspire that pastor and congregation into saying and doing things that will have impact for the good in the life of the person you are helping.

I have been in services where I heard from the pulpit things I felt were just for me. This has not always occurred solely in my own denomination. And it is not only from my own denomination that counselees have come to a session bubbling with enthusiasm over a blessing from the pulpit delivered just for them.

I am part of my denomination because I believe it to be closest doctrinally to the scriptures. But when perfect knowledge comes, and we join together in heaven, I realize a diversity of denominational backgrounds will be represented. Don't let differences interfere with your ministry.

Pastor's Plan

III. Codependency

Learning to Recognize and Refuse Codependent Behavior

The first thing that must be accomplished in helping a person reject codependent behavior is to teach them what codependent behavior is. The next step is to train them to recognize their codependent behavior when it is going on, even when they are just beginning to initiate it. All of the things connected with counseling and supporting it are directed toward that purpose. The counseling process includes the personal counseling, the 12-Step Support Group, selective reading, audio and video tapes. All of this should be designed to sensitize the member so that he recognizes the codependent pattern of error in himself, and to realize when others are promoting such a response from him. Without being armed with this knowledge, how can the codependent hope to recover?

The codependent Christian should be encouraged to pray for and depend on the Spirit of God to help him recognize wrong or improper behavior. A codependent cannot correct behavior he cannot see. Surely, for the person suffering with this problem, this is a distinct area of spiritual warfare. A study of the character of spiritual warfare reveals that the Holy Spirit is absolutely essential for victory. When we see with the eyes of the Spirit, when the Spirit of God reveals to us codependent behavior in our lives, we must detach ourselves from it.

Detaching is simply the act of separating ourselves from a person, situation, circumstance, thought and so forth. This separation allows us to take a better look at whatever the codependent behavior is centered around. That is exactly what is made possible through the salvation experience and surrender to the Lordship of Christ. We become detached from sin. And as we do not allow sin to any longer reign in our lives, for we are under the rulership of Christ, so we do not allow codependent behaviors to reign in us, for they are contrary to our freedom in Christ.

The objective Christian view sees things in the Light of Truth. This is a new experience for the codependent, for he is not accustomed to seeing things in the light of reality. Detaching helps prevent reacting without thinking. Whatever the focus of the codependent behavior, it is now responded to with thought. A new experience, a new response.

> *For God hath not given us the spirit of fear;*
> *but of power, and of love, and of a sound mind.*
> ***2 Tim. 1:7***

Codependent's responses can be ingrained almost to the point of seeming an animal-like reaction without consideration for the total ramifications of the action. What is learned is not to lose reasoning objectivity. In short, to think the situation through. For example, let's say our friend Mike has been jailed for public drunkenness for the one-hundredth time. The phone rings, and Mike is on the other line asking to be bailed out. We jump into the car and drive toward the police station. Enroute we remember that this is the hundredth time we have made the trip. Boy does poor, old Mike have bad luck! We know that to bail Mike out will cost. As a matter of fact, our entire family will suffer financially because the money we are using to help Mike is necessary to cover household expenses or even the house payment. Oh well, if we do not help Mike no one will, so we may just as well get ready to suffer...

But what if we do reason the thing out when the attack is made on our individuality. Again, the telephone rings, and Mike is on the line asking to be bailed out of jail for the hundredth time. Now we think before we move. We remember that bailing Mike out of jail has not helped him or improved his behavior in any way. The truth is that he has grown progressively worse and more demanding. This time we say no, remembering that our wife and children should never suffer want of what they need, and besides, everyone should be held responsible for their actions. We love Mike, but it is not right for others to suffer for his irresponsible behavior.

Telling Mike no may cause him discomfort. It may even make him enraged. But which one of the responses do you think is likely to get his attention and make him think? Which is likely to encourage him to do something about his problem? Which is least likely to cause others to suffer for Mike's sins? Which is most likely to help the codependent being used to become free from being a victim?

Even genuine need by someone should not be met at the expense of the well-being of others. The good Samaritan account shows no evidence of the family of that Samaritan being harmed in any way. Evidently he was well able to do that which he did, and he was willing to do more if needed. Clearly then, his act did not require the deprivation of his loved ones. It also was not done to gain status. When he had finished doing good he knew that he would still be a Samaritan. In short, he did good because it was simply the right thing do, and not because he was codependent.

It takes time and effort to learn to detach from situations in life in order to see them clearly. It takes practice, practice, practice. At first, giving thought and consideration, not only to circumstances, but also to people and motivations before reacting will seem very unnatural. Discouragement is what blocks surrender as the codependent suffers the stress of learning new ways of dealing with the things in their life. This is important because the desire to cave in will often be very strong.

In detaching, too, one is learning not only of how to react, but when not to react. This may be the hardest lesson of all. But it has a familiar base for the codependent. That is, they must refuse to take responsibility for what is not within the scope of their genuine obligation, and at the same time, insist on un-interfered with control of the life God has given them. Demanding, from those who would ensnare them, the right to lead their own lives and have authority over it.

Pastor's Plan

III. Codependency

Assessing For Addictions

In the segment on causes, we mentioned that the dysfunctional home, out of which the Codependent generally comes, usually has some types of addictions present. Generally the same thing can be said for the person who comes into your counseling room with codependency problems. In fact, we would go so far as to say that it is the rare person who has a problem with codependency that does not have some type of addiction present in their lives. The addiction must be uncovered and dealt with accordingly if this person is going to be whole.

We usually think of addictions only in terms of drugs and alcohol, but remember food, sex, and unhealthy relationships can all fit into the category of addictions. Not only these but other forms of addictions also exist. Consider that addiction is fundamentally the giving up to or abandonment to a habit. When a person is involved in any type of unhealthy activity to the point it has a dominance in their life, they are clearly addicted.

Sections of this book that deal with specific problems that show up as addictions in the codependent should be utilized to assist the codependent in gaining victory in their lives. You incorporate those parts into your Pastor's Plan for Codependency. You may find that issues such as some sexual addictions, and so forth, need referral to specialists who counsel in that area of need. However, in most cases, as the codependency issue is dealt with, the addictive behavior will also subside. The addiction responds to having been handled as part of the codependency issue.

Eliminating an addiction that is part of a codependent issue is virtually impossible, if the basic problem is not taken care of. Since addictions are generally a type of medication for the pain fostered by the codependent problem, the response that grants some relief will be persistent. Even if a form of addictive behavior is abandoned by the codependent, without victory over the root issue, other responses will take its place. Some philosophies of psychology may accept the replacement of some socially unacceptable behavior pattern with another less onerous, but this is not acceptable in Christian Counseling. This substitution is both contrary to the Gospel of Christ and the life in Christ that believers are called on to experience. Therefore, addictive/compulsive behavior on the part of a codependent is treated as part of the total codependency problem, not as a separate issue.

There is a tendency among people receiving counseling for codependency to pass off addictive behavior by just pointing out that it is part of their codependency as they learn the terminology. This gives them a way of justifying wrong behavior. They are blaming the problem and not facing the responsibility they have for their actions in these cases. People can be really subtle about doing this. Now we know that addictive behavior is based on choice. This basic truth remains, no matter what other problem promotes it. So, while you do recognize that the problem does have a base that it is founded on, don't allow your client to delay their recovery by avoiding responsibility. After all, codependents love to be responsible for other than what they should be responsible for, which means they are avoiding responsibility for their own lives.

In the event that you discover addictive/compulsive behavior as you go along and the individual unfolds themselves to you, which is likely, do not be alarmed. You have now been forewarned, and, therefore, are forearmed with the knowledge of why it is and how to approach it. In working through the issues of codependency you do well to remember that the person did not get into the problem overnight, therefore, it will not be eliminated suddenly. As the codependent grows through recovery, they will learn to experience their worth, acceptance, affirmation, and love in a new way. They will replace performance oriented behavior, tied to acceptance by others, with positional oriented self-esteem, based on their relationship with Christ.

Pastor's Plan

III. Codependency

When to Refer

There are times when a person's needs in recovering from codependency requires referral. Emotional immaturity is a foundational disorder to many other disorders, yet it also can be a facet or the symptomization of another basic issue. It can be a very complex problem. Since genuine codependency problems are progressive as well, it is nothing to be taken lightly no matter how foolish some behaviors might appear to someone watching what is going on from the outside. The intensity of codependency problems can be great enough to necessitate in-patient and/or out-patient hospital care.

When evaluating the member for codependency, you may find issues that require immediate referral. Sometimes the difference between whether you refer because of what you discover, or continue to counsel yourself, is dependent, not upon the issue, but the intensity of the issue upon the hurting member. The judgment to refer or to work requires wisdom that depends on the guidance of the Holy Spirit. However, the Lord has given you signposts that allow you to gauge whether continuance or referral is the order of the day. Be open to reading the indicators. Counselors are neither heroes or wimps. We are not out to prove anything with people's lives. We merely serve the Lord by serving our fellow man in need. The decision to refer or not to refer is based solely upon what is best for the client.

Issues such as deep depression, especially depression that never subsides, is a prime candidate for referral to someone who spends their time counseling and is, therefore, more adept in responding to the need of such a person. Such depression associated with thoughts of suicide for escape from the problems codependency produces is virtually a red flag to get a move on with getting your member professional help.

As you will see in our discussions on suicide issues, any and all talk about suicide is always to be taken very seriously. This is especially true when there is obvious depression present. Crisis situations that commonly promote depression being present in a person's life, coupled with negative remarks about life, are to be seen as a time to find out where any member is. When the individual is codependent, don't be superficial in your investigation. You will likely never experience a repercussion from being too careful of a codependent's well-being, but you can regret being careless for the rest of your life.

Codependency has its own brand of pain. Its effects are not to be taken lightly. The pain of codependency is immeasurable, even though it is not physical. Respect the fact that the codependent is going through real and continuing trauma in their lives until they begin to have victory over their situation. When no progress is being made in helping someone through utilization of your Pastor's Plan, it is time to refer. It really does not matter what the reason is for the lack of progress. People get into counseling and then go into denial that they have a problem. Some are out and out resistant to recovery in spite of their protestations to the contrary. Whatever the reason, when you see you are going nowhere, give them a second chance with someone else.

When you are spinning your wheels, two people's time is being wasted. Your time and the client's time has been misapplied. Sometimes the difference is a change of counselor, or the emphasis another counselor puts on a particular approach. But when you are at a stalemate, it can't be broken without a move. Refer.

Pastor's Plan

III: Codependency

Booklet Recommended:	*Learning More About Codependency*
Authored by:	Pat Springle Senior Vice-President of Rapha Resources
Published by:	Rapha Publishing/Word Inc. Houston and Dallas Texas

Excellent for acquainting the busy pastor with the basics of codependency.

Most useful as a tool for helping the client recognize himself in the codependency dilemma, thereby laying the groundwork for recovery.

Booklet contains four chapters:

1. Family Systems of Behavior

2. Characteristics of Codependency

3. The Codependent Christian

4. Handles on the Process

Two items would make the book worthwhile if it contained nothing else:

1. A chart to help explain the causes and effects of codependency within the two possible environments; a functional and dysfunctional family. Located on page 8.

2. A questionnaire which allows the client to determine for himself whether he is codependent or not. Located on pages 29 and 30.

This book is recommended for placement in the client's hands at the first Codependency Counseling Session.

Minister's Notes

Pastor's Plan

III. Codependency

Book Recommended:	*Close Enough To Care*
	subtitled: Helping a Friend or Relative Conquer Codependency
Authored by:	Pat Springle
Published by:	Rapha/Word Inc.

This book explains the codependent to the one who cares and gives the person near enough to help some tools in responding correctly with what they really need to break out of the manner of living in which they are trapped.

At the same time the friend or relative who is close enough to care and close enough to be hurt is equipped for survival, even victory, within the situation they find themselves.

Must reading for the pastor since he is often brought in as a friend to the need and, also, because he must minister to the whole situation for success within his church family. This is also a resource to give to help those within the circle.

One distinct value of this book is its usefulness extends into situations where substance abuse recovery is an issue, and where these types of codependent situations are set up, as well. Not only that, but you will find that because of the pervasive nature of the codependency affliction, this book will be useful to many who have hurting loved ones.

Minister's Notes: ____

____

____

____

____

____

Pastor's Plan

III. Codependency

Book Recommended:	*Codependency* Subtitled: Breaking Free From the Hurt and Manipulation of Dysfunctional Relationships
Authored by:	Pat Springle
Published by:	Rapha Publishing/Word Inc. Houston and Dallas Texas

Presents seven common definitions of codependency:(pg. 22 & 23)

1. Codependency is bondage to pleasing somebody.
2. It is being controlled by someone and trying to control him or her.
3. It is being dependent on making someone else happy.
4. Codependency is the responsibility to make others happy, successful, and good.
5. It is a hurting child in an adult's body.
6. It is feeling guilty when you don't do everything just right-and that's all the time!
7. Codependency is trying to make a sick person well, but ending up sick yourself!

Discusses the different facets of codependency with the reader in a Christ-centered manner. The book is so broad, not every chapter is likely to speak strongly to the client. But every chapter will serve to benefit their understanding, and warn them against exchanging one type of codependent behavior for another. It is a workbook in the sense that it asks questions at the end of each chapter. It is highly personalized because the material in the chapter must be related to the reader's life in order to answer.

This book is worth purchasing just to obtain self evaluation appendixes in the back. They explore how the user's family shaped their view of God, self-concept, and relationship with others.

The pastor who studies the book, Codependency, will benefit personally from it in his relationships with others and understanding of himself. Chapter Nineteen, "Enjoying the Lord", is both wonderfully devotional, and a sermon skeleton on a topic every Christian needs to consider. Several other chapters have passages that will also strike similar responsive chords and lend themselves to expository preaching that will meet needs of people who never enter the counseling office.

Going back and considering the charts, graphs, lists, and illustrations from time to time will not only refresh your knowledge, but will broaden your understanding. The thoughtful pastor will find this book one of those most cherished in his library.

Pastor's Plan

IV. Suicide

Define

"The taking of one's own life."

Pastor's Plan

IV. Suicide

Defined

Suicide, simply defined, is the taking of one's own life. In all probability, suicide should be defined as an act of escape. Most of those who commit such an act are clearly looking for a way out, an escape from their pain. It is absolutely astounding how many people actually die every year in this manner.

It is not uncommon for someone to have had personal experience of suicide in the death of a family member, a friend, or acquaintance by the time they reach mid-life, themselves. My own experience was the death of my mother. I recall vividly finding her dead from a drug overdose. She was only thirty-seven years old. Why did she choose to die? The answer is that she chose to die to escape from the pain in her life.

Suicide has no boundaries. It intrudes into the lives of the rich, the poor, the educated, the uneducated, the old, the young. It is a story that goes on and on. Suicide is devastating to those who are left, to say the least. It reaks havoc on families and individuals. It is an event that goes on daily. It takes no holidays. On holidays suicides, like car wrecks, increase, but with far more pain for those left behind. In the next twenty-four hours, multitudes of lives and homes will be shattered by this event. Even as you read this, many are contemplating taking their own lives. More than likely some of these are within the bounds of your ministry.

It is not comfortable to contemplate, but right now someone in the area you minister in may be through thinking about suicide and going ahead with the very act. If your ministry has not been touched by suicide yet, more than likely it one day will be. Whenever we start to prepare to minister in this area, no certainty exists that we have started soon enough. Therefore, now is the time to begin getting ready for a day you hope, against all odds, will never occur in your ministry.

Sometimes there seems to be credible reasons why the person has taken their own life. You look at the circumstances and things seem clear. Then at other times no explanation appears to even begin clarifying why this ultimate act took place. No other kind of tragedy can leave people feeling so puzzled, helpless, and abandoned.

Each of us has his own thoughts about why suicide occurs. The ideas are conditioned both by old-wives tales and scientific explanations we have been exposed to. The why is just the first of the questions we ask, but the emotions will continue to refrain; Why? Why? Why?

I remember looking for suicidal notes after my mom had taken her life. I must have looked for days and days to find answers to the "whys" she left behind for me to deal with. I was convinced there were clues that could lead to answers. But in all my searchings in those agonizing days, I never turned up any. Twenty-two years later the pieces of the puzzle finally came together and the reasons became clear. Reasons? A multitude, banding together to make possible the most desperate act a human being is capable of. Depression, fears, anger, hurt, a wasted life, poverty, illness, and an absolute need for relief and escape. This is what made it possible in her case.

Left behind for the survivors to deal with is the stigma of suicide. Many families feel marked by the act. It is as if something is wrong with the family; with them personally. Maybe they have bad genes. And, of course, the old idea of a general craziness in the family tree of a suicide has not left our thinking at all.

The shame and embarrassment that suicide produces in those the victim leaves behind are very real to me. You must understand that these feelings stem from a viewpoint of their world, the reality of which is inconsequential. The issue remains in the individual's life and must be dealt with as the legitimate issue it is. You must see what the person feels as a real issue, not to be casually dismissed, if you are to be a blessing in the hurting survivor's life.

I remember telling people that my mother died of a heart attack. I did that for years. Another reason I sometimes gave for her death was that she died of a broken heart. Perhaps that is true. Her heart was broken. Even as I write this it is difficult to hold back the tears. It is hard to think how great the pain must be for someone who takes their own life. It was years before I could share publicly that my mother died at her own hand. Why? Shame and embarrassment. I felt suicide was totally unacceptable, and quite frankly, it is.

Our society rejects such behavior, but that does not mean it doesn't happen. Because of attitudes towards the survivors, real and imagined, many deny that the act of suicide occurred. People actually live for extended periods, even a lifetime, in denial. Even the obvious gunshot wound, clearly self-inflicted, I have seen denied by those nearest to the victim. "No," says mom and dad, "someone else did this." Or, the reaction goes, "Oh, it was an accident!" Like suicide itself, accounts of failure to deal with a loved one's self-destruction continue to be added every day.

What is the motivation in denial of suicide? Perhaps it is done to protect the pride of the deceased. Always the need is felt to protect the ones left behind for the reasons already mentioned. Yet more motives for rejection exist. I don't pretend to know all the answers to why people refuse to face up to suicide. That question alone could keep a Suicidologist busy for a lifetime. But one thing is clear. Refusing to face the reality of a suicide, refusing to talk about it and trying to sweep it under the rug will not make the pain and hurt go away. Today, I feel free to talk about my Mom's suicide. I am still left with the load of unanswered questions extending beyond the why. But I can talk about it. Because I have faced the issue, I don't have to lie about her death or pretend she did not die the way she did.

So, pastor, how are we going to define suicide? Simply as the taking of one's own life. We will not treat death as accidental when it was not. No, some ghostly assailant was not responsible for this deed. It was a living person that took their own life. They were an integral part of those who need you to minister to them after suicide. You will seek to assist those who are hurting to not go into denial greater than normal. We are going to help them identify reality and separate fact from fantasy so that they can recover from grief in a healthy manner. We are going to be there to encourage the survivor to talk and find the way through the why of it. The quicker they begin to do this, the sooner they begin to heal.

How to tell when a person is suicidal is the "twenty-four thousand dollar question" that occupies no little part of our discussion on suicide. If we had pat answers, it would be wonderful. We do not. But what we do have, we share with you. Armed with a little knowledge and the leadership of the Holy Spirit, wisdom in correctly analyzing situations is possible.

If you are going to recognize someone when they are suicidal, you must first have some insight into what it is to be suicidal. You can say a person is suicidal when they are involved in actions or mental processes that have a leaning or tendency toward suicide as an outcome. A person is also suicidal who simply has the urge to commit suicide.

Case History

Actions which have a leaning or tendency toward suicide are very often things that alter or change the world as the individual knows it. So, a young girl in her early teens has finally come into a relatively stable home life living with her natural father. After years of dysfunctional home life with her mother, who is involved with several men, she has been able to break away and go to Daddy. It's true he is no prize, from an outsider's viewpoint, but he has given her love and acceptance. For the first time in her life much daily turmoil has been removed. She feels happy at last. Then daddy's drinking and driving catches up with him. He has to go away for a year to prison. Tragedy has again entered into this young girl's life. She is a codependent, hero type. Her good grades in school actually go up, instead of down, as you might expect. It is as if to say, "If I am good enough, I'll get my daddy back." You see, in her mind, it is somehow her fault that he's gone. Every day she hurries home from school. She will not leave the house for anything. Daddy might be able to call and she could miss him. Isolation and loneliness attend her days as she struggles to get daddy back....

When hope runs out and perhaps false-guilt gets too great, suicide can be the result. The above illustration of actions are coupled with wrong thinking, but it is the isolation from others, as well as what she has endured in her dysfunctional family life, that we are focusing on. This example is resistant to change in established pattern because it is based on a hope. When it is revealed as false hope the fall can be great. You need to understand this little girl is not a fictional character. She is real. There are many like her. Some die.

Case History

Mental processes that lean or tend toward being suicidal focus on the negatives, sometimes, but not always, blowing them out of all proportion to reality. Picture in your mind a Deacon's wife. Her husband, quiet, dependable; a simple, but devout man who loves her dearly. She has two children of above average intelligence. Two cats, one definitely retarded, that she has cared for since birth, are her constant companions. She lives in her pretty little cottage cut off from much outside contact, even church. The center of her attention is the ailments of the cats, her children and herself. Minor illnesses are frequently viewed with no resemblance to reality. In spite of the doting care of her husband, she has attempted suicide twice. And now she must medicate herself daily to try to stay on an emotional even keel. She is so neglectful of that medication that her husband has to call home from work to remind her, but then he has to call home to check on her anyway, just to keep her reassured about things. In spite of the medication, a gloom is ever present with her. Maybe it is because she constantly thinks in negatives. The whole family believes one day she will try suicide, again. That hangs over them and affects their lives.

Her attitude is infectious. Her son feels the social stigma of his mom's condition. He finds it hard to establish friendships. Since he is tall, gangly, a little homely, and socially ill at ease, people do not naturally gravitate to him. He thinks everyone knows he has a crazy momma, when in reality her situation is little known, even in the church. Maybe people really think there is something wrong with him, too. Maybe there is, he suspects. Lately he has had thoughts of suicide, too. Is he crazy? Better to die now than to live like Mom.

Do you get the picture? These people are real. They are not made up. They are people who are hurting, each in their own way. If the condition is recognized soon enough by people who care and have an idea of what to do, a tragedy of life might be averted. These situations do not always get that recognition.

A man of international renown has built an empire from scratch. In the course of getting to where he is, he has frequently taken chances that brought him again and again to the very brink of ruin. He would risk all to continue to amass the properties he wanted and to grow. At times, some of those in financial circles wondered if he did not have to keep going, wheeling and dealing, to cover his truly insolvent condition.

This man is in many ways his father made over. A high roller, his father made and lost two fortunes in the course of his life. However, when the second fortune collapsed, faced with insolvency and no hope of return to the financial circles of the elite, he took his own life. The son is very like his father, adopting many of his attitudes and beliefs as his own. The son has no place for a Living God who has every right to control his life.

The son's belief system embraces a view of euthanasia based on life being worthwhile only as long as it can be defined according to his concepts of quality of life. He believes this so strongly he has gone out of his way to speak out on the issue publicly. He promotes the idea that people have a right to decide when life is no longer worth living.

Each time a crisis threatens his business empire a profound change has taken place in his expressions and demeanor. Now, when those things occur, he even looks worn and haggard. As people sometimes say about tragic figures, he has the smell of death about him. This man loved and admired his father. His father used the suicide route of escape when life became intolerable. Since it was a valid option for the man he most admired, it is also a valid option for him. He has already known the urge to commit suicide.

These examples are not the only scenarios where a proclivity toward self-destruction might be played out. Hopefully, they will make you sensitive to seeing what lies behind facades that get erected and to realize the possible outcomes of conduct, attitudes and mindsets. As you read on, remember that it is a greater thing to minister to the individual whose life might be cut short than to the survivors of the tragedy. Why do we say this? It is because somebody, perhaps you, recognized the danger and saved a life, by getting them help. Learn to recognize dangerous behavior. It is just fine if a person goes through recovery, getting help for their problems, yet denies how close they might have come to an ultimately wrong decision.

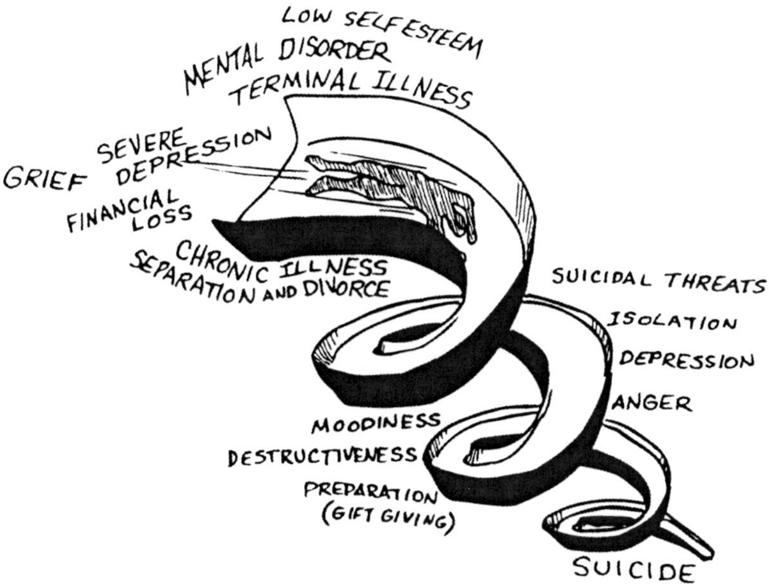

The Downward Spiral

Pastor's Plan

IV. Suicide

Signs and Symptoms

Quick Look Sheet

1. Is the member having thoughts of suicide?
   He is making expressions like wanting to end it all.
   He is talking of wanting escape.

2. Is the member isolating himself from others?
   This is a change from previous social habit. (places frequented such as church etc.)
   He has withdrawn from others he previously associated with.(family or friends)
   He is possibly staying alone.
   Has there been a sudden loss of interest in previous activities?(hobbies, sports, work, etc.)

3. Is the member showing marked signs of depression?
   Does the member have a sad or depressed look?
   Is the member evidencing self pity?
   Do they have an inability to focus on a subject?
   Are they exhibiting low self-esteem?(making self denigrating statements)
   Does the member refuse eye contact or have difficulty establishing/maintaining it?
   Does the member have feelings of guilt about past or present?
   Are feelings of helplessness or hopelessness being expressed in any way?

4. Does the member openly talk about taking their own life/wanting to die?
   Has the member formulated a plan for taking his own life?
   Does the member know the method he would use?
   Is the plan worked out in detail?(location, who will find them/timing, etc.)
   Is the member able to explain his plans to you?

5. Has the member been giving away prized possessions?

6. Has the member a past history of suicide attempts?
   Has the member experienced suicide in someone close in his past?

7. Does the member refuse to talk or communicate feelings?
   Has there been an obvious change in character?
   Does the member evade the subject of suicide when asked?

8. Behavioral change: General unhappiness with life and failure to see good.
   (May be coupled with occultic interest 9).

9. Occult behavior: This includes game such as Dungeons and Dragons and music.

CONFIDENTIAL

Pastor's Plan

IV. Suicide

Assessment Guide

Member's Evaluation *(write on back anywhere you need the extra space)*

Name____

My primary problem as I see it is__________________________
____
____
____
____
____

It all started when ____________________________________
____
____
____
____

Since then I have had feelings of: *(circle all that apply)*

guilt/remorse	depression	uncontrollable mood swings (happy/unhappy)
sadness	hopelessness	angry/get angry all of a sudden
helplessness	oppression	feel need to cry often/all the time
unhappiness	sorrow	my mind being mud dled/can't think straight
worthlessness	trapped	

Do you feel that things will eventually get better?
*Explain*____

In what way have you been responsible for what has occurred in your life? *Explain.*

What have you done to try to improve your situation? *Attach paper for this.*

COMPLETE THE FOLLOWING STATEMENTS:

I often have feelings of wanting to run away or get away from it all. This occurs

I would like to escape from my trouble. I believe this can only be done by

I believe God views my situation as

I believe my family sees me as…*(you may want to attach a sheet and write about several family members specifically)*

I believe my friends see me as *(you may want to attach a sheet and write about several relationships specifically)*

I believe my spouse sees me as

I have returned to some old habits that I thought were out of my life forever

I have taken up some new habits that I never thought I would do

I am avoiding certain people because

I do not see myself as worth what I once was because

I am having difficulty being with people and enjoying their presence. It seems like____
____
____
____
____

What do you think the counselor can do for you to help you?____
____

I am willing to work with you because____________________________
____

Please write on additional paper to explain as fully as you are able.

Pastor's Plan

IV. Suicide

Signs and Symptoms

The signs and symptoms of a potential suicide are not always easy to detect. Some who are contemplating suicide are open and very direct about their plans. However, many become closed mouthed and secretive. Two things are working here and they are disastrous in both cases. When an individual is open about their plans, they are not likely to be taken seriously. Therefore, proper help for that individual is not sought by those near to him. The second thing is that the people around a person who is secretive usually do not recognize the signs and symptoms that convey that the loved one is suicidal.

Exploring the signs and symptoms that convey a possible suicide in the making is too large a task to be dealt with, completely, here. Any such claim, in any work, would probably be proved lacking in the long run, and it certainly would not be beneficial to a pastor who has a full plate of concerns pulling him in a number of directions. For practical reasons, the pastor must concentrate on the more obvious indicators. Two things are at work against you identifying the potential suicide in a pastoral setting: The first is that you are not going to be living in the environment of the person desiring to escape. The second is related to that. You are likely to be getting your information about the growing situation second hand.

Because your input is buffered, you must take every suicide threat seriously. The correct response to the threat is to get proper help for the hurting member. Your assessment information in this section will help you get a feel for the situation. You must do this quickly and not delay implementing a positive response. It is highly likely that you might feel a referral is in order. If you have already built your Personal Referral Resource for this type of situation, you won't be wasting valuable time, now that you need it. The potential suicide is not likely to put their pain and despair on hold unless you show them something that gives them what they are most lacking. Hope!

It is important in this block that we define what we mean by the terms "Signs and Symptoms" a little more clearly than we have thus far. You will see as we go along how the two relate, yet are distinct in the message being conveyed to you by the member. A sign is something you or someone sees. A symptom is what the member expresses.

In defining signs and symptoms, we've come a long way in acquainting you with the major indicators of suicide, as well. It is very difficult to try to give a feel for the difference between what is a disorder that needs ongoing assistance from you in a recovery process and a situation requiring major intervention with no delays or interruptions. When depression is an indicator being displayed as a sign, it might well keep the individual in bed with curtains and blinds drawn and closed. Depression as a symptom is something that is felt, that won't go away, and the emotional pain that might find expression could only be described as unbearable. Both aspects of depression, as far as the individual is concerned, makes them feel that life in general is hopeless and whispers continually that the situation is without any hope or help. Depression that leads toward suicide is a depression that isolates the individual from the world around him and tells him he is all alone.

Case History

In another country, half way around the world, the pastor of a small local congregation struck up a friendship with an American Baptist pastor who had been in his country just a few short years. One day during a social visit in the local pastor's home, an astonishingly intimate piece of information was revealed, contrary to normal social custom. The information was that the local pastor's wife had attempted suicide twice, some two years apart, as a result of depression. The most recent attempt had been only about a month previous.

The circumstances leading up to this revelation seemed quite casual, but in retrospect it is easy to recognize the local pastor had guided the discussion, looking for answers. As was their custom when together, the two pastors discussed the Word of God, comparing the English with the German texts. The wives would make casual comments or chat about other matters to the side. On this occasion, the topic was Eternal Security or what is sometimes called "once saved, always saved". The two pastors held differing positions. After the Baptist demonstrated in English and German Scriptures an agreement in his proof texts on the issue, the local pastor introduced into the discussion the belief that those who commit suicide are damned because there is no opportunity to repent. Again the Baptist responded, pointing out the history of that belief and its lack of support in Scripture. It was at this point the revelation of the suicide attempts was made.

The wives had stopped their talk as the conversation had taken the turn toward suicide. The German wife was merely, quietly, listening to the flow of talk, but the American wife was feeling her discomfort. The local pastor confided that his denominational leadership had given him some unpleasant times over the subject of his wife's problems. The poor wife sat there, her hands in her lap. That picture of isolation and aloneness is engraved on the American minister's mind to this day. Less than a month later, this poor abandoned woman drove her car to a deserted spot, ran a hose from the exhaust system to the passenger compartment, and died.

The Baptist pastor fancied himself a counselor. He did financial, marital, and career counseling as a matter of routine. How he wishes he could have read the signs that day and ministered to his friends. It could have been so, if only he had been prepared to correctly read what was being displayed.

The section on depression in this book is fairly large and well worth being familiar with. Often depression is a root cause. Sometimes it is a symptom of another problem. But depression is very common to most issues that adversely effect the human mind. Having a grasp on the kind and depth of depression can be helpful in illuminating what you are dealing with.

Lets clarify signs and symptoms a little further by considering some of the signs you might observe. An oft repeated sign of impending suicide is watching as an individual who is depressed begin to give away their most prized possessions. They don't plan to either need them much longer, or they are making sure that those whom they would like to inherit them actually get them. Then, too, it is a way of saying goodbye, isn't it? Another sign would be observing a person having mood swings. Up one day and down the next. All of this without apparent explanation. Observing someone withdraw completely from normal interests and activities, a normally communicative person becomes sullen and withdrawn. These too could be signs that a helping hand is needed, and quickly. So what are signs? They are something you see.

A symptom is something the member tells you. "I hurt." "I feel sad." "I feel overwhelmed with pressure." "I just don't see a way out." A symptom is subjective, because it is the individual looking out from their situation, and expressing it. It does not have to be logical to be real to the person hurting. Suicide is not an expression of logic; it is an expression of hopelessness. Suicide as logic only appears so to the suicidal. It does not consider that it creates multiple victims.

It is important to understand that the signs and symptoms listed on the Quick Look Sheet or discussed in the text are not always a sure indicator of a potential suicide. They are items of information to give strong consideration when dealing with those you suspect might be potentially suicidal. Judgment is involved in making a determination of whether what you are observing is just signs of other problems or the indicators of the trend that ends in death.

Two examples of indicators that could be saying suicide are depression and isolation. This can be considered to illustrate the point. Depressed people are not uncommon. Many people could even be called chronically depressed. It is a fact recorded in history that many very gifted and outstanding people either suffered from chronic depression or periods of deep depression. Yet, they do not ever attempt suicide. Some even express the desire to die, but they never make a single attempt to do so. A great number of people enjoy being isolated from others, or they enjoy withdrawing from time to time for their own reasons. Perhaps these are periods of creativity or preparation for some creative endeavor. They have nothing at all to do with either suicide or depression. But man is by nature gregarious, and depression is synonymous with melancholy, the enemy of hope. Some do attempt suicide, and many succeed.

Our purpose is not to diagnose, but to help you become aware of some more common indicators of potential suicide situations. It is not unusual for people to see in retrospect that things were tending toward suicide. That does little good, though. When you pick up on the trend before hand and take steps to forestall an unhappy outcome, you have done what many with hindsight wish they had. For example: A person comes to you seeking help for depression and during your session they begin to share they are having thoughts of just ending it all. What you have then is depression associated with feelings of helplessness and hopelessness, with suicide being contemplated as a means of escape. Therefore, strong consideration must be given to getting immediate care for this individual.

Everyone who says they are going to kill themselves does not do it. I've had many people come through counseling who made statements such as, "I'll just kill myself." They said it, but they did not do it. As a pastor, my function and responsibility would not be to sit around trying to figure out who is being honest about suicide. After much training and experience in counseling and working with people in crisis situations, the one thing I know for certain is that the most experienced person can make a wrong assessment when it comes to suicide.

Case History
You'd scarcely think anyone would know a man better than his wife, after a goodly number years of marriage. One such woman had her husband come home drinking, just as he had done many times before. He came into the house and said, "Give me a hug, or I'll blow my brains out," just as he had done many time before. You would have thought this wife, of all people, would have known it wasn't a joke this man was making, but a serious statement. But, she did not.

Our responsibility to a person threatening suicide is to provide the proper help to meet their need. If they refuse the help, then we can be assured we did what we should have done. And also, we did all we could do. In pastoral ministry, failure is always heartbreaking, but even in suicide as in other areas, the knowledge of having done all you could is a comfort.

This is a sign, you can see it

This is a symptom, you can feel it

Pastor's Plan

IV. Suicide

Analyzing Signs and Symptoms

An old myth is that the person who talks about suicide does not do it. We cannot tell you who introduced that idea. We can tell you what they were. They were wrong. Probably, the most reliable indicator that suicide is being contemplated is the verbal or written pronouncement. People can be very direct about it. When someone starts making statements about killing themselves, when they talk about death, dying, getting away from it all, it is time to listen.

Case History
The girl is in her mid teens. She feels alienated from her mother and step-father. She does not feel that they have any trust in her. They grudgingly allow her out of the house for anything outside of school hours, whether it is to visit a neighbor or go to church. And when she returns, it is usually to unhappy circumstances. Her parent's interests have no relationship to her life or interests. Her new found faith in Christ has only deepened the gulf between them. Since she has become a Christian, she had brought to surface sexual molestation that occurred six years before by a family friend. She wants to tell her parents, but has no confidence they would believe her. A friend from the church shares her secret. She tells her friend that she has been contemplating suicide because her life situation seems so impossible. She has written poetry about her feelings.

Would you consider this person suicidal? What would be the catalyst that would push her into putting into action what has only to this point been thought about?

Our young girl's statements should be taken very seriously. You would think that parents who are this suspicious would discover the suicide writings and give them serious consideration. We cannot say that they have seen the poetry, because we are on the outside looking in. What we can consider is the strong possibility that they are so busy with their own problems, they are neither considering what is going on in her life, nor the impact their decisions have on her.

Can we say our subject is depressed? Certainly. That which we know about in her life gives us several good causes for her depression. These things are impacting on her at a time of life when young females are prone to feel things with special intensity. The young girl is reaching out in developing a friend, but even so, she is experiencing withdrawal because the people she most desperately wants to communicate with are withdrawn from her. Talking with her friend about her problems, even about her suicidal inclinations, has not pushed her over the edge. It very possibly has saved her from taking her own life.

We can begin looking at a person by asking ourselves what behavior is within the boundaries of normal behavior for them. This requires an understanding of the individual. People have similarities, but they are not the same. We briefly discussed under Signs and Symptoms the variations in withdrawal and depression as they occur in individuals. We now realize that the meaning of actions are dependent on the individual. Forced to rely on common sense and sound judgment, with no absolutes, what do you do? Let us suppose you see a person intentionally withdrawing from his normal associations. It is clearly being done willfully. Believe it or not, the most obvious and best answer is the most overlooked. Ask them why? It's not going to hurt to ask. Most people will appreciate you caring enough to ask, even if no problem exists. If it does exist, the person's sign that said, "I need help!" has been read. We did not say it in words, but the unspoken communication of inquiry was, "I observed your behavior as unusual for you, and I cared enough to ask why."

Seeing a non-user of alcohol or drugs get involved in either is a clear indication of trouble. But the question we are dealing with in this chapter is whether we are looking at a symptom and sign of the downward spiral toward suicide. We are not talking about long term degeneration ending in suicide. We are discussing a short term fall off the cliff of life. Information about what has been happening in a person's life recently gives clues that help define what you are looking at. A person who has simply fallen into bad association, by their own foolishness, may inadvertently take their life by chemical overdose. However, the person seeking escape may see suicide as their next option. When such an extreme personality alteration is coupled by speaking about suicide, listening to depressing musical lyrics, or other negative expressions, it is time to take things very seriously.

One effect of drugs and alcohol on a person is a weakening of inhibition. Many a person has confessed to slashing a wrist or some other suicidal act, when visited by the impulse of the moment, while intoxicated. Any person using a substance that impacts the mind, particularly in heightening depression, whether prescribed or not, might have a latent suicidal thought find action. When a person has attempted suicide previously, they have demonstrated that their innate inhibition against suicide is low. It doesn't matter if the previous try was considered a ploy for sympathy, or not. Chemicals and a weak inhibition are a deadly combination.

In counseling situations, I've personally confronted individuals with the question of their thoughts of suicide. Many times I've done this with no ill effect. When a person has reached out and come to you for help, you enjoy an added advantage in being forward with such questions. It is fair to say that anytime anyone comes to you with depression, the counselor should inquire about thoughts or preoccupation with suicide.

You may remember studying about Edgar Allan Poe during the "good ol' days" of school. Some of us thought things like American Literature were great burdens to be endured. Now, I find that that semester has provided a good commonly known example of abnormal behavior. Preoccupation with death and dying is not normal. It is an indicator that something is seriously wrong. The dominance of these thoughts is a person's mind sending a message that there is a presence of helplessness and hopelessness in an individual's life. Help is urgently needed. The depression, moodiness, and withdrawal of Poe is well documented. It has been speculated that Poe's emotional problems were heightened by the influence of hallucinogens. Others suggested that Poe might have had a murder weighing on his conscience. Whatever his motivators, we know the pain of this mind was intense.

This dissolute figure of American Literature cannot be ignored when potential suicides are being considered. It takes far less of similar pressures to drive many people to commit themselves to eternity. Take, for example, the man whose wife has left him once again because of his alcohol and drug abuse. The son of an alcoholic, he patterned himself after the father, except that he does try to be manipulative, as is his mother. He has chosen a wife who attempts to manipulate, also, by with-holding approval and affection.

Case History

Our subject has the moodiness associated with abrupt changes in personality. He abuses prescription drugs, and has used illegal drugs in the past. His history, under the influence, includes aggression so violent he once took several police officers on at the same time. Because of his problems with emotions, induced by the side effects of prescribed drugs, he is "up one day and down the next," resulting in his relationships with other people being distorted. The effect on the job means he is the first person to be laid off. Self-esteem is in the pits.

Even if he did not have the problem with emotional swings, the effects of prescribed drugs clouded his mind and interfered with higher functions, like mathematics, that he needs to do his job. Part of his mother's manipulation has been to compare him with her other sons whom she always presents as more successful and more considerate of her. Each time he proves her assertions, his self-respect plummets.

Because of the combination of poor interaction with people and declining job performance, he is finding it harder and harder to get jobs in his technical specialty. His wife has left him because of the confusion he throws into her life and to try to force him to quit drinking. She has more problems with his conduct under alcohol than with his problems related to drugs. However, she also abuses prescription drugs. His children are not only gone, they don't want to live with him. The only person content to take him any way he may be is his poor old drunken sot of a daddy and he is in jail right now. Nothing exists in his life to say that he is worthwhile.

Once before, when feeling low, he had slit his wrists superficially. Now he is talking about suicide on a daily basis. What is holding him together? He gets in touch with a minister who counsels.

So many things have to happen in this man's life it is difficult to know where to begin. It will be no easier because he has a tendency to play games with the problem. Remember he is manipulative. Genuine desire to overcome his chemical problems will have to be developed. But before he can have real victory in life he much begin to understand self-worth is not determined by people but by a Person, the Lord Jesus Christ. Our subject must desire to enter into a real relationship with Him. Even if the minister refers out this person to other agencies, he will benefit the man by standing by him and aiding him in his search for significance. One thing should have been clear to you as we developed our subject's signs and symptoms in this instance; if he does not go forward, a good possibility exists he will die out of season, and very likely by his own hand. Did you see the signs?

Pastor's Plan

IV. Suicide

Causes

Writing on topics related to people's innermost being, we find ourselves coming back to respect issues we've once explored or touched on. We present a little more that will hopefully prove insightful and of benefit to you, our reader. People are like flowers. When viewed from different angles, you are seeing the same flower, but you learn new things about the shape of that flower. Perhaps from one angle you might see evidence of assault the flower has endured by insect or weather that is hidden from all other views. This might be the sight you would omit in enjoying the flower's beauty, but it is the area of concentration when helping a human being unfold their beauty in God's creation.

Like a worm hiding inside a fruit, eating out the good, like causes lie hidden under such issues as depression. Causes of depression leading to suicide include the death of a loved one, divorce, feelings of rejection and failure, and failing health. In fact, virtually any cause for depression has the potential, given the right person and circumstance, to be able to leave someone feeling so hopeless that suicide appears the only way out. Since 90% of all depression is treatable and curable, it follows when the right person opts for suicide as the relief of choice, a terrible and unnecessary waste has occurred.

We can never underestimate what depression can lead people to do. In my lifetime, I have known of several in Christian work who gave it up. The Bible names several prophets, such as Elijah and Jonah, who both, depressed for entirely different causes, wanted to die at some point. Depression coupled with anxiety attacks is virtually a flag to say that the person is going through periods of suicidal thought. Failing a biological reason for these episodes, learning to rely on the Lord Jesus for that which is outside our ability to control is essential to halting the downward spiral. The reason our chapter on depression is extensive is because it impacts on the other disorders so heavily. In fact, depression, regardless of its initial cause, can become a cause in itself when suicide is the issue. Never forget depression can and does lead to suicide.

Many times the losses experienced in life can be the cause for a person committing suicide. The losses of life are well recognized, even categorized, in the study of human grief. Common losses experienced in life have even been studied so that we understand what represents normal grieving and reasonable recovery times from various types of loss. When loss becomes the cause of suicide, we can say loss has been experienced abnormally.

Loss can be experienced in many areas, and this is discussed in our recommended material on grief. So not to be redundant, we recommend you be familiar on the subject of loss related to grief. This will provide the proper background to understand what we mean when we say losses can be so emotionally and mentally crippling suicide seems far easier than having to deal with living without what was lost.

Remember the stock market crash of the Depression Era? It is hard for most people to believe that men were jumping out of windows of tall buildings because of the crash. Why did they do it? Loss. The loss of their finances struck at the root of how they defined themselves as people. When the money or power was gone, so was the reason for living. In fact, not living appeared preferable.

A prime Biblical example of what loss can do to a person can be found in 1 Samuel 31 in the account of King Saul's battle with the Philistines. King Saul chose suicide rather than surrender to his enemies. What he had already lost, combined with the indignities he was in expectation of suffering, made suicide preferable to life. In Saul's particular case, his losses had been multiple. Often, in people's lives today, losses are multiple. More than once you have undoubtedly heard of an elderly person who, having lost a mate or alone with failing health, has opted out of life. Frequently, murder/suicides occur with ailing marriage partners to avoid such multiple losses, as well.

Recently a so-called "Suicide Doctor" has preyed on the pain of people in poor health, wasting away from some incurable chronic or terminal illness. Fearing having to spend year after year confined to bed or wheelchair, such people have been easily encouraged to follow through with their contemplations of suicide. Ailing health has so worked havoc in the minds and emotions of those seeking his services, they have yielded themselves to his wicked purpose of cheapening human life by promoting euthanasia.

Having to be dependent on others is very demeaning to some people. We can recognize the embarrassing aspects of having others care for our personal hygiene and bodily functions. But do we also see that such things as dependency for food preparation or the supply of a place to live might cause some to be so embarrassed they might take their life?

Case History

Take for instance a woman who had spent her life doing for others. This was how she found her sense of importance in life. Other people came to her for help. She had given of herself, and with limited means, sometimes to the detriment of her own well-being. We can talk about her codependency, or simply note that though she had met the needs of others, asking others to help her when in need was out of the question. And she was in need. Various reasons, one of which had been the continuing cost of caring for her husband, had finally taken her limited resources past the breaking point. On a Sunday she was at the altar looking for a miracle. Even her husband did not know the home was soon to be foreclosed upon. God does not grant the miracle she expects, and she will not tell her need to the church. She waits but a few days. When she does not get what she wants, the solution she thinks she needs, a bullet, helps her avoid facing the issue further. A month later, the husband who depended on her to add structure to his life, gives up and dies, too. The whole church is shaken by the loss of one who had always played the self-sufficient role, who seemed so strong.

Sometimes fear is the cause of suicide. I recall many years ago, while working as a paramedic, responding to a call where an elderly lady of about eighty years had taken a pistol and shot herself. During the search for cause we discovered she had been diagnosed with cancer just the day before.

A well-known horseman was diagnosed with cancer. Coming home from the doctor's office, he sent the family off on a pretense. Sitting down in his rocking chair, he pulled out his six-shooter and put a bullet through his brains.

The common denominator between the cowboy and the octogenarian was fear. The motivation of that fear was different. Fear of being a financial burden; fear of losing independence; fear of losing the appearance of hearty vitality and manliness; fear of pain.

A well-known mass suicide called Masada had at least an element of fear. Fear of the retribution of Rome in a lifetime of future servitude. Fear of the torture that might come with capture. Of course such motivations might have been distorted in the suicidal bravado. But even Jim Jones developed fear and then preyed upon it to perpetrate his mass suicide. Oh yes, fear is a cause of suicide. Even oriental ritual suicide had the element of fear. Fear of being shamed. Fear of living with an embarrassment.

One outstanding area of fear as a cause for suicide is the fear of medical costs. These fears have prompted many so-called Living Wills which say life-support systems should not be used to prolong life, Fear of medical costs often keep people from seeking medical attention when they suspect a serious problem, and that same fear can prompt a person to take their life when such a problem, or even the hint of that type problem, is possible in the diagnosis.

To conclude the section on causes, we must give recognition to the effects of addiction as a cause. But to that we have to add other issues such as mental illness, homosexuality, abortion, and a host of other things that afflict mankind. Anything can, as we have said, with the right person and the right time , be a cause for suicide.

We must complete this segment with a look at one of the world's most memorable suicides, that of Judas. Judas, faced with the enormity of his deed, committed suicide out of remorse. But remember Satan had entered into Judas prior to the act that brought about his fall. This brings us to the true source of all suicidal motivation. I believe that all suicide is motivated by the devil. Suicide represents one of the greatest attacks upon man as the representative image of God. It steals from the Lord, His chief tools on earth, men and women. Satan's desire has always been to destroy mankind. Can you imagine the perverse pleasure he gets when he prompts someone to do the destruction by their own hand?

Pastor's Plan

IV. Suicide

Care

As we mentioned earlier, the primary objective of the pastor initially in suicide intervention is to prevent the suicide. This is so much more gratifying than after-tragedy care giving. Of course the pastor must plan an immediate referral for any one where suicidal processes are indicated, but the story is not ended there. What we do and why we do it is our consideration in this segment.

One reason for referral is that individuals who appear suicidal need professional evaluation and treatment. Professional evaluation helps to determine how serious the threat of suicide is and whether underlying conditions not readily apparent are present. Professional treatment provides, at the very least, twenty-four hour care while the suicidal threat is being eliminated.

When the threat of eminent suicide exists, attempting to remedy the situation by scheduling counseling sessions days or a week apart is not realistic. In the intermissions between sessions where you are seeking root causes, the client is still struggling with the urge to follow through with the act of suicide itself. It does very little good spending time trying to remove the causes when the member returns home only to again have opportunity and possibly reinforced motivation to kill themselves. Since your objective has to be to keep the person alive long enough to help them, you must get them to people who can do that.

Timeliness is of the essence. Having developed your referral resources in advance of the need (we hope), a review of options can help you select an appropriate resource for the situation. After finding available space for your member, an important introduction has to be made. You must introduce the hurting person to the resource in such a manner they are a willing recipient of the service the resource offers. The success of that will depend a great deal on whether or not you have the member's confidence.

The conscientious pastor has been working to gain his people's confidence in him from the first day of his ministry among them. But we understand that a person who is suicidal has an abnormal mental state. They are suspicious of people they might ordinarily trust. As we write this, we cannot predict that the person who will be in your presence in such a state will even have the benefit of past association with you. You must assume that confidence must be won. Do not presume upon the past.

The principles discussed in our segments on building relationships are important to you now. If the client must understand anything it is that the pastor is there to help. He must realize the man of God is concerned and will do everything he can for the sole purpose of helping. If they do not believe that, you may fail in getting them to help. Remember that when people are at the point of suspicion common to those suicidal, anything phony or insincere on your part will be greatly enhanced in their mind.

Your listening skills, patience, love, friendliness, and acceptance will go a long way in potential suicide situations. Winning them to yourself will help you guide them into rediscovering a reason to live and not die. What the person must see in you is genuineness.

Gentleness and cautiousness must be used in acclimating the member to the idea of referral. Do not push the potential suicide when suggesting referral. Instead gently pull them to a place they can understand referral is absolutely necessary. Remember, pull is better than push.

Talk of referral awakens fear very often. Since fear is generally already present it does not take a lot to get it to become very active. Often people who present themselves for help already fear that they are crazy. Referral can sound an awful lot like institutionalization in such a case. Being institutionalized means to them being locked away and left alone, abandoned. They can think this is going to happen to them at this point. That has no appeal to a person who feels isolated, as it is. You can see how important that trusting relationship can be in removing fear. The client, knowing that he can trust the pastor, finds the pastor's introduction to another resource easier to accept.

So, your relationship and your referral are the two key elements in initial suicide intervention. It is no discredit to acknowledge that suicide involves things that often go beyond the pastor's boundaries as they exist within his church resources. His referral resource system is an extension of his boundary and he should view it as such. If that mental adjustment cannot be made, at least remember referral is better than having to give an account to family, friends, or even the court about why referral was not made.

Because of the mental turmoil of the client, you will probably have to handle the referral procedure along with a family member. Disarray of emotions makes people ill-equipped to deal with the peripheries to their recovery. Pick up the phone and start the arrangements with the person in your presence. You don't want to appear in a panic or anxious, neither do you want the client to feel something is happening or being said behind their back. You might want to say something to the resource like, "I have John Doe here with me now. They would like to get some help from you...." This clues the person at the other end that you don't want to have questions asked, the answer to which might be unsettling to your client, and that you don't want to be put in a situation of having to sound evasive either.

An advantage to immediate action is that it does not give the suicidal person an opportunity to change their mind about following up on the referral. After the referral is complete, you are then free to encourage and assure the individual that everything is going to be okay and that they have made a wise decision, while you wait for transportation to be ready. This is also a time to reassure that you are not abandoning them, just recruiting some help. Don't abandon them either, build the relationship for when they come back.

The ideal situation is to include yourself in the transportation arrangements if at all possible. If a family member who has a positive attitude is available, they should also be included in the transportation plans. This way the trip to the resource becomes more reassuring. The wise minister can become the one who introduces the client and the resource on the other end.

Having experienced support and concern, through what is for the distraught individual a trying ordeal, thoughts of abandonment have been somewhat short-circuited. The basis for your follow up support has been strengthened. Your involvement with the referral from start to finish is the best way to solidify your ability to work, in the future, with all the family affected by the problem.

What should you do if a counselee appears suicidal, but refuses referral? The answer is simple, but the practice of the answer will be hard. You remove yourself from any commitment to counsel. That sounds tough when you are looking at a person threatening to end their life, but we have to be realistic. It does not take a genius to figure out if they will not accept your counsel to get competent help, they are not likely to accept any other counsel you have to offer.

The problem you might be saddled with, in a situation where a person has rejected your best offer of help and you have continued to try to intercede, is being caught in the middle of a blame game. Your client takes his life and the friends and family blame you for it. It is foolish to try to band-aid a fracture. The injury from trying to give unresponded care could be unhealable to your ministry or to your family's future.

There was an elderly lady, many years ago, who had a saying that was profound in its simplicity. "Some people you just can't help." It does not hurt to explain to the potential suicide why you are removing yourself from the counseling relationship. Let them know you do take their situation seriously and reassure them of your willingness to help them if they would like to treat it seriously before it is too late.

Case History

A woman in her third marriage, with three children from the failed marriages, had a history of six suicide attempts. Her past, almost from birth, was a painful experience to contemplate, much less to live through. We could see how she wound up an emotional mess. In fits of anger she had been known to physically assault her present husband, scratching and gouging with all the fury of a little wildcat. Her husband, no weakling was engaged in work that challenged both courage and stamina. He could easily have hurt her and violently subdued her as had previous husbands, but he did not. Some nights, because of the threat of her attack, he slept locked inside the car because he dared not sleep where she could get to him easily. He wanted desperately to help her and sought their minister's assistance in this. The minister had worked with her of some months, recruiting neighbor women of the church to assist.

Her rages were preliminary to bouts of depression. The depression would find expression in criticisms of others of a most sharp and virulent manner. At this point she was not far from lapsing into a despondency that would precede the next suicide attempt. It was at this part of the cycle an attempt at intervention was made to get her into more serious help at her husband's request. It was plain she was trying to avoid the issue and continue the cycle. Suggestion that she receive help was rejected with fervor. She became so angry, she was scarcely coherent. Her words were to the effect, "Get out of my house and don't ever come back!"

The minister's reply went like this, "Okay, I am leaving. But I want you to understand what is going to happen to you if you don't receive help and go on like you are. Six times you have tried suicide. Sooner or later you will succeed, whether by accident or on purpose, you will succeed. These children of yours have gone through the experience of your wrecked marriages, violence, and suicide attempts. You have said that they would never have to live through the hell your childhood was, but what have you given them? How will they react to their problems when they are grown? If you decide you want help let me know, I'll be there for you. But you need to consider what you're doing. Good-bye."

This farewell dose of reality was such that she began to work at controlling her outbursts and attitudes. It took a year before she was ready to come back for help. But cutting her loose from counseling with a nouthetic approach broke the cycle for a year and brought her to a point where she was ready to receive further help. Of course, the tough love formula done in this manner might send another personality the other way. For her, the terminal confrontation pointing out the effect of her actions on her children pushed the right buttons.

How the separation from a person who refuses help is accomplished depends very much on your knowledge of the person and the leadership of the Holy Spirit pushing the right buttons in you. But the client who is being dismissed from counseling needs to know you are not taking their problem lightly and you are available if they want help in the future.

Always, counseling should be documented carefully. But in issues of suicide the importance of documentation cannot be over-emphasized. Within Comfort Care Ministries, documentation is done both within and after the counseling session, depending on the individual counselor. What matters is that it is done thoroughly.

Anytime the counselee refuses referral you should carefully document that occurrence. It is good to include in the notation whom you planned to refer to. Document the client's response to the referral suggestion explicitly. Also note all contacts, including familial that you have made on behalf of the client.

Most of the time documentation is useful as a history of exploration and discovery about the individual. But it can also be a source of vindication, demonstrating that you did your best for someone.

Pastor's Plan

IV. Suicide

Counseling the Counselor

Sometimes, in spite of everyone's best efforts, people die. There are some people who go through numerous rounds of referral care, yet they eventually take their own lives. Too many times loved ones and even counselors blame themselves as did the American pastoring overseas in an earlier account. People are left thinking, If only I had done more they would still be alive. It is possible to walk around for weeks or months, perhaps even years shouldering blame that really does not belong to you.

Guilt feelings have been experienced by pastors, counselors, psychologists, etc. A degree does not make you immune. When you lose someone you know so much about, and whom you have invested a part of your life in, you will experience loss. But if you allow guilt, then you can become crippled emotionally and unable to help anyone.

It is so important that you do the best you know how to do. But some people will experience a time when that will not be enough to stop the act of suicide. I recall very vividly blaming myself for my mother's death. I carried the guilt for years. Was it something I said, or something I did not say? Was there something I could have done and did not do that provoked my mother to take her life? For years I said in my heart that it was my fault. The guilt became so bad I ended up in the hospital being treated for an intestinal ulcer, anxiety, hyperventilation, and depression. I remember, after a series of tests, a doctor came into my hospital room and gave me some very good advice. He told me to get on with my life. I did not listen. I had spent weeks locked away and isolated at home shouldering blame that did not belong to me. I could not eat or sleep, and when I began to sleep, I would wake up hyperventilating. After being dismissed from the hospital, I started medicating my guilt with alcohol. That way I could at least sleep enough to remain functional. This went on for years.

Even after receiving Christ as my Savior, I continued to blame myself for my mother's suicide. It was only through attending a seminar by Dr.

Norman Wright that I found deliverance. During the seminar Dr. Wright explained that suicide was not the fault of anyone but the person committing the act and we, no matter who we may be, are never to assume that responsibility. Know what? Dr. Wright was correct. No matter how one looks at it, there is absolutely no way we can Biblically blame ourselves for someone else's behavior in the area of suicide. I never will forget the relief I discovered that day. I will always be grateful to God for how Dr. Norman Wright was able to minister to me.

Pastor's Plan

IV. Suicide

Resources

Book to Read: *Why Suicide*

Pastor's Plan

V. Self Esteem

Verbal Abuse Grace Ketterman
The Search For Significance (book and video) Robert S. McGee
Beyond The Darkness Kubetin and Mallory

Pastor's Plan

V. Self Image/Self Worth

Defined

Self esteem is commonly simply defined as self-worth. It is couched in such expressions as belief in one's self, or referred to as self-image. How ever it is defined, what it boils down to is how a person perceives themselves, whether they consider themselves to have value or not. It does not matter how others see the person in self worth; it matters how they see themselves. Virtually everyone has value to someone, but that does not guarantee the individuals see themselves as worthwhile.

Everyone has a need for a sense of self-worth, but it has become a scarce commodity in our day. Never before has there been such a famine of self-worth, and it is working havoc in our society. Not only are adults suffering from low self esteem, but youth, as well. The fact belies what often appears. People act as though they are on some ego trip. They are very self centered, even as they seem, but the assertions of their greatness belie how they actually feel about themselves.

> *...Thou shalt love the Lord thy God with all thy heart,*
> *and with all thy soul, and with all thy mind, and with all thy strength:*
> *this is the first commandment.*
> *And the second is like, namely this,*
> *Thou shalt love thy neighbor as thyself.*
> *There is none other commandment greater than these.*
> ***Mark 12:30,31***

People do not really love themselves in a healthy sort of way. Healthy love is not encountered in the context of either pride or selfishness. Healthy self-love is an appreciation for who and what an individual is apart from the trappings of the world, job, possessions, etcetera. It is a difficult issue for a secular practitioner to properly deal with because of where the root of the problem of self-esteem lies. Whatever the route one followed to arrive in their condition, the problem is an alienation from the life in Christ. Whether the person who comes to you for counsel has been saved or not, this is invariably true.

The life in Christ is an affirming life. Certainly if God loved us so much that He was willing to give His only begotten Son for our sins, then we must realize it is His intention for us to love ourselves. Since John 3:16 summarizes our value, there is no question whether or not a person should have a genuine sense of value, only whether or not we can acknowledge emotionally that value exists in us. A person who does not have this sense of his own worth cannot possibly have the right attitude toward others. The commandment was that he should love his neighbor as himself. An individual cannot love God and live in wonderful relationship with Him if he is incapable of loving his fellow man.

> *If a man say, I love God, and hateth his brother, he is a liar:*
> *for he that loveth not his brother whom he hath seen,*
> *how can he love God whom he hath not seen?*
> *And this commandment have we from Him,*
> *That he who loveth God love his brother also.*
> ***1 John 4: 20, 21***

Except for humanistic philosophies and liberal theologies there has been little attention paid to the need to develop an attitude of self-worth in people. This problem has come home to roost in the 1990's. Today, a lack of self worth is literally destroying millions of lives. Not only are our problems with alcohol and drug addictions tied to low self-worth, but promiscuity, suicide, and abortion all have ties to this condition. The humanist claim that he "is somebody" becomes more a hollow denial of what he really believes as he sanctions ideas that dehumanize man. He does not really believe he "floats like a butterfly", but he feels the "string like a bee."

Everyone has an inborn need to have a sense of being valuable or worthwhile. When that does not exist nothing is left but feelings of worthlessness or uselessness. It is as if man has an inborn understanding of the impossibility of atonement for sin by any means of compensation on his part. And when this sense is not relieved with the knowledge of their value to God, or distorted by demeaning remarks or actions by parents or peers, the individual falls into a pattern of believing he is without merit, and therefore, without value. In fact, like a garden untended grows weeds, a man uncultivated has a natural inclination to wrong self-image. It is the legacy of man's fall, of his inherited sin condemnation.

That they should seek the Lord,
if haply they might feel after Him, and find Him,
though He be not far from every one of us:
For in Him we live,
and move,
and have our being:

Acts 17: 27, 28a.

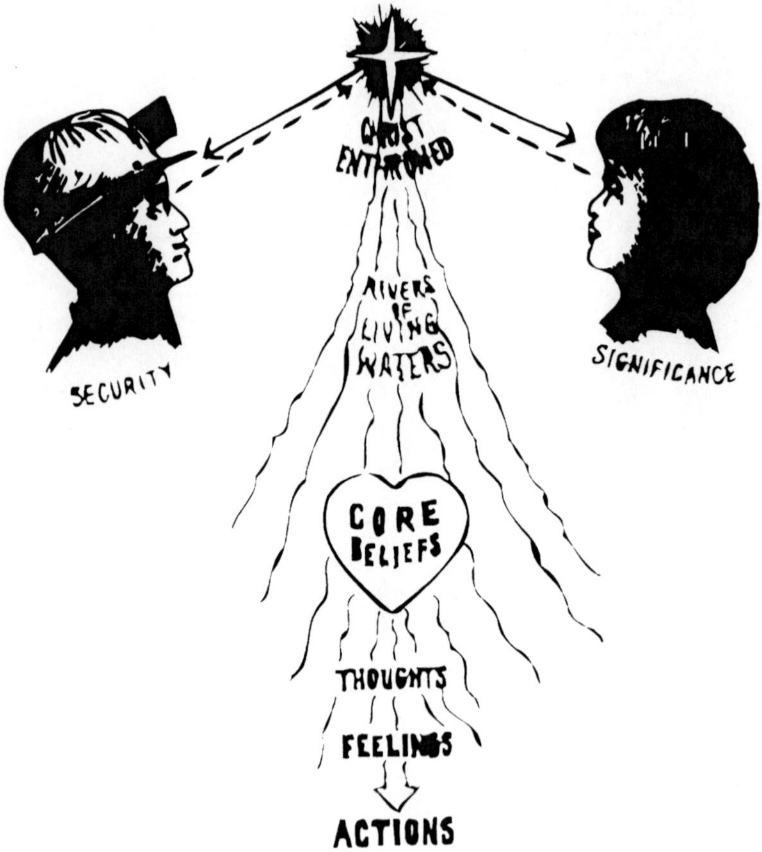

Correctly Placed Dependence For Self Esteem

The Pastor's Plan

V. Self Image/Self Worth

Signs and Symptoms

Quick Look Sheet

1. Negative Comments about self.
   a. "I'm no good"
   b. "I'm worthless"

2. Improper/Inappropriate behavior. (Purpose probably to gain attention)

3. Inability to Interact comfortably with others.
   a. Are feelings of inferiority indicated?

4. Addictive/Compulsive behavior.

5. Over attention on Dress.

6. Overwhelming need for others approval.

7. Fear of being rejected by peers, authority figures, etc.

8. Equating self-worth with successfulness/finances, popularity, etc.

9. Feeling that no one cares for them.

10. Lack of Self Confidence.

11. Sense Of Worthlessness.

12. Sense of Uselessness.

13. Reluctance to Accept Challenges.
    A. Fear of failure indicated.

14. Inability to see positive qualities in self.

15. <u>Suicidal attempts or thoughts connected with above attitudes/emotions.</u>

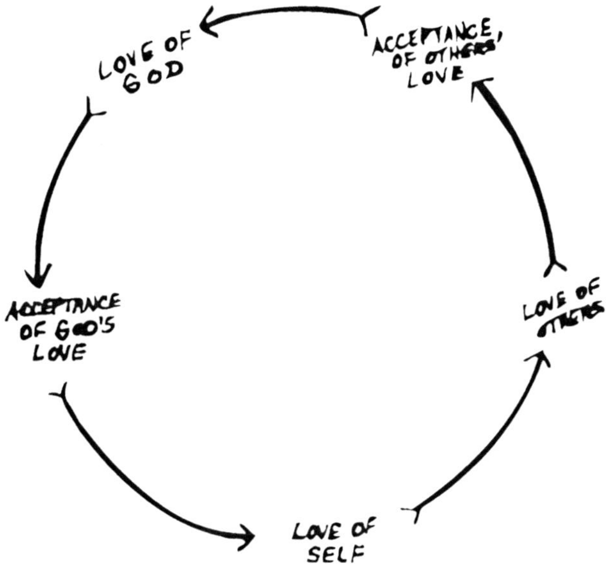
LOVE OF GOD
ACCEPTANCE OF OTHERS' LOVE
ACCEPTANCE OF GOD'S LOVE
LOVE OF OTHERS
LOVE OF SELF

Pastor's Plan

V. Self Image/Self Worth

Signs and Symptoms

The signs and symptoms of low self-worth are absolutely too innumerable to expound on in depth in the area we have allocated in this work. Therefore, we will focus on those that are most obvious and most commonly seen in the counseling setting. We will leave it to you to explore the many books on the subject, written by well known sources, for in depth development. The information we give you will be of great benefit for the general pastoral counseling scenario. In complete candor, it does not take an individual who is trained or untrained very long to figure out when one has a sense of worthlessness. It is not at all uncommon to hear an untrained individual remark that someone they are in close contact with is having problems with low self-worth.

The skill that is needed to recognize struggles with these types of feelings is just good common sense. That does not mean that professional help is never needed. Quite the contrary. Sometimes low self-worth can so devastate an individual's life that even in hospital care is needed. The hurt and pain sometimes can only be dealt with by professional care that can be provided by the Christian Psychiatrist or Psychologist. To say that professional help is never needed is definitely an incorrect statement to say the least. A little knowledge of the basic issues makes determination of the more intense cases quite a bit simpler.

It is interesting to note that God has so uniquely designed man that what is going on in the inner man is usually manifested in the outer man. In the discussions in this book we have hit on the subject of body language. Virtually, no part of the human physiology fails to communicate the feelings and attitudes of the inner man. Additionally, people will often express verbally where they are in relation to themselves. They will do this either by direct or indirect choice of words. Picking up on when people say things that have the effect of "cutting themselves down" is the type of thing that can be sending a clear message. That message is, "I don't like myself."

Often people come to me for counseling who are filled with negative statements about self. On occasions they can expend thirty minutes expounding on what a failure they are and how they will always be a loser. They seem to be obsessed with focusing on their negatives and hiding away their positives. Quite honestly, we all have our negatives, but it is unfair to us, God, and others if that is all we find worthy of our attention. Just thinking about your experiences of people in the past should affirm what is being presented to you here.

A person with a healthy self-image will at least have a few positive things to say about themselves. There should always exist at least a healthy balance, a fifty-fifty mix, if you will. A person who never has anything pleasant to say about self definitely has a problem. The words we use to describe ourselves are like the strokes of an artists brush on a canvas. As we utter the words, we paint them upon our lives. Stroke after stroke until the picture is completed. So, what is conceived in the mind becomes displayed on and in our person.

So many people do not realize what they are communicating about themselves, or what they are talking themselves into feeling about how they are as a person. They just talk. Their words remind you of an artist who never cleans his brush in between exchanging colors. Their words are all mixed up, just like the paint. They become too busy trying to complete the picture of self to focus on what they are saying. If most can be induced to slow down and be more selective in thinking about the person they are painting, they might end up with a few positive statements and a much better picture of self.

I believe it was William Shakespeare who said "To thine own self be true. Then, as follows the night, the day, thou canst be false to no man." Whether that is a true statement or not, it is true that an indicator of low self worth is problems interacting with others. Those who isolate themselves from others are generally hiding behind a wall of fear. The fear is they will not be accepted; the belief is that they do not deserve to be accepted. That fear of rejection will keep people from fulfilling the God given desire for fellowship with others. This is a very strong need, and when they choose isolation instead of risking rejection, they reinforce the negative self image with the lack of meaningful interaction in their lives. People who tell themselves lies about their value as persons are being false to themselves, and we suspect this not only makes them false with others but also, with God.

How many times have you contacted a person having difficulty interacting with others who excused their behavior of withdrawal by claiming to enjoy being a loner. Many a wife has a husband whose non-communicative and withdrawn behavior from her is excused by the statement, "He just doesn't talk much, that's his nature." All the time the problem is he will not trust his wife any more than anyone else to enter into an intimate relationship because he fears rejection even by her. He then denies her the affirming interaction that is supposed to be a part of marriage and her needs go unmet, as well. The truth is he perceives himself as worthless. It is a false truth, and in this case, at least Shakespeare's axiom is correct in the negative. Having been false to himself, he has then been false in his most important human relationship.

If you have ever entered a room and felt isolated from everyone, you have some idea of how people suffering from low self esteem feel. They often watch and envy others who interact. They desire the interplay, but fear that someone might try to strike up conversation with them. Often they do not know why anyone would want to reject them, they just know they would. Sometimes people have built these attitudes because they were not as tall, short, thin, as well built, or pretty as they thought they should be to be worthwhile. Maybe it started out because they could not afford to dress as others, or because they moved into a strange culture where people saw them as out of place. Who knows? They do! Somewhere behind it all is root cause. It may not be obvious, but it is there somewhere until it is rooted out and exposed to the light of reality. Until the person develops new habits of thinking and reacting to relations challenges, the person with low self esteem lives in a combat zone. They are crouched in their foxhole of isolation, and prying them out takes real effort.

People do run into rejection in this life. It takes courage for them to face their fears and begin to move out into healthy relationships. Rejection, real or perceived, can send people scampering back to the foxhole. So, part of the recovery is changing the attitude toward other people's actions.

The following **case history** will spread light on the subject:

A mother brought her daughter in for counseling because of the child's refusal to interact with others. The girl came in and sat down quietly with her head down as her mother explained the problem. For the mother it centered around the fact the child refused to play or have anything to do with children her own age. She would play with children four or five years younger than her. When asked why, the child could not explain. However, during assessment it was discovered the young lady did not feel threatened by younger children. It was also revealed that she had previously been taunted by her peers. Her fear of rejection got to the point that she had been removed from public school and educated in the home. It was also noted that she spent all her time in the home, with no interest in attending or participating in sports or other activity with kids her own age. The majority of her time was spent alone at home or at home with her parents. The child also acquired obsessive/compulsive behaviors. The mother volunteered that she had been diagnosed by medical doctors as having obsessive/compulsive disorder, however, it did not respond to medication, treatment by psychiatrist, or other medical doctors. I inquired what other type of therapy the child had received besides being medicated? The answer was nothing other than weekly counseling sessions that were nothing more than sessions of interrogation. The child volunteered that in these weekly sessions the same questions were asked every time. At this point it became obvious that no one had focused on finding the root cause for the girl's difficulty in being able to interact with her own age. But it lay openly visible after just the initial assessment. Her peer group had reviled her calling her names such as ugly, clown face, stupid, and so forth. Over a period of time these statements developed into a belief. A belief in the child that she was worthless. The obsessive/compulsive behavior, shyness, refusal to have anything to do with her own age group, and of course, isolation, was all signs and symptoms of a root problem of low self worth.

Lack of confidence is also a common sign of low self worth. Those who are controlled by this problem are generally afraid they will fail at whatever they do. They tend to avoid accepting challenges because, if by chance they do fail, their self-worth will be affected. What does this mean, you may ask. First of all, it means the person's self-worth may be based on their ability to perform. Therefore, if their performance is poor, their self-worth could be damaged. So, in order to avoid running the risk of damaging their self worth, they avoid challenges. The threat here could result in the individual never functioning at their full potential. I'm sure, even as we write this book, there are many who are settling for a common laborer's job who have the potential to be a medical doctor, school teacher, etc.. The reason they are not is that they are being controlled by a lack of confidence in self.

Pastor's Plan

V. Self Image/Self Worth

The Pastor's Value

Since society abounds with wrong definitions to describe what makes a worthwhile man or woman, it is no surprise that modern civilization, like a multitude of individuals within its bounds, is on a self-destructive course. It is possible for the individual pastor or counselor to feel overwhelmed by the enormity of the need he surveys. If he is to be successful in his ministry, he must have a proper perspective of his place within the parameters defining self-worth and the ministry to the individual.

To obtain perspective, two books of the Bible really stand out. They are the books of Daniel and Revelation. It was Daniel who recorded the angelic prophecy; *"...And they that be wise shall shine as the brightness of the firmament; and they that turn many to righteousness as the stars for ever and ever."* In the Book of Revelation each invitation is offered to the individual that overcomes from his particular situation. That's how people must be looked at when you open your hand to help. One by one they are to be met within the framework of their need.

There are two groups of people you cannot help. The first you will not help either from the pulpit or the counseling chamber. That is the person who refuses to accept that the Word of God speaks to the human condition in every aspect of its existence in the world. This may be the person who sits in the pew and hears, but separates sacred from secular. We may know that any difference is an illusion, but they reject that. These will reject anything you have to show them about successful living in this world. They are without help and without hope as long as they remain in that category of people.

The second group, who cannot be helped, is those who come for counseling but refuse to accept the counsel you give them. They hear what is said about value. They may even discuss with you the things in their experience that contributed to their harmful attitudes, but they will not put into practice in their lives the conclusions and insights they arrive at in counseling. They can be guided to see truth, but they will not make it a part of themselves. These are particularly frustrating because you expend more energy, as a rule, upon them than other individuals whom you see in ministry.

You must understand that in a society that has rejected what its very existence was based on, the God of the Bible, these people are being bombarded with propaganda in the schools, media, workplace, etcetera. It is a special work of God, desired and received in the life of a person, when anyone overcomes the barriers to Biblically based healthy self-esteem in a sinful society.

When you understand you cannot help those who do not receive it, and that the response is individual as is the invitation of God, you can get on about ministering without being overcome by those who do not so choose to experience victory in their lives. This is very important to you and your family because the pain of hurting people, particularly in the area of self-esteem, is often incomprehensible. Your own self-image must be complete, for you must be able to understand their condition without being overcome by it. Never underestimating the damage a sense of worthlessness can cause must first begin with you.

We are beginning to understand that the sense of worthlessness or mis-directed self-image is destructive to both youth and adults, but actually its influence reaches to those who have not even begun to approach their teen years. Early in everyone's life the desire for approval of those around us is evidenced. What happens in these formative experiences often lays the groundwork for the future. Without the value that is Christ-centered being prepared and realized in their lives, a miserable or unsatisfying existence lies ahead until it is relieved or cauterized in some way. Our streets are filled with men and women still wandering aimlessly looking for a place to find worth.

Would to God everyone looking for self-worth would head to Calvary. It is only at and through the cross does any man, woman, boy or girl find everlasting, genuine value. It is a shame how badly it is needed and how hard man makes it to be found. I recently talked with a school superintendent about the increase of teenage problems. He said, "The greatest problem in our schools is so many youth with a lack of self-worth." He went on to say that the lack of self-worth was turning many to all types of negative behavior in an attempt to feel good about whom they are. Furthermore, he went on to say, it was not just the poor or underprivileged who suffered from low self-esteem. They came from all types of economic and environmental backgrounds. This affirms what we believe about the influence of societal propaganda upon our lives.

People will do almost anything for acceptance, approval, affirmation, love, or just attention. They want to get their needs met even if it means doing something wrong or unacceptable. We do have a problem in this world with self-esteem, and we need to do something about it. From the pulpit the issue can be addressed without violating the Scriptures. In counseling, souls will be redeemed, one on one, one by one.

Pastor's Plan

V. Self Image/Self Worth

Causes

The self-image is seen as a person's conception of self. It is tied to self-esteem because the image is what people base their estimation of worth upon. It is, as we have seen, a fact that worth and esteem go hand in hand. As noted before for all practical purposes the terms are used interchangeably, but the nuances of meaning give insight.

Self-esteem, like many other emotional problems, has experienced its period of being a "fad disorder", but notoriety does not mean the reality is any less real. The image is really everything, but not in the way the world defines it. From the world's definition we define ourselves by the kind of work we do, the recreational activities we invest our spare time in, the house we live in , the clothes we wear. We even define ourselves by the person we marry or the physical appearance of our bodies. All of these are both illusive and transitive conditions. A person who seems secure in their attitudes toward self, who has a false self-image based upon such fleeting conditions, is a candidate for a very serious fall. The evidence of this is the increasing numbers of senior/older citizens who are now making their way to the counseling office.

One of the reasons people experience grief in their lives is because they tie their definition of whom they are to something other than their relationship before Christ. When the worldly definition fails, they experience a genuine sense of loss. Probably one of the greatest of these loss reactions in recent times is self-image tied to work. People now find involuntarily changing careers as many as three times in a lifetime a common experience. Sometimes these changes means also adjusting income and social standing to fit new realities. The problem these changes can cause in the life of a person can be terminal. We desperately need to get the self-esteem of people back on track and headed in the Godly direction.

One society where the value of human life seems to have been diminished radically is the Chinese. Here the individual became nothing, and individual life value diminished. While this is not uncommon where the Buddhist religion holds sway, the Chinese condition has held a particular prominence. Here the loss of individuals, even by tens or thousands does not move the society. It has been a fertile breeding ground for philosophies that subvert the individual for the so called "collective good." One image in Western thought is the opium den. It was tolerated because the value of life was not great. Moves to make drugs legal, abortion acceptable, and suicide palatable mark a society headed down a similar path. It is little surprise that Eastern and Asian philosophy has encroached upon America when you see attitudes accepting the same moral code. The reason this is possible is not because the attitude toward self has moved toward the Asian model, but rather, it has found a common point where people lose value as persons.

The drive by shootings and senseless acts of violence in the perpetration of crimes are testimony to the growing disrespect people have for themselves and consequently toward others. To play on a popular title; "I'm No Good! You're No Good!" With that attitude is always the suspicion that the "I person" is a little more no good than the "You Person". If you remember the story of Joseph and his brothers from the Old Testament, you will remember that his brothers had every reason to consider Joseph above them. Joseph demonstrated his feelings of superiority in his attitude, and the father of the boys showed his favoritism. The brothers sought to elevate their position by eliminating the one who occupied a higher place in their little society. This is the way of the world. Instead of dealing with the personal conditions found intolerable, the world strikes out at what they secretly suspect really is above them.

Many lessons can be learned from that early example of a dysfunctional family environment. On a familial level we might realize we should not put children into competition with one another, but treat all our children fairly and with equality. Within the extended family of a church we might see that each person should feel secure in their role in the body. As a society, we should not try to eliminate differences or glorify them, such as by promoting "ethnic diversity," but rather be accepting of people as they are while encouraging them to be all they might be within the framework of their talents and abilities. Since these things have not happened in the past and will not happen in the future without the redemptive power of Christ holding full sway, people will need to be lead into being whole in their beings. Only one kind of man can answer this challenge. He is the mature man of God.

The most common cause of low self-worth expressed in adults is the result of being reared in a dysfunctional environment. Homes, where childhood growth and development is distorted with parental abandonment and neglect, offer little to be desired when the challenges of child-rearing are considered. When the environment increases in a negative direction more than simple neglect is experienced. Lessons of life in homes that say to the child that they are less-than, or not-as-good, and even outright condemnation are commonly experienced by many growing up in families that don't quite work. Stunted misshapen adults are the general product. Since most adults enter marriage unprepared for their new life with another person, let alone sharing that life with third parties, a great deal of tension can be generated in the most well-meaning of families. It is easy to see how easily people can be hurt where people either do not care to, or do not know how to be well meaning in their relationships.

Unfortunately in some homes the experiences of a child entail more than careless treatment. They experience abuse. Two kinds of abuse exist. One kind never has any physical violence. It is verbal. The tongue is a deadly weapon, we learned in the Book of James. It destroys people's self-esteem, just like it can destroy people's reputations. Now verbal abuse can be accompanied by physical abuse, but physical abuse is its own category. It doesn't matter how big the adult is, to the child the parent is bigger than anyone else. When you have a six foot three parent with hands as big as the child's face, as I did, hurt and humiliation makes the impressions on the soul that last a lifetime. Impressions that most people do not turn into positive experiences that can be used for the benefit of others.

I recall as a child having to listen to verbal abuse on a daily basis. Constantly being told I would never amount to anything has affected my life. It affected me as a child and it affected me as an adult. In our home no one communicated, they just screamed a lot. Having a different opinion or giving expression to ideas was considered rebellion, and rebellion demanded discipline. The kind of discipline I now recognize as all along having been abuse.

Very often for abused children there are three rules present:
1. Keep your mouth shut.
2. Keep your opinions, thoughts, and feelings to yourself.
3. Expressions can get you killed or make you think you are going to be. Control them.
Do you wonder that anyone who develops in such an environment has a self worth problem? The wonder is when they do not!

Physical and Verbal abuse are studies in themselves, but the important thing to be grasped here is that these things are two evils deadly to people's self-esteem, no matter at what age they experience them, but especially are they destructive to the young. A person who has been the victim or the abuser will, generally speaking, be in positive recovery for about a month for every year they were involved.

Living in an environment where no one ever says, "I love you," or "I think you are okay," or things like "you're as good as everyone else," means a very basic human need is not met. When parents are not present, either physically or emotionally, problems are inevitable. In the formative years, children are dependent on others for the development of self-concept. They are dependent on others for showing them what the standard is. The standard should be that the person is important simply on the basis of being wanted and appreciated for whom they are.

Within the educational system today very little education actually takes place. What does occur is that individuals are often laid open for victimization in their self-esteem. In the little societies of school, kids weaknesses and tender points are often discovered by their peers and preyed upon. Remember, some people need to diminish others to try to feel good about themselves. Teachers often come down on the hurt child who responds to peer baiting instead of the person causing the problem. There is a reason this occurs. In responding to "being picked on", the hurting individual appears to the teacher more disruptive than the person actually inflicting the pain. What results is a youth being doubly victimized. First by the peer, and secondly by an adult who should represent order in his life. In such a situation of lose-lose, it does not take long to produce a life-long victim.

The child who is a victim of abuse, particularly verbal abuse in the home, is more likely to become a candidate for victimization outside the home. Sometimes it seems like a sixth sense exists that points out the potential victim, but the truth is almost everybody is a candidate. The terrible thing about self-esteem victims is that they produce more victims in succeeding generations, because they inflict the suffering they have experienced on others.

When a person's self-worth is low, it will affect his ability to express worth to anything or anyone else. People have a difficult time realizing how much God loves them and values them when they do not love or value themselves. We find a principle in the observation that our relationship outwardly with man mirrors upwardly with God and Vice-versa. When the child becomes an adult he cannot live out *Ephesians 5:28:*

> *So ought men to love their wives as their own bodies.*
> *He that loveth his wife loveth himself.*

Living that Scripture out requires self-esteem. The alternative to that is finding someone lacking in self esteem who can be the target for abuse that makes the deficient person temporarily feel better about himself at a long term price to his victim. We have now brought an endless chain to its greatest point of tragedy when the greatest gift God has given to man outside of salvation is degraded. Needless to say, there can be no communion with God when such conditions exist.

Spousal abuse grows out of self esteem issues, whether the abuser is a man or a woman. People frequently seem to select people to marry who will continue patterns of abuse they experienced in early life. And people who are abused become abusers as well. They leave wounded egos that see themselves without value.

An emotionally healthy person, after being subjected to ongoing abuse, in the particularly vulnerable environment of marriage, can find they have surrendered their once healthy self concept in very short order. Many a marriage has started out with partners who felt good about whom they were that ended with one, or both, feeling worthless because of something in their life that set up an attitude that demeaned the person.

Many a vibrant woman (or man), who once shined as the sun, has ended up looking and acting like a whipped animal after enduring months or even years of abuse in some form. Every type of abuse, or even misuse, of another person strips them of their dignity and self worth. Usually by the time such people arrive in a counselor's office they only have depression, shame, humiliation, and guilt left in their self image. A person cannot live and recover in a combat zone. Let me be perfectly clear. Both men and women can give and receive abuse and destroy their mate's self esteem. Usually, but not always, men are more physical in expressing abuse than women, but how ever abuse comes, men, too, can wind up in a counseling setting looking like a "whipped puppy".

It is not uncommon for male impotence to be tied to a pattern of abuse, and like other physical signals, alert the counselor to self esteem problems arising from abuse. It is also true that abuse seems to also inhibit conception. These are results that sometimes point to a cause.

Case History

One case I am very familiar with involved a woman married to a man for five years who abused her emotionally and sometimes physically. She was in constant stress about what would happen next. On one occasion she woke to find a drunken man climbing into her bed because her husband had lost a bet. During the whole course of their marriage, no contraceptive of any type was used. Yet, she never became pregnant. After her divorce and remarriage, she was pregnant within a year even though her second husband had a low sexual drive and intercourse was infrequent. This was followed three years later with a second child. This case is interesting because even though the woman married again and conceived, after breaking the pattern of abuse against her, she carried her low self esteem into the second marriage. The relationships in this scenario were also notable. The first man she had married was a drunk, just like her father. She married, in her second marriage, a man who had been reared in a home with a drunken father, who suffered from low self worth even though he was a highly intelligent and thoroughly competent technical person. Like her mother before her, she became verbally abusive of the second husband, who finally became totally non-responsive sexually. Both of the two children of that marriage suffer from low self worth problems. The younger child, which had been most pampered, becoming pregnant as an unmarried teen.

Probably the most valuable asset a spouse has to give is self worth. When that is taken away, there is nothing left to give. In the process of being robbed of self worth, there are also other things that get lost. Feelings of love, concern, compassion, affection for others all pass away. Usually the relationship is terminated, sometimes after many years of marriage. But, without a recovery process, the divorce itself may only serve to heighten the sense of failure, ego worthlessness. When you think that self esteem, in one or both spouses, is one of the greatest contributors to one out of every two marriages ending in divorce, it becomes clearer why this point deserves special emphasis.

Sexual abuse is another work of Satan that destroys self worth. Sex abuse includes rape, molestation, and harassment. It has many characteristics that are common and some that are unique in what this category of abuse can do to a person. Nothing leaves a person so humiliated, degraded, and violated as sexual abuse. Survivors of sexual abuse deal with long term problems involving their self worth including shame, quiet fears, desperation, recurring intrusive nightmares, and so on. Individuals who have had to endure such violations tend to view themselves as objects rather than humans.

It is easy to understand how a depersonalized mentality can be acquired if you stop and think about it. Those who were sexually abused were considered as objects to be used for another's self gratification or revenge. Whether for a long time, or in a single traumatic event, they saw someone take authority over their being to use them; to dehumanize them; to make them less than others. They were robbed of their ability to feel good about themselves because the person who exercised such power over them saw them as a thing.

A person who has to endure continuing sexual abuse or harassment comes to think that the only time they are wanted involves using them. Is it any wonder that anyone who experiences these things have problems with a sense of worthlessness? Children who experience such things wind up being robbed of both childhood and adulthood. They are stripped of pride, self confidence, courage, as well as emotional, mental, and physical health. Each of these conditions can impact people's feelings of worth. So, you see the validity of saying sexual abuse may actually be the most devastating attack that can be launched on a person's self esteem.

As this book is being written, an estimated thirty thousand persons will take their life. The reason for that is they have weighed themselves in the balance and found themselves wanting. What was lacking. A sense of their own worth.

Pastor's Plan

V. Self Image/Self Worth

Meeting the Need

In our dialogue we hit the main causes of poor self-esteem, such as the dysfunctional family failing to provide the emotional needs of its members, the tensions of society, and the challenges of survival as a person within the work place, etcetera. We must acknowledge that self esteem causes do not always come neatly packaged. The more subtle causes of acquired self esteem problems often take time to dig out. Some counselors have argued that finding causes of low self esteem is not really important. They believe that with self-esteem issues it is sufficient to deal only with the present condition and go on from there. Certainly this might be possible in some cases, but it is not a good idea to state categorically that it is always the case, because every person is not the same and every self esteem scenario is not the same. Plainly, it is obvious that self-esteem can be an issue among other issues or the root cause of other issues. Likewise, the means of addressing self-esteem must be as varied as the conditions it can be found in.

The one certainty in a self esteem issue is that the problem for the individual does not go away when the conditions that bred the loss of self esteem goes away. Over time, the method of expressing the feelings of inadequacy and so forth change ways they find outlet into a life as the environment changes, but the problem remains unchanged. That is, the problem remains unchanged unless you want to call the possibility of the problem getting bigger in a life change. Once the pattern of negative response to adversity, or just to themselves, is established in a person, it is a very hard habit to break. No matter how a person overcomes self-esteem issues in their lives they must inevitably confront them and identify them for the enemies within that they are.

If popularity or success, riches or fame could make people feel good about themselves, we wouldn't have so many movie stars in therapy; rich men who had taken their own lives, or athletes on drugs. Why do so many people establish the wrong standards on which they base their self-worth? Perhaps it is because as a little child they had to figure the standard out for themselves, and is often the case, they figured it out wrong. The substitutes for the real thing purchase momentary good feelings, but they are fleeting illusions. The movie star with an Oscar strives for two. One box office success must follow another if they are to stay on top, and even then they must deal with the valleys between. The millionaire must make another million or initiate another leveraged buy-out and so forth. The kid who must always be the honor student, cheerleader, football hero, and so forth can be as big a mess emotionally as the one who walks stoop shouldered and sits off to himself on breaks at school. Some people actually become addicted to popularity and other such crutches, using them as a kind of medication to make them feel good about themselves.

It is great when a parent who has grown up with their own self-esteem problems makes a wonderful recovery. Perhaps it has been through preaching and counseling, life experiences, or some of the better self-help books that they figured out the self worth issue in their life. Now wanting to turn into affirming parents, they likely find problems have already begun at home. Usually this scenario has come too late in the life-cycle of the children to spare them. The child has already begun to suffer as the parent once did, in accord with its age, within that environment. The problem, like other emotional problems, passes from generation to generation and does not get better in its effects as it is passed on.

When the adults in the family do see the errors in the standards they have held in life, and speak of those errors openly with their children, it is a far better thing for the whole family than simply trying to cover it over. But it would be a foolish assumption if the adults expect to solve all problems that have resulted. The role they could not play in positive development before, or the role they did play in negative development is a part of their child's history and problems. Developing a relationship where this can be discussed openly and without recrimination can be of good benefit when it is possible. At any point in life, becoming an affirming parent or even grandparent will be a way to stop or alter the passage of self-esteem problems to succeeding generations.

Even though many Christians do suffer from this problem, we affirm that it is at Calvary where self-esteem is obtained. It is possible that some who come to Christ in the counseling encounter have an advantage over the Christian who has fallen victim to this malady or who has continued to suffer from it for years after their salvation experience. Failure to go into the new life in Christ carries with it a load of guilt that can burden tender sensitivities. No doubt this burden has impelled believers to proclaim spiritual experiences or attainments falsely.

It is astounding the number of born-again believers who are struggling to gain a sense of self worth. Our heart-felt hope is that this section will help the pastor to not only recognize the problem, but gain insight on where to start at resolving it. Realize this. Grace has been abundantly manifested toward the person, who though suffering from low self-esteem, has experienced the love of God sufficient to receive His salvation. They are miracles in which God wishes to reveal Himself.

Coming to an understanding of the Love of God that was displayed at Calvary for them, and has been kept for a pouring out upon their lives, can alter a person's whole perspective about themselves. No more wonderful passage exists than John 3:16, when applied by a person to himself:

> For God so loved me
> that He gave His only begotten Son for Me
> that I could believe on Him,
> and not only live forever,
> but live an abundant life right now.

This is the personalization of the word. It is soothing balm for our doubts and fears. It makes us whole.

Just as God takes us in salvation right where we are, that is how you will have to take people who are going to be helped in self esteem/self-worth situations. That is, if you are going to take them anywhere. Take them first to the cross, and then on to becoming whole persons in Christ; you have to meet them where they are, just as Jesus did. We have really emphasized this point throughout. You cannot expect hurting people to meet you where you would like them to be. Most often it is going to take some time to work with people suffering in this area. Generally, when the root is self-esteem, whatever the cause of feelings inside them, they have afflicted them for some time. This scar must be healed on the inside, not just the outside, or the infection will soon break through to the center of their lives. The minister who will help the hurting in this area must have patience. Feelings of rejection by you can seem some of the most devastating of rejections to a person who has turned to you for help. It is in the power of a pastor's hand to be the greatest counselor to the individual hurting in the area of self esteem, or the most devastating.

Even when you refer a person with self-esteem issues out to a Christian Counselor, they are going to continue to look to you for affirmation. After all, you are their pastor.

Pastor's Plan

V. Self Image/Self Worth

Healing in His Wings

The main source for building self esteem is the Word of God. It far exceeds all other books written on how to obtain a healthy concept of self. Just studying and reading God's love letter can change our attitude about ourself. In essence, the Word is a tool that can constantly be used to remind us of what great worth we have and the great value God places on us.

Those who come seeking help in building self worth should immediately be directed to the Scriptures. Too often, self help books are utilized to assist ministers in ministering to the victim of low self worth, to the neglect of the Scriptures. The Word of God, too often, is totally neglected by people who say they are doing Christian Counseling.

I'm not implying all books on self worth are useless. We recommend books to you on the subject. But the one thing that is certain, and you should understand this when you are preparing for counseling, is that of all the books you can get, God's Word is the best book. Scripture has a way of building a positive self worth that has a correct foundation and viewpoint, like no other book.

The role you will play is two fold:

1. You will introduce your counselee to the Book. Many people do not realize the value of the Book. Too many have no acquaintance with it other than finding Scripture on a Sunday.

2. You will guide them to appropriate passages for their need. It does not matter if the counselee has been a deacon for thirty years, he still might not know where to go to have his problem ministered to in the Word. That is why he has come to you.

You don't want clients to select their passages at a chance. They might wind up like the fellow in the story about such chance Scripture selection who, looking for guidance, opened the Bible haphazardly and read, Judas went out and hung himself. Then he flipped again and read,

"Go thou and do likewise." You are the guide to the Scripture that gives the best and fastest result for the specific need. You are the promoter of daily and specific Scripture reading.

Sometimes the only pill that we need is the Gospel. A great deal of medication is prescribed for people suffering from low self esteem. In genuine conditions of simple low esteem, not compounded with other organic problems, this has only the effect of numbing the spirit and ultimately results in increased symptomatic depression for the hurting member. The mind is the target, but drugs are not the means of cleansing. The mind often needs a good washing with the Word to produce a change in the thoughts of the heart.

Positive thinking is a term we almost hesitate to use for the abuse some men have done to it. But positive thinking in the truly Christian sense is a way people can boost their self esteem. I have a saying that I like to use when working with people with self esteem problems. It goes, "we are not what we hear, but we are what we think." Negative thoughts about self have to go. Most who have self esteem problems spend the majority of their time thinking about the wrong things. They indulge in what we describe by a term you have already encountered in this text, "Stinkin' Thinkin'."

God's Word tells us to concentrate on the good things:

> *Finally brethren,*
> *whatsoever things are true,*
> *whatsoever things are honest,*
> *whatsoever things are just,*
> *whatsoever things are pure,*
> *whatsoever things are lovely,*
> *whatsoever things are of good report;*
> *if there be any virtue,*
> *and if there be any praise,*
> *think on these things.*
> ***Philippians 4:8***

Why do you suppose He said that? Because God knows negative thinking has a very destructive effect on how we feel. Especially how we feel about self.

Pastor, it is a must that instruction be given to the hurting member to change their thinking about self. Negative thoughts are to be replaced by positive ones. One of the important steps in doing this is getting the counselee to listen to themselves. They need to start to hear in a conscious way what they are telling themselves about themselves. People with self esteem problems have quite often spent months, even years, saying all the wrong things to their own person. This is where the input from without has its damaging effect, when the individual agrees with whatever was the root cause of the issue and ingrains it into their being deep enough that they believe it, and it becomes a stronghold in their lives. It is when the belief is established that they act on it, and it is manifested in such things as lack of confidence, depression, withdrawal, and the host of other negative emotions and behaviors.

It is urgent that the negative thought be replaced by the positive. This is done by the counselee learning to be in control of his thought life. Listening more carefully to what they are telling themselves is a key step to replacing negative thoughts with more positive ones. This may sound impossible, but it is not. It may be frustrating to the client at first, but they must be encouraged to work at it. We are created as creatures of choice and, therefore, we choose what we think about, and that includes self. You may call it an act of mind control, but the fact is that if you do not have control of your mind someone else does, and we can surmise from scripture, god is not a promoter of negative thought, so who is left?

People who come for counseling on self worth issues are already in mental warfare. It is territory that must be reclaimed and regained through the power of the blood and the working of the word. It demands choice on the part of the client. They must assume responsibility for their thinking. Until they do that and go forward to begin the struggle, it is not likely they will ever be able to change how they think, feel, and ultimately act out about anything.

The use of handout material can be used in conjunction with the Word of God and positive thinking exercise. This material must be loaded with positive biblical reinforcers. What we mean by biblical reinforcers are things that do not contradict the Scripture, things that are not fundamentally humanist or new age in their philosophy. Many helps are available, and have even been produced for duplication by other authors, but you will notice we have sought to save you time by providing some resources in our own text. The client can turn their house or personal areas into reminders that they are special possessions of God of great worth so that they get reinforcement that is proper. When you have chosen and provided the material you can also have confidence that it is not the "hogwash" the world offers.

Written material of all types that are consistent with Christian principles can be used very effectively to remind the member to consciously change from negative to positive perspectives about self. Handouts and books are not the solution, they are very helpful tools. One of the finest of these is "The Search For Significance," recommended in this text. It is the premier man produced work in helping people to recover from self esteem problems.

Avoiding two types of people is also helpful for you client. The two types of people to be avoided are negative thinkers, and the verbally abusive. Sometimes this means a person has to limit contacts with members of their own family or even household. Many people surround themselves with absolutely too many negative folks. "You can't hang out with buzzards and soar with eagles!" Those struggling with these problems need to be around positive thinking and positive acting people. There is not anything that will take the wind out of a client's sail (or your sail, too, for that matter) than negative people. People who think and act positively are not only a joy to be around, but a definite boost to low self worth. Encouraging a client to develop their own support group of friends, who look at things on the bright side, who will affirm them and encourage them, is a great step.

One question that will arise in reference to negative family influence is how do you overcome it. It is not a question that has an easy answer and must be worked out in the context of varying situations with such factors as age, finances, and relationships. But in every case you will have to be constantly reinforcing the thought with the client that other's negatives are not to be allowed to be transferred to themselves. Considering the sources "bad vibrations" are coming from and mentally choosing to disregard the negatives of others, no matter how close they are, may be the only solution possible. But the best possible procedure is to extract them from the negative environment until they become strong enough to counter it.

People suffering from low self worth need to laugh and look at things that are positive and promote a lighter attitude. For this reason much television is off the list of things to bombard the client's senses. Getting out and going to places of peace and tranquillity, and places of fun and positive excitement are good for people. We have such places close to our Center (within two hours driving). One of my favorites is Callaway Gardens. Here a person can go to a quiet spot and reflect, ride a paddle wheel boat, sit in a beautiful Chapel and pray, ride a bicycle through the woods, explore an old log cabin home, enjoy the beauty of a butterfly conservatory, visit a variety of plants and vegetable gardens, or take a horticulture class. Get the picture. Peace and tranquillity of soul is promoted, providing an atmosphere where a person can be at peace with the restless self. Here, healing of the soul can occur, the outlook can become lighter. Such a place may be close to where you live, too.

Finally, the person suffering from low self worth should be instructed in how to become spiritually fit and how to stay that way. This can be accomplished first of all by encouraging prayer. We have given you our choice for the tool best suited for promoting this in an earlier section. In every case a tool might not be necessary, but in many cases they are. In our book you find much discussion on the value of prayer, but even so, we feel that this topic has not been overemphasized. At this point two observations are made on the value of prayer. The first is that the supplicant, asking God's help with their problem, releases God to exercise His power to enable them to be victors instead of victims. And the other point is that a necessary element of prayer, thanksgiving, benefits the supplicant by focusing them on the positive. Being thankful to God for the person that he created can lead to genuine love of self.

Being thankful for self acknowledges that God did not make a mistake when He created the person we are. When we realize we are not a mistake and that we are special, unique, and greatly loved, we begin to feel better about self. We need to recognize that and so does our client.

Church attendance, along with the positive friendships that can be built, provides much needed love and affirmation. Not everyone who attends church is positive, but you will find more positive upbeat people at church than at a funeral home. I venture to say that the things going on at church are more positive than negative. It was at church that I personally learned that I was greatly loved and that I did have great worth. Some of the very finest, encouraging, loving people can be found at God's house. So it is to the House of God the pastor should direct, even insist, the individual go who is seeking help in the area of self worth.

I recall years ago a young man started attending church where I was serving. As I began to get acquainted with this young man I discerned that he had a very poor concept of self. I found out he had a speech problem. He stuttered. He was poor, had poor hygiene, wore old and worn out clothes, all of which earned him taunting from kids his age. It was apparent that his poor life style and speech problems had been the vehicle of his loss of self worth. But the church members encouraged him to keep attending and get involved. In other words, these church members received this young man with open arms. As time went by this young man began to blossom. In spite of his stuttering he would from time to time stand in front of the church and speak about how God had helped him.

He eventually became very involved in youth work. This young man could and would go fill up a church bus with other unchurched kids and bring them to youth services without even being prompted. He learned sign language and began to minister to the hearing impaired by serving as their interpreter during preaching and other church functions. What changed this poor, ragged, stuttering young man's outlook? The church! A church that did what God designed a church to do! I've seen many enter God's House with a sad look and a hanging head who left with a smile and lifted chin. That is as it should be for it is in those who attend that house that the Word both living and written should richly dwell!

Pastor's Plan

V. Self Image/Self Worth

Resources

Book Recommended:	*Verbal Abuse*
Authored by:	Dr. Grace Ketterman, M.D.
Published by:	Servant Publications Ann Arbor, Michigan

This is one of those books which should be referenced in several areas of our text. The thoughtful pastor will find it useful for helping people in several areas of counseling where abuse of the verbal kind has affected attitudes and perceptions. After reading this book the minister will appreciate that verbal abuse is often part of the basis for other problems.

The book has the capacity of speaking both to the abused and abuser. Dr. Ketterman points out that they are often the same person. You will understand how the one person can either be both at the same time, or at different stages of their lives.

In the area of spousal abuse, Dr. Ketterman makes it clear that the abuser can be either the husband or the wife. It can also be both.

Even though we might wish more detail and depth to the defining of categories of verbal abuse covered by the book, it is certainly an adequate primer on the subject. It has an added advantage of offering a 12-Step outline for recovery from verbal abuse and a 12-week guide for support group meetings. It can form a key part of an effective pastor's plan for abuse recovery.

One criticism we have is that the book has a shortage of Biblical reference. In keeping with Comfort Care Ministries' philosophy of bathing counseling in the Word, this discrepancy will require pastoral augmentation of the text with Scripture. Until the text is expanded and a workbook is available, providing appropriate and adequate Scripture reference will have to be done by the pastor. But with Scripture augmentation, the pastor can use the text with its end of chapter questions as a workbook of sorts.

The pastor who recognizes the implications of what Dr. Ketterman reveals from a theological perspective can use much of the book within sermons for the benefit of the lives in his congregation. It has been my experience that such use promotes individual responses of a very positive nature.

Video Recommended:	*The Search For Significance*
Authored by:	Robert S. McGee Founder and President Rapha Treatment Centers
Published by:	Rapha Resources Houston, Texas

Useful in nearly every counseling encounter because of its reinforcement of right thinking (God's Thinking) in the conduct of life in every situation. Reinforces the value of the person in God's eyes. Expounds the necessity of salvation to victory in living.

Video Outcome: Individual realizes that they are not unique in what they are experiencing.
Video Seminar is divided into four parts:

Part I. The Search Begun
- The Importance of Relationships
  - Believing a lie.
  - Self Worth = Opinions of Others + Performance
- Where God fits in

Part II. Overcoming Deception: The Four False Beliefs
- Being overwhelmed by emotions destroys lives
  - God thinks correctly, is not overwhelmed
  - We should think as God thinks
- Only God's acceptance can fulfill our need for acceptance.
  - The love of Christ is not conditional.

Part III.	Pathways to Freedom Continues the four false beliefs. Thinking God's thoughts He bought our freedom at great price You are somebody in Christ Facing your deception.
Part IV.	The Search Concluded God's answer for permanent change There is nothing you can do in life more satisfying than doing what God is into. Jesus paid the price on the cross so we could have a brand new start. He desires for us to have that freedom right now. The rest of life is a learning/living experience.

Based upon the book: The Search For Significance.

Book recommended:	*Beyond the Darkness: Healing for Victims of Sexual Abuse*
Authored by:	Cynthia A. Kubetin & James Mallory, M.D.
Published by:	Rapha/Word Publishing Houston & Dallas Texas

The book is filled with accounts of incidences of child abuse that illustrate important issues in that type of abuse. The author, Cynthia Kubetin, presents these as one who can identify, having had to overcome this trauma. Reading this book will help the pastor to understand what is going on in the life of the member who turns to him for help. The material is thoroughly Christocentric.

"Beyond the Darkness" given to an abuse victim will, first of all, let them know they are not alone. Secondly, it will continually reassure them of their value. Third, it will demonstrate that others have come away from being victims to being victors. It will show them how it was done and reassure they can do it too.

While the book may be given to some individuals who have suffered abuse to read and work through on their own, the wise pastor may decide to use it as part of his Pastor's Plan of counseling, following the Study Guide in back of the book. If the hurting member stays on track (some lessons may need repetition), the abuse victim can move to reinforcement counseling at the conclusion of the program, lasting approximately twelve months.

Each chapter is, or at least has the potential to be, the most important chapter of the book. Special attention should be paid to the list of Special Helps on page xi. You will find these useful tools when other parts of the book are not needed.

To this list should be added:

The Healing Process/Safety Consideration pgs 20-22
Learning to Interpret Messages pgs 49-50
A Prayer for Perseverance pg 68

Minister's Notes: ______________________________

Pastor's Plan

VI. Marital Conflict, Separation, and Divorce

Love Is A Decision, Gary Smalley
If Only He Knew, Gary Smalley
For Better Or For Best, Gary Smalley
Love Life For Every Married Couple, Dr. Wheat
Passages of Marriage, a Minirth Meier resource

Pastor's Plan

VI. Marital Conflict, Separation, and Divorce

Causes

The fundamental cause of marital conflict, separation, and divorce is unmet needs. These needs are diverse and vary in their emphasis in different persons' lives, but they orbit around the core needs of people. These core needs have two aspects in which they manifest themselves in marriage. They are:

1. Security in love
2. Significance in relationship

As Christians, we know that people are supposed to draw their security and significance from God. But we have to ask ourselves, is it then wrong that we depend on a mate to meet needs in these areas? The answer is no. And the reason we must answer that way is because God designed marriage and marital relationship to be the school room in life that teaches of our greater relationship to Him. In fact man's duty to his wife is described in Ephesians 5 as being likened to Christ's response to the church.

> *For the husband is the head of the wife,*
> *even as Christ is the head of the church:*
> *and he is the savior of the body...*
> *Husbands, love your wives,*
> *even as Christ also loved the church:*
> *and gave Himself for it...*
> *So ought men to love their wives as their own bodies.*
> *He that loveth his wife loveth himself...*
> ***Ephesians 5:23,25,28***

In like manner, the response of a wife to a husband is on a par with what the church response is supposed to be to our Lord Jesus Christ:

> *Therefore as the church is subject unto Christ,*
> *so let the wives be to their own husbands in every thing.*
> ***Ephesians 5:24***

In the Ephesians, teaching the foundation for understanding the differences in focus of need between the husband and wife is illustrated. The husband looks primarily for the need of significance to be met by the wife and the wife is searching for need of security in love to be met by the husband. Each, also, has a corresponding need of security and significance, but the dominant need varies according to gender. Therefore in the conclusion of the chapter we read:

Nevertheless let every one of you in particular so love his wife
even as himself;
and the wife see that she reverence her husband.

This statement recognizes the unique difference between the focus of men and women and commands that the spouse render unto the other in the area of that focus. Thus a statement opening up the thought is clarified:

Submitting yourselves one to another
in the fear of God.

Ephesians 5:21

Unmet needs in marriages, whether the need falls in the aspect of significance or security, exists in two characteristic categories. They are in the area of some activity present that needs to cease or they dwell in the realm of something absent that needs to be present in the individuals practice of their lives. It is just like sin. Sin has only two types: That thing which we ought to do and do not, and that which we ought not to do and yet do:

For that which I do I allow not:
for what I would, that do I not:
but what I hate, that do I.

Romans 7:15

Therefore to him that knoweth to do good,
and doeth it not,
to him it is sin.

James 4:17

That is right! Failure to meet the needs of the person one has pledged their life to is sin, whether it be through something they did or did not do. Husbands and wives so very frequently lack a realistic conception of the importance of their joint undertaking, both to this life and that to come. It is not only because that failure is a sin issue, but it is also an issue of understanding spiritual things and of serving God, as we serve one another.

The relationship that is lived with the idea that mutual conduct should glorify God, by the care shown for each other's needs, can be heaven on earth for those so embarked. The marital partners who look at their responses in godly love being responsibility they have regardless of the performance of the other, find marriage instructive and satisfying, even if demanding. Thus they live out in the flesh the example of God, who commended His love toward us, while we were yet sinners.

> *But God commendeth His love toward us,*
> *in that,*
> *while we were yet sinners,*
> *Christ died for us.*
>
> ***Romans 5:8***

Real love, Godlike love, commended love, is love that is a decision, not an emotion.

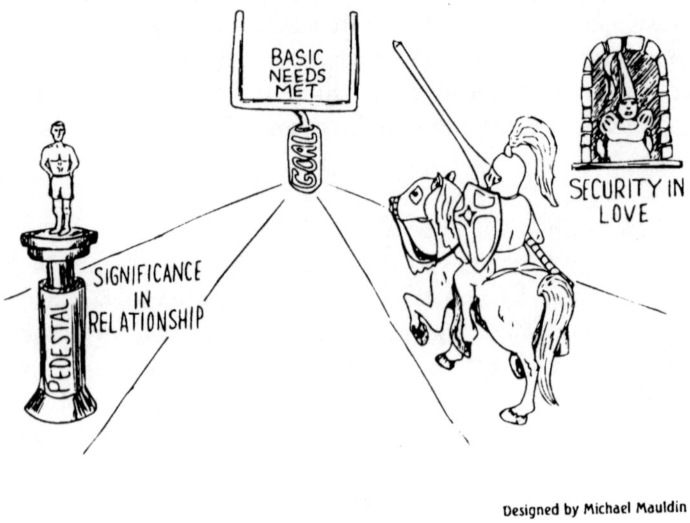

Goal Illustration

Why do people fail to meet the needs of a person to whom they have pledged a lifetime of faith and love to? It would be easy to shrug the shoulders and chalk it all up to original sin and stop at that point, but that does nothing to meet the needs posed by the problem. To understand a little of mankind's marital difficulties, we must remember that he or she is a multifaceted being with all six areas impacting on their relationship with the world, and most particularly, the person they have married. Remember, these are:

Spiritual
Physical
Emotional
Social
Mental
Volitional or Self Will

We all have the capacity of being "out of whack" because of our carnal natures, but we all do not fail in our marriages, even though we may not be perfect in them. When marriages are in distress, the problem goes beyond our fallen nature into areas where there are strongholds contrary to God's plan established in those lives. For even lost people can have satisfactory marriages even though they are separated from the Gospel of truth, if they obey certain common rules.

The variations of how people express their failure is overwhelming. Can we sum up these excuses; lump them into certain key groupings that make sense of it all? The answer again is yes.
The three general headings or repositories into which people's excuses for failure really fit are:

1. <u>Alienation from Christ, or at least the life in Christ:</u>
Even though it is possible for a lost person to have a good marriage, it is an abnormality. So why is it that a lost person can have a good marriage and a saved person can have failure? The answer is that even though they do not have the word of God on how to live out the marriage relationship, they nevertheless do those things, whether they have learned them by observation or practice them by virtue of their personality makeup.

For there is no respect of persons with God...
For when the Gentiles which have not the law,
do by nature the things contained in the law,

these, having not the law, are a law unto themselves:
Which shew the work of the law written in their hearts,
their conscience also bearing witness,
and their thoughts the mean while accusing or else excusing one another;

Romans 2:11,14,15

The individuals who do not practice the principles of God's Word in their lives have corresponding problems related to it. It is the law of the harvest, sowing wind and reaping whirlwind tempered by the factor of the other member in the marriage.

2. Developmental failure-Failure to learn skills that contribute to being a good marriage partner during the formative years of life.

This failure can be the result of bad example. Such as the bad example of a mother or father who did not practice good marital principles in their own lives. Divorced parents have more children that divorce than do parents who stick together and work out problems.

Failure to develop marriage skills can come from parents who are abusive to each other or their children. They then produce children who think this is the way to live out their lives. Parents who do not respect their mates also produce children who enter marriage defensively, determined not to be the victim they saw the parent they identify with being.

Some developmental failures result not from the relationships within the parental marriage that was over, but from the atmosphere of coddling and placating within family life that allowed the child to grow into the self centered and selfish adult.

Developmental failure, caused by the intentional or unintentional wrong teaching about sex and other areas of marital relationship, carries over from generation to generation.

And, finally, there is the developmental failure of the individual who, though given every opportunity for success by environment and proper care, hard headedly decide they want to have their own way in all things to the exclusion of the other. These are the worst of all possible mates and utterly contemptible in their performance within the marriage.

3. Failures caused by obstacles- Obstacles are things that have intruded into a person's life, either through wrong decisions or by the actions of others.

Two big obstacles that keep rearing their ugly heads throughout the modern history of man are alcohol and drugs. Just like drinking and driving, alcohol, drugs, and marriage do not mix. It is not too surprising, since the word for drug use is translated witchcraft in the Scripture, that the holiest of exercises and one of the unholiest of activities, should be antagonistic to one another. The exercise of a genuine relationship, in the marital context, places demands on all parts of our being. This precious possession can survive the hardships of impairment only when they are not self-induced.

Low self worth is both an obstacle and a developmental failure. Very often it is an induced failure rather than the conscious decision of an individual. But, it is virtually impossible for a human being to meet another person in the area of their need if they don't believe that they are worthwhile. The reason this is true is if they are not worthwhile, then anything they have to offer another is not worthwhile either. And , in the extreme, anyone who considers them worthwhile cannot be worthy of respect and genuine consideration. It is easy to see how large and painful this obstacle can be in the context of a marriage.

Sexual difficulties and sexual development in a marriage are two different issues as long as the sexual development progresses in the relationship. The best estimates of average growth into satisfying sexual compatibility is twelve years. But as long as the relationship is being worked at and developed in such degree that utter frustration is not overwhelming either partner, continuing sexual development should be considered promising at any year in the marriage relationship. Problems of sexual difficulties are not promising and are genuine obstacles when the issues involve:

(1) Inordinate desire for activities that cause pain to a partner;

(2) Fails to respect them as a person;

(3) Violates the sanctity of the marriage bed;

(4) Limits the satisfaction to either mate in the sexual relationship either by frequency or function;

(5) Is not entered into freely and joyfully as an expression of their mutual caring for one another.

Career difficulties used to be centered only in men as an obstacle to marital success. However this is not longer the case. Some people have gone so far to maintain separate houses in different parts of the country for the sake of following careers at the sacrifice of marriage. It is small wonder that such arrangements break down relationships. That this was likely should have been clear to people who study society when they had opportunity to study military people, who often have recurring and prolonged separations as part of their occupations, but if any sounded a warning, it went unheeded. It is still most often that men use career to try and achieve feelings of significance they have missed in marriage and in other relationships, but the women are coming on strong.

Finally, the last issue we will mention is codependency, itself. Tied to self esteem, yet separate, its controlling and being controlled nature does not reflect the freedom that we encounter in Christ. It goes without saying that the codependent cannot enter fully into the life in Christ, neither can they enter fully into a marriage relationship. It is easily seen for the enormous obstacle it is.

When looking to understand the causes of marital discord, you can find no substitute for knowing the people. You must know them not only as they are outwardly today, but know them for where they have been, as well as knowing how they are inwardly. The pastor, who knows his people and invests a lifetime in ministering to them, can save much heartache in doing effective premarital counseling. This is the best time to identify and deal with causes, before they become tied up in the marital relationship.

Pastor's Plan

VI. Marital Conflict, Separation, & Divorce

Quick Look Checklist

Marital Issues Checklist

There are many issues around which marital problems turn, but they seem to be in common categories of conflict. For the sake of time and expediency, this list represents the common issues you will encounter.

1. Infidelity
2. Jealousy
3. Poor Communications
4. Poor self worth
5. Sexual Abstinence
6. Physical Abuse
7. Emotional Abuse
8. Mental Abuse
9. Lack of Affection
10. Financial Problems
11. Role Reversals
12. Parenting Issues
13. Control Problems
14. Sickness

15. Death of a Child

16. In-law Interference

17. Blame

18. Unable to Resolve Conflicts

Pastor's Plan

VI. Marital Conflict, Separation, & Divorce

Quick Look Checklist

Checklist of Divorce Issues

1. Infidelity (adultery) and Sexual Issues
2. Communication Problems- (lack of skills)
3. Alcohol and Drug addictions
4. Personal Issues- such as immaturity, poor self worth.
5. Parenting Differences (children involved may even be promoting conflict)
6. Jealousy (between spouse and family members)
7. Finances (spending differences; financial insecurity)
8. Spousal abuse
9. Chronic and Terminal Illnesses
10. Lack of Quality Time Together
11. Codependency
12. Unresolved Conflicts Prior to Marriage.
13. Lack of Christ/Holy Spirit
14. Absence of Partner (spouse chronically gone hunting, fishing, sports, etc.)
15. Role Reversals

16. Career Differences (Spouse concentrates on career or job too much)

17. Interference From In-Laws

18. Wrong Influences (from outsiders)

19. Lack of Honor (marital partner does not demonstrate respect for the other)

20. Lack of Appreciation/Affection (demonstrated by marital partner)

Pastor's Plan

VI. Marital Conflict, Separation, & Divorce

Signs and Symptoms

The Signs and Symptoms of marital conflict are varied. Fortunately, people only have so many ways they can express themselves or give vent to emotions. This gives the counselor some stable ground on which to make observations and assessments. The danger is that the counselor will place his values upon the signs and symptoms observed rather than seeking to understand the client's meanings. Drawing the participants into dialogue, both with you and with one another in a controlled environment, helps to define what those meanings are even as progress is made in healing relationships.

Emotions, when they occur as symptoms, include anger, hopelessness, despair, sorrow, bitterness, disappointment, and so forth. It is the nature of people to resent what they see as the source of pain in their lives, and this resentment may be expressed in continuing or transitive ways. This manner and range of emotions experienced is based on factors separate from the marriage itself, but remember you are dealing with the whole person, not just the part.

Physical illness of a debilitating nature may even appear as symptomatic of marital conflict. For instance, by unconsciously deciding to become ill, an individual avoids confrontations and responsibilities within the marriage. Many a dollar has been spent paying doctors to find and treat illness whose origin lay in the marital relationship. It is important when people are expressing their emotions that the cause of the emotion be uncovered, because the feelings of today can destroy the person tomorrow.

An illness may be a sign, just as sudden outbursts of unexplainable anger, vicious cutting remarks, physical violence, expressions of bitter and cynical attitudes, and so forth, may be. In a women these things become signs of a "closed spirit," which signals that she has lost faith in the person she was prepared to make her hero. The man she wanted to view as her knight in shining armor, so to speak. The saying, "hell hath no fury like a woman scorned," might have been intended to be applied to the lady whose affections were not returned, but they are far more appropriate to that unhappy damsel who has been wooed, won, and wasted.

The silent treatment can be a sign of trouble both in men and women. Sometimes, it is the instigator of problems in a relationship. Men, more often than women, cause problems by failure to communicate. This is probably because most women focus their activities in the creative side of their brain where emotions primarily dwell. Men do not feel that need to communicate about things as much as women do, as a rule, hence, this is fertile ground for friction. But when relationships break down, men and women can both withdraw from the other and "clam up." Then, lack of communication can be a signal that the other partner would do well to heed. The problem with genuine clamming up, that is not always done as a control method to manipulate the mate, is it is often indicative of lost hope that must be restored. When people are in this mode, it is often very hard to get them to participate in counseling.

Needless to say, the silent treatment has its opposite component. As one fine Christian lady said to me about her husband many years ago, "I wish he would have an opinion about something. Everything I do is fine! He makes me so mad I want to scream! Whatever I cook is fine! Whatever I want to buy is fine! I just wish he would tell me what he really thinks once in a while!" Here was a woman doing all the right things and doing them very well, who was turning into a harridan with her husband because he was too passive. She wanted him to take a bigger part in her life and for him to include her, where he could, in his affairs. In short, she wanted a relationship on a continuing routine basis. That really was not too much to ask. Unfortunately, she had married a man who had been trained that the lines of responsibility and authority were very clear cut and distinct in marriage. She became aggressive because she felt uncertainty in her search for security in love. She equated his taking notice of her activities and showing approval of them into his approval and acceptance (love) of her, which then comforted her that her world was secure and safe. Her changing attitudes threatened his feelings of significance in the relationship, which he tried to compensate for by concentrating more on developing his part time business to win her approval. Their relationship was then on a roller coaster ride where both were communicating through signs that the other could not correctly interpret.

Pastor's Plan

VI. Marital Conflicts, Separation, & Divorce

Quick Look Checklist

Signs and Symptoms of Marital Problems

1. Outbursts of Anger
2. Saying Mean Things (One or Both Members)
3. Prolonged Pouting
4. Falsely Accusing
5. Blaming One Another
6. Lack Of or Withdrawal Of Affection
7. Resistant To Communication
8. Nonspecific Or Indeterminable Illness
9. Looking For Needs Resolution From Another Source:
    1. Alcohol and/or Drugs
    2. Sex Outside of Marriage
    3. Workaholic Seeking Recognition
    4. Substitute of Church for Family

    This list of relationship substitutes can get very long. People are ingenious at trying to resolve pain in their lives.

In reading Signs and Symptoms correctly, there is no substitute for experience, however, common sense and willingness to commit the energy required to be a keen observer are equally important. Even experience has its weakness, for in it lies the danger of supposing that what has been observed before is always true in every case.

Pastor's Plan

Marital Conflicts, Separation, & Divorce

Marriage Issues

It has become apparent, in the little discussion we have had here, that the subject of why people fail is large, but not unmanageable. People who want help in their marriage can be helped, if genuinely, they want to receive help. However, some of the people who come to you will want you to solve their problems without them having to do any investment of themselves in their problem resolution. Nowhere else is this lack of commitment by people to their own recovery any more evident than when marital issues are the subject. An individual, or individuals who have this type of attitude, need a good healthy dose of reality to confront them, as soon as you become aware this is their attitude.

Other people come wanting the pastor to fix the problems of the person they are married to, but have no thought of correcting, altering, or modifying anything in their own lives. Every marriage has issues where the other partner must, or should grow, into wholeness, even where severe dysfunction exists in the other mate. Frequently, a blaming mate is a contributor to, or even the source of trouble for the person having overt problems affecting the marriage.

Until marriage partners get past those types of attitudes, they cannot be helped, because it is not help that they genuinely want, but escape from responsibility. In marriage counseling, where only one mate is actively seeking counseling, the pastor should be very clear that they can help the individual only to fulfill their responsibilities in the marriage. They can teach techniques to make their marital situation happier, but they cannot help them to solve all their problems. The old saying is "it takes two to tango", and marriage is very much a dance. It is the dance of life.

Pastor's Plan

VI. Marital Conflicts, Separation, & Divorce

Bringing People Together

The goal of the pastor is to enable each marriage partner to become able to meet their partner's needs. Sometimes, this requires reeducating people about false beliefs or assumptions that they have brought with them from their childhood.

Some needs are not legitimate needs and enduring attachment to those false needs are indicators of the need for specific counseling in those areas. The reason those needs are not legitimate is because of the kind of desires they are, or the impact they have on the person they marry. It is reasonable to say, needs that are not legitimate needs are those that are sinful, repulsive, hurtful, or demeaning. People who insist on holding on to needs or desires that result in these kinds of feelings in a partner can be generally said to be in need of specific counseling.

There is always an over-riding purpose in marital counseling for the Christian who counsels. The purpose is to help the parties involved bring their lives together into conformity with the image of Christ that is supposed to be displayed in them. Pastors are often squeamish about dealing with the subjects marital counseling must touch on. The reason is that they do not understand the relationship between the sacred and the secular in marriage which can be summarized simply that all of marriage endeavors and relationships are intended for sacred purpose.

Subordinate purposes do exist. What are they? They are whatever is the need in the lives of people who come to you for help. The counselee may not recognize the sacred aspect while they are busy focusing on the subordinate issues. A couple might come to you looking for help in learning how to disagree with one another without getting into a fight. Others will come wanting to resolve problems in their sexual relationship. An individual may come looking for ways to deal with an unresponsive or undemonstrative mate. It could be that they come because they have a mate who is chronically unfaithful. In every situation, they come wanting not only help with the problem, but a perspective that has originated at the throne of God.

The purpose must be supreme. It must overcome your own prejudices an inhibitions. You must be willing to look at situations from the genuine perspective of how the Creator, who established our physical as well as our spiritual being would view them. To do this, you must have a healthy view of what the Scriptures teach, as well as the complementary testimony of God's purpose in His Creation. Not only that, it is good to understand how humans develop throughout their lives together, so that you can understand what stresses have some normalcy about them and what troubles and degrees of stresses are abnormal in the lives of your consulting members.

An example of how this might work out is when you find it necessary to explain, very kindly, to a young bride, taught by her mother that sex was a thing to be put off as long as possible, and endured when forced upon her, that sex in marriage is not only good, but intended by God to be enjoyed. Or perhaps, when a couple comes to you, frustrated, after ten years of marriage, that some sexual problems still exist in their relationship, it will require an understanding of development in sexual relationship to give you tools to identify and explain this is not necessarily an abnormality, and they still have two more years to hit the average for working out sexual relationships. It's probably unlikely that any couple will ever come in worried because their marriage seems to be so much more stable than their friends.

If you live out so close a relationship with you parishioners, they feel comfortable coming to you for help in marital relationships, you will find the other facets of your ministry and work with them also to be greatly satisfying and profitable. For you will be what a pastor is truly supposed to be, a guide who watches out for the souls entrusted to you, as one who must give account, Hebrews 13:17b.

To assist you, some books have been recommended to you, but they are by no means exhaustive of what you need to be exposed to. They are simply intended to be a recommendation of the very best starting point that comes to mind. We have given you a foundation you can build on, no more. As time goes by, you will undoubtedly discover many fine sources, but with a good foundation our hope can be that you not be misled by the multitude of material that is lacking or tainted with ideas that run contrary to the Word, while maintaining a guise of being Christian. You will discover that much we have not mentioned is out there that will be of considerable use. Please, as a faithful servant, never accept blindly, but always test what is proposed by the final standard, the Word.

The enclosed forms are not intended to be used in every case. These are simple and self explanatory tools that hardly need more comment than what exists on the forms themselves, however, some observances are made in the hope that they will be beneficial:

1. The Background Survey of Marital Relationships, used correctly, will save time getting to the core of matters. It can also be a confrontational tool to cut through barriers when people come wanting to get help, but play games with the counseling. At such times, they often misrepresent why they came to you. The strong point is that this form gives you more tangible background on the person allowing you a better understanding of where they are at and why. As you develop understanding, you can lead the client to understand the wheres and whys, as well.
2. The Letter To My Beloved form is designed to open up dialogue between people. It can be used in the Premarital and Marital Communications segments of counseling.
3. Exciting Expectations is useful in either premarital or marital counseling. It is a tool to get people to express their perceived needs in the marriage relationship. It is nonverbal and potentially non threatening and very useful in situations where ill-chosen words have led to explosions.
4. The Positively Popular Page is useful for redirecting a person's thoughts about the person they have married by requiring them to think about the partner's positive attributes instead of their negative qualities. When too much "stinking thinking" is being indulged in this can be very useful.
5. The Survey of a Previous Marriage is a tool to help you organize a person's biography so you can deal with it. In a busy counseling ministry, you must stay organized about people you work with, or you will wind up either looking confused or inattentive. But more than that, you will fall short of helping the person who has come to you. This form has an added benefit in showing people, who have had multiple failed marriages, how they have gone about setting up recurring failure patterns as well.
6. Survey of Extended Residences helps to organize information about people who have experienced very dysfunctional environments,

growing up. Today, many children live in uncertainty and rootlessness as parents indulge in many marriages, refusing to accept responsibility to their offspring, pawn them off on others, or behave so poorly they lose their children to government agencies. This survey helps you put that trauma together in an understandable form.

Pastor's Plan

VI. Marital Conflicts, Separation, & Divorce

Checklist For Counseling

1. Has a clear commitment to the counseling process been elicited from each member before starting into the sessions?
   Has both members agreed to participate fully?

2. Do I have enough background information on both clients to proceed with marital counseling?
   This may need reassessment as counseling progresses.

3. Have I set clear boundaries for the couple in the counseling setting?
Examples:

    No Nagging
    No accusations
    No blaming
    No dominating; conversationally, physically, or otherwise.
    No interruptions of the other mate when it is their turn to speak.

4. Have I defined clearly the options the partners face?
   A. Work on resolution and live together in peace.
   B. Solve nothing, come to a treaty between camps, and tolerate one another.
   C. Forget resolution, go on as is and live in a hell.
   D. Get out, and possible repeat problems with someone else.

5. Have I gotten the two to each define the problem as they see it?
   Needs list solicited from each member

6. After assessment did I clearly define the problem to the couple as I see it?
   Includes discussion of real and perceived needs

7. After problem definement has a renewed commitment to resolution been achieved?

8. Has the procedure towards resolution of problem been mapped out for couple?
   A. Behavioral changes.
   B. Specific studies/Integrating new life principles into lives and marriage.
   C. Homework- Videos, audios, written assignments

9. When separation of mates is absolutely necessary for counseling on member specific issues, have I made it clear to the excluded mate what is being discussed is not them?
   Have I reinforced this understanding by spending some time with the excluded member discussing things related only to them?
10. Have I laid emphasis on individual responsibility to fulfill needs of other as not based on performance of the mate?
    Has this concept been emphasized equally to both?

11. Am I maintaining my objectivity and not intruding my own prejudices into the counseling process?

12. Have I separated the counseling relationship from all other church relationships related to these clients?

LETTER TO MY BELOVED

Dear_______________________________

Because I love you and want to share my life with you, I have prepared this for you to read.

In these pages you will find me, warts and all, and I write this hoping you will love me the more for sharing myself with you.

(Having begun the foreward to this sharing of self, encourage the client to add whatever words they might wish to the foreword)

My biggest memories of childhood were_______________________________________

(This statement should include both the good and bad memories. What is wanted is those memories that are most dominant. A good description should run not less than a page. If it runs to five or six, you should examine it closely. You may have encountered a life in turmoil, or it could be that your instructions have been misunderstood.)

I want to tell you about my parents.

If for some reason the potential mate does not know the parents of their intended, encourage more in depth description of them.

I did/did not get along with my parents.

Describe the relationship with them and why you saw it to be the way it was.

My biggest hurt and my biggest disappointment as a child were.

This may very likely be two separate events.

I was/was not in trouble a lot. I usually got into trouble for/because

____

I usually got out of trouble by

____

This can be quite humorous, but it must be honest.

The pets I had as child were: *tell how old you were, their names, and type*

My favorites were...*tell why*

My hobbies were..*tell how old you were and what you felt each one did for you.*

My favorite toys were...*do you remember what happened to them?*
My favorite games were...*why did you like those games?*

The thing I enjoyed most about school and related activities was ______________________________
The thing I least enjoyed about school and related activities was ______________________________

When I was a child I used to dream of being a ______________ when I grew up.
I thought this would be the ideal occupation because______________________________

I want to tell you about my talents as a child...
I could also do______________________________.
How did you see your abilities in the things you excelled at in relation to others?
I won ___ awards for:
Other special achievements I received recognition for was...
This can also be a place to write down special achievements that went unrecognized.

My nicknames were:
At what stage did you have each nickname?
How did you feel about each nickname?

My best friends were:
We used to do ______________ together.
They are now:
Be sure to record at what age they were closest. Tell what has happened to them.

When I was a child I was afraid of

____

Do you still have any of those childhood fears?
Today, I am sometimes afraid of

____

As a child my feelings toward myself were...

As a teenager I felt about myself...
Did you like or dislike yourself and why?

Who did you date?
How long did you date?
Where did you go on your dates?
How did you feel when you liked someone and they did not return your feelings?

What I thought about God as a child was

____

How I have come to feel about God now is

____

Include explanations about how you view God's involvement in your life.

What has been you greatest disappointment in life so far?
What did you learn from it?

When you first met your intended, what was the first opinion you had of him/her?
How was this influenced by the things going on in your life at the time?
What most influenced you to decide you wanted to marry and spend your life with this one person?

What are your hopes and dreams in this marriage?
What quality about your intended has thus far brought the greatest satisfaction?

CONFIDENTIAL

All information asked for is completely voluntary. It is required to assess your problem properly. All communication about yourself will be treated as confidential. We recommend you do not discuss your counseling with others.

Background Survey for Marital Relationships

Your name ______________________________age________________
D.O.B. ____

Are you a Christian? Y___ N___ How long have you been?

____

Give the name of the church where you are a member

____

Attendance: regular ___ occasional ___seldom ___holidays only ___
almost never ___

Do you hold an office within the church? Y ___ N ___
If so, list them on the back of this form.

What type of work do you do?

____

How long have you done this? _____________ How many hours per week? _____________
What hours do you work? ________________________________

If you are in a profession or in work requiring you to be on-call, how often is the family disrupted by the demands of work?

____

Name of mate ____________________________________age ______
D.O.B ___________
anniversary date _______________How long have you been married?

____

How would you characterize your current relationship with you mate?

Stormy ___ placid ___ non-communicative ___ cold ___ difficult ___ tense ___
truce ___ uncertain ___ up and down ___ intense ___ verbal ___ interactive ___ sexual__
separated ___ heading toward divorce ___ we're only together for the kid's sake _______

Describe your relationship:

____

____

____

____

Areas of difficulty: finance ___ sexual interaction ___ hobbies ___ child discipline ____
other ___
Explain

____

____

____

How did you meet you mate?

____

____

____

____

How long were you dating/engaged?

____

By whom were you married/where?

____

Were you counseled prior to marriage? Y___ N___ Where?

____

____

Have you been married before? Y ____ N ____ How many times?

____

 If the answer to the above question is yes, get a survey sheet on previous marriages (one for each marriage) and complete those questions.

Do you have children in your current marriage? Y ___ N ___ Are all ____, or some ____ of the children born by your marriage union? (Write in number)
If you have children in the home from previous marriages, indicate who brought these children into the marriage. If several children are involved, give full circumstances on a separate sheet and attach to this form. ____

____

____

____

How does the children in the marriage affect you and your mate? Consider also those children not living with you.____

____

____

____

The following questions probe your background:
Who are your parents?

____

____

Did you grow up in their household? Y ___ N ___ (If the answer is no, ask for the survey sheet on extended residences. Get one sheet for each situation you lived in growing up.)
Describe your parents relationship with each other when you were growing up.____

____

____

What is their current relationship.____

____

____

____

Did alcohol or drugs have any hold in your parents household?
Y ___ N ___
Describe if answer is yes. ____

If your parents are divorced, what was your age when they were divorced? ____________________

How did their divorce affect you? ____________________

Did your parents take you to church? Y ___ N ___

What part did God play in their home?

How do you get along with your parents today?

When you came to counseling you had expectations. What do you think we can do to help you have a successful marriage?

What are you willing to do to make your marriage work?

Pastor's Plan

VI. Marital Conflict, Separation, Divorce

Marriage Enrichment:

Exciting Expectations

Too many people do not know what expectations their mate has of them in the marriage relationship. Everyone goes into marriage with ideas about what the marriage relationship will mean to them. Many or most people would like to meet expectations of their spouses, if they only knew what they were. List your expectations of your spouse.

____
____
____
____
____
____
____
____
____
____
____
____
____
____
____
____
____
____

Pastor's Plan

VI. Marital Conflicts, Separation, Divorce

Marriage Enrichment:

Positively Popular Page

Write down every good thing about your spouse that you can think of. Have you ever told them what you can see good in them? How can they know unless they are told? Don't you like to be genuinely complimented? So do they!

CONFIDENTIAL

The questions on this page refer only to the previous marriage with the person whose name you write on the page. Do not use this page to discuss any other marriages to any other people, use a new sheet for each one. If you were divorced and remarried to the same person more than once, write in beside the name the number of times this occurred and describe the situations on a separate sheet of paper.

Survey of a Previous Marriage

Your name ____

Name of previous spouse

____

At what age were you married? _____ Spouse's age? ____ How long wed? _________

Describe your relationship in that marriage.

____

____

____

____

Were children a part of that marriage? Y ____ N ____
If yes, what are their current ages, and where do they now live?

Name	Age	Reside
______________	________	_______________
______________	________	_______________
______________	________	_______________

Use space on reverse side if needed.

What is your current relationship with children? If the answer is different with each child, use a separate piece of paper to write your answer. Describe in detail.

____

____

____

Why was the marriage dissolved?

____

____

____

Describe your current relationship with former mate.____________________________________

____

How does the relationship during this former marriage compare to the one you are now in? Are you re-experiencing the same problems that caused failure before?

____

____

CONFIDENTIAL

These questions are not intended to cover the whole subject of your background, but to give enough insight to the counselor for him to begin the journey of recovery counseling, without delaying, for several sessions.

Survey of Extended Residences

Name ______________________________________

I lived with ________________________________and

____

from age ____ to age ____ their relationship was: (check one) aunt/uncle _______
grandparents ____ other ______________________________

____

Describe your life there.

____

____

____

____

(complete statement) When I lived there, I always felt

____

____

____

I was treated: good ___ bad ___ indifferent ___ other

____

Was violence or abuse present in that home? Y ___ N ___
Was alcohol or drugs present in that home? Y ___ N ___
Was church attendance part of the life there? Y ___ N ___
Describe the part God played in that residence.

____

____

My current relationship with these people can be characterized by the word: good ______bad ___ none ____ hatred ___ genuine affection ___ growing ___ lost contact ________
don't want to ever see again ___

Please comment in your own words.

____
____
____
____
____

Pastor's Plan

VI. Marital Conflicts, Separation, Divorce

Resources:

Book Recommended:	*Love is a Decision Thirteen Proven Principles to Energize Your Marriage and Family*
Authored by:	Gary Smalley with John Trent President and Associate Director of Today's Family
Published by:	Word Publishing, Dallas

Oriented mainly toward helping the married man, but could prove useful in helping a woman understand why she has anger in her marriage relationship.

Most valuable material is, "The Incredible Worth of a Woman," which actually spans more than the one chapter by that name, and "Discovering the Secret to a Close-Knit Family."

No part of the book should be ignored, including Notes in the back.

Video is available.

The book contains fourteen chapters:

1. Planning on a Great Marriage?
2. Honor: The Foundation for all Healthy Relationships
3. Love Is a Decision
4. The Incredible Worth of a Woman
5. Energizing Your Mate in Sixty Seconds
6. A Closed Spirit: Overcoming a Major Destroyer of Relationships
7. The Tremendous Value of a Man

8. The First Aspect of Nurturing: Adding the Sunlight of Security to Your Relationships
9. Meaningful Conversation: Life-Giving Water to a Relationship
10. Keeping Courtship Alive in Marriage
11. Sex is Much More Than Sexual Intimacy
12. Discovering the Secret to a Close-Knit Family
13. Finding Fulfillment: More Than Our Cup Can Hold
14. The Source of Lasting Love

Minister's Notes ____

____

____

Book Recommended: *If Only He Knew What No Woman Can Resist*

Authored by: Gary Smalley

Published by: Harper Paperbacks New York

This book is designed to explain to the man a woman's needs and give insight into how to go about meeting them. Promoted to appeal to the man's self interest, it asks the questions on the cover:

Do you want your wife to:

- understand you
- appreciate you
- be more responsive sexually
- support you during hard times
- admire you
- share your interests

The chapter titles tell it all:

1. How to Drive Your Wife Away Without Even Trying
2. Where Have All the Feelings Gone?
3. If Your Wife Doesn't Win First Place, You Lose!
4. Your Wife Needs Your Shoulder, Not Your Mouth
5. Climbing Out of Marriage's Deepest Pit
6. What No Woman Can Resist
7. What Women Admire Most About Men
8. If Your Wife's Not Protected, You Get Neglected
9. Arguments... There's a Better Way
10. A Successful Marriage...It's Easier Than You Think
11. So You Want a Perfect Wife
12. Watch Out! It Can Happen to You

This book can serve, very well, as an endeavor in male sensitivity training of a positive sort.

Minister's Notes:____

____

Book Recommended: *For Better Or For Best Understand Your Man*

Authored by: Gary Smalley

Published by: Harper Paperbacks New York

This book is designed to explain to a woman how a man is very different from her and help her to understand what motivates the husband. The emphasis is on what she might do to properly motivate her husband to meet her needs, but the text promotes the woman's growth in appreciation for her husband as a person.

The book is divided into two parts:
Part I
The Foundation For Building A Better Marriage:

1. Lasting Relationships Don't Just Happen
2. Eight Ways Husband Hurt Their Wives
3. The Hidden Reasons Men Act the Way They Do
4. Helping Your Husband Become More Sensitive
5. Motivating Your Husband to Listen to You
6. Motivating Your Husband to Change

Part II
Building A Better Marriage

7. How to Increase Your Husband's Desire to Spend Quality Time With You
8. How to Gain Your Husband's Undivided Attention on a Consistent Basis
9. How to Increase Your Husband's Emotional Sensitivity to Your Emotional Needs and Desires
10. How to Gain Your Husband's Comfort and Understanding Instead of Lectures and Criticism
11. How to Motivate Your Husband to Receive Your Correction Without Defensiveness
12. How to Gain Your Husband's Appreciation and Praise
13. How to Help Your Husband Share Responsibility
14. How to Motivate Your Husband to Meet Your Material Needs
15. How to Increase and Deepen Your Husband's Affection for You
16. How to Become Your Husband's Best Friend

Minister's Notes:

Book Recommended:	*Love Life For Every Married Couple* *How To Fall In Love And Stay In Love*
Authored by:	Dr. Ed Wheat, MD Gloria Okes Perkins
Published by:	Harper Paperbacks New York

Ed Wheat is an unsung hero of marital counseling. He brings his years of experience as a physician into his work as a Christian Counselor of both patients and counselors. This text deals with questions on the physical, psychological and stress related issues of marriage. In his page dedicatory, Dr. Wheat says, with characteristic sweetness and love, "It is our prayer that you may learn, not just to hold your marriage together, but to become united as lovers, experiencing a living, growing, romantic love which becomes more wonderful every year, making every month a honeymoon (literally a month of sweetness)."

Pastor, if you do not read behind Dr. Wheat for your own sake, making copious notes, you are the poorer.

Minister's notes:

____

____

____

____

____

____

____

____

____

____

Book Recommended:	*Passages of Marriage*
Authored by:	Dr. Frank and Mary Alice Minirth Dr. Brian and Dr. Deborah Newman Dr. Robert and Susan Hemfelt
Published by:	Thomas Nelson Publishers Nashville, Tennessee

This book discusses the five growth stages through which all marriages should pass, and the approximate times in which such passages normally occur.

The five growth stages given in the text are given as follows:

Young Love-the first two years-overcoming idealistic notions and molding two individuals into one unit.

Realistic Love-third thru tenth years-recognizing the subconscious reasons you married your spouse, the hidden agendas and secret contracts.

Comfortable Love-eleventh thru twentieth years-establishing and maintaining individual identity along with marriage identity.

Renewing Love-twenty-first thru thirtieth year-grieving and accepting inevitable losses of marriage, i.e., lost youth, unrealized dreams, sexual intimacy.

Transcendent Love-thirty-one years forward-unveiling new reasons for existing after major life tasks have been completed.

Notes:____
____
____
____

VII. Grief Recovery/Follow-up

Grief-*The mourning experience that occurs when loss or anticipated loss is experienced in a life crisis.*

Life Crisis-*Any change or transition that takes place in a person's life and alters their personal world and how they live in it.*

Grief Recovery-*The process by which the past is rationalized and reconciled with the present.*

Follow-up-*Continuing to be a care giver through the recovery process when others less effected by the loss have continued on with their lives.*

Video: Love Is A Choice Minirth Meier Clinic
Book: *Recovering from the Losses of Life,* H. Norman Wright
A Curriculum Resource on Recovering from the Losses of Life
No Wonder They Call Him Savior, Max Lucado.
Materials provided by: The Radio Bible Class/Day of Discovery.
Care Notes Abbey Press

Pastor's Plan

VII. Grief Recovery/Follow Up

Defined

Grief is simply the mourning experience that occurs when loss, or anticipated loss, is experienced in a life crisis. Grief is normal and even healthy in most cases. It is only when grief is experienced abnormally, either by duration or intensity, out of proportion to its cause, that grief is a hurtful experience.

We usually connect the topic of grief with death, and that is one area pastors are intimately connected with. It is easy, especially with aging congregations or long-term ministering in the same area, to feel a bit like Moses must have in the wilderness, when, for forty years he was undertaker to a generation of Israel. But grief is not confined to death, or is it confined to a particular age group. The discussion in this section is aimed at defining grief from a pastoral perspective. We hope the guidance in ministering from that perspective will also prove valuable.

Having defined grief as *the mourning experience that occurs when loss or anticipated loss is experienced in a life crisis,* we find it necessary to also define what a life crisis is to make our meaning clear. A life crisis is any change or transition that takes place in a person's life that alters their personal world and how they live in it. So, the loss of a person who is close to an individual, in some sense, is a life crisis, as is a job change or loss, marriage, divorce, graduation, and so forth. Each one of these losses brings with it similarities, but its own unique set of challenges, as well.

We contend that real pastoring of the flock is best served by the man who is present at the life crisis experienced by the members of his congregation. You will notice that it is to his own flock that I point to in mentioning life crisis. The nature of the shepherd is to herd his own sheep, not those of someone else. Ministering to life crisis grief requires an intimacy that is virtually impossible outside the congregation, and downright hard, inside the congregation. Except when called upon by someone hurting, attempts to minister outside the congregation should be confined only to those cases where the people are directly related with your congregation. As our discussion develops, I am sure this will become clearer, if you don't already recognize the truth of what is being said.

One point needs to be made on the subject of defining what we are talking about. Ministering in a time of life crisis, and hence, in a time of grief, is not an option to the successful pastorate. It is an absolute necessity. Most of your people feel, either openly or unconsciously, that if you cannot be there for them in a time of crisis, you need not be there at all. That may sound harsh, but I think it is correct. The man of God is to be a guide, and who is in greater need of guidance than those who are hurting?

> *They that be whole need not a physician, but they that are sick.*
> **Matthew 9:12**
> *The spirit of a man will sustain his infirmity;*
> *but a wounded spirit who can bear?*
> **Proverbs 18:14**

The title of this section is Grief Recovery/Follow-Up, and that title was chosen with purpose. We have already:
(1) Declared grief to be normal and even healthy in the tribulations of this world.
(2) Asserted that the pastor has a primary role to play in grief recovery and follow-up. Now, we must define what those things are, if we want to be able to explore how to go about doing them.

Grief Recovery is the process by which the past is rationalized and reconciled with the present. By that we mean past memories of what was to be faced and disposed of in a way that makes the present life bearable. Follow-up for the pastor means continuing to be a care-giver, long after others less involved in the grief process have continued on with their lives. This requires understanding, whether by knowledge of statistics or intuitively, whether the process taking place in an individual is normal or abnormal for the type of grief they have experienced.

> *Thine own friend, and thy father's friend, forsake not;*
> *neither go into thy brother's house in the day of thy calamity:*
> *for better is a neighbor that is near than a brother far off.*
> **Proverbs 27:10**

The pastor's position is unique. It is his position, and consequential ability, to prepare and guide people through the grief process. With an understanding of grief, and his special role in people's lives, he can prepare people for living life from beginning to end in a thoroughly Christian and, therefore, satisfactory manner.

If you have reviewed the preceding six segments, you have surveyed in this text a multitude of areas where grief is taking place in the world, today. But it is only with those with whom you have a relationship that you can give pre-emptive, care which is the best for accomplishing grief recovery in harmony with God's purposes.

In closing our segment defining what we are talking about, in reference to grief, let us consider for a moment God's purpose in grief. Since grief is a result of sin having entered into the world, it is realistic to believe that grief should be, first of all, a testimony of God:

A man that hath friends must shew himself friendly;
and there is a friend that sticketh closer than a brother.
Proverbs 18:24

In grief, people have the opportunity to realize the power of the Lord Jesus Christ in their lives or to reject His divine hand. I love that passage in Isaiah that begins; *"And I have put my words in thy mouth, and I have covered thee in the shadow of mine hand..."* (51:16). It speaks of both adequacy and protection, both for the one who comforts and the one in Christ who receives comfort.

A friend loveth at all times, and a brother is born for adversity.
Proverbs 17:17

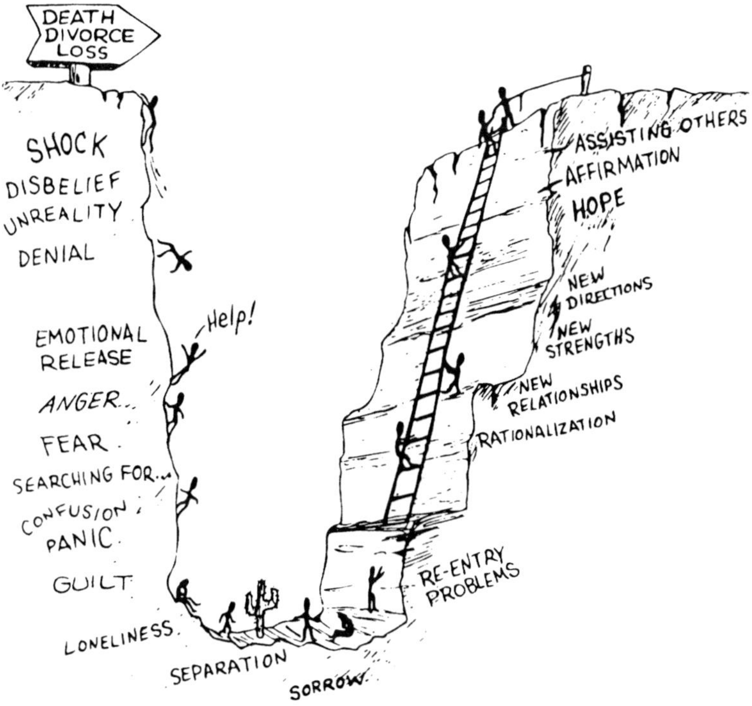

Grief Recovery Process

Pastor's Plan

VII. Grief Recovery/Follow Up

Causes:

People suffer from prolonged grief because of unreconciled issues that are in some way connected with the source of their grief.

For instance, a person might experience prolonged grief at the loss of an occupation, because their feelings of significance have been derived from what they do. This is more common in men than in women, but with the increase of women professionals, we might expect some increase. However, since women focus on security more for their sense of self esteem than on significance, it is doubtful that it will ever become as big an issue for them.

Case History

Very frequently, guilt is also associated with prolonged grief. An example is the retired soldier, of my acquaintance, who experienced severe feelings of anxiety, guilt, and grief as Operation Desert Storm geared up and was carried out. He literally lived between news broadcasts and watched all reports he could about the war. The problem became so severe, he could scarcely think about anything else, scanning each news release for people he knew. He was anxious because he knew some of his friends were over there. In this group were men he had trained to do the jobs they would be carrying out. He experienced guilt because they were there, and he was not. He was anxious, for these lest he had failed in some area of training that might cause them to be hurt. His grief at the loss of profession, that had been experienced after retirement, was renewed with vigor.

With, virtually, any grief causing condition, you may see similar scenarios being played out. Little children, being forced into the new environment of school, often go through grief, as they are being forced for a long period away from their "safe" home. Many protest loudly, at this challenge to their feelings of security. The young person who is graduating from grade school, high school, or college is going through a life crisis, which involves some grief at the leaving of familiar environment and associations. Some of these breaks also include breaks with family environments, such as when people leave high school or college to enter the work force and begin homes of their own. These occasions can be swallowed up in excitement of expectation or they can be truly traumatic.

The crisis in life surrounding the transitions of children also impacts on parents. They pose their own challenges, and again, become prolonged grief opportunities when people have incorrectly placed their own inner person's value in the wrong things. People do not readily accept change in their world, and when that world is challenged, how they feel about themselves comes into jeopardy. The experience of loss causes grief. Even the threat of loss can cause extreme grief, when it challenges the center of a person's being.

So, we see that grief originates from more than death in a house. But, even the experience of death does not have to become part of an inordinate grieving experience, unless there is a malfunction in a person's inner makeup. People who live in dysfunctional environments, have harbored anger and guilt, or been neglectful of the deceased are more likely to not recover in grief than a person who has experienced a healthy relationship with a similar loss.

Case History

An example of death resulting in an inordinately prolonged grieving experience would be the daughter, who after a rebellious and trying childhood, was married and living a goodly distance from home at the time her mother declined and eventually died. Unlike the other children who all lived close to home, she was unable to do things to help out in those last years of her mom's life. Because of her financial circumstance, she was not even able to contribute much monetarily. When the mother declined suddenly, she was unable to get home till after her death. By the time she arrived, even the funeral arrangements had been made. Several years of grief, resulting from guilt and unresolved issues, resulted.

The conditions described in preceding sections of the Pastor's Plan each can contribute to the experience of prolonged grief, and the symptoms evidenced by grief have strong relationships with the symptoms expressed in each one of the conditions. Grief very seldom is a root cause, unlike the other problems we have described. It usually is a sign or a symptom of other problems which need to be redressed in a person's life.

Low self esteem and codependency are prime contributors to unresolved or prolonged grief issues. Fundamental to this problem, like the contributors themselves, is dependency upon something other than the relationship with God they have in Christ to provide their lives with Security and Significance. Hence, a weakness in their core beliefs puts their thoughts in jeopardy. And, where the thoughts are, feelings and actions are sure to follow.

This book opened with a Scriptural statement:

For as he thinketh in his heart, so is he:

Proverbs 23:7a.

It remains just as true in grief, as it has in any other part of our discussions about man's problems, that we cannot escape the ultimate outcome of wrong thinking.

Pastor's Plan

VII. Grief Recovery/Follow Up

Signs and Symptoms:

Again, we must remember the basics when we speak of signs and symptoms in regard to prolonged grief. Remember, a sign is something that you see. A symptom is something that the member experiences or feels and, consequently, expresses. The problem with signs and symptoms in relation to grief was reflected in our discussion under cause. Since grief, prolonged, is most often with adults a symptom itself, it is very understandable that we should observe that the signs and symptoms are very similar to what is exhibited in other problems. This poses a problem in assessment as you SOAP out your member.

What makes the difference in whether you will correctly identify what is going on with your member is usually how well you know him. Today, Christian Counseling is often overloading itself with technicalities and losing its touch with the fact that things are usually pretty simple. Like salvation, men try to complicate it. The Lord Jesus said, *"My sheep know my voice."* The undershepherd must know his sheep. What makes for good understanding of problems is what makes good pastoring in other areas. Involvement with the people you serve is a must.

If there is any area in counseling that the pastor should come to the forefront in, he should dominate here. The understanding of what grief is, coupled with his knowledge of those he serves, gives him the tools to read and observe the facts. What he does with them is the subject of other discussion. Remember, your assessment is a combination of what you are told, from the inside looking out, and what you observe, from the outside looking in.

Intuition is important to you in correctly categorizing that what you observe is true. But, it is not blind because your intuition is based on these two categories of input that we have discussed. Furthermore, we presuppose a continuing relationship with God and a sensitivity to the guidance of the Holy Spirit. This relationship is very important because it will help you always keep from allowing your genuine love for the flock to interfere with your understanding of what is occurring. Should you impose what you desire for the people into what you observe to be the facts, then you are unable to be the guide they need you to be. Too many pastors have allowed their desires to disguise the facts. Good intentions and best wishes mean nothing without understanding.

Reading the signs and symptoms is not something you begin when the member comes to you for counseling in grief issues. For the pastor, this is something you should do as part of your loving care for the people of God. Remember, you watch for their souls, as one who must give account (Hebrews 13:17).

> *But there is a spirit in man:*
> *and the inspiration of the Almighty giveth them understanding.*
> ***Job 32:8***

Pastor's Plan

VII. Grief Recovery/Follow Up

Signs and Symptoms Checklist:

Delayed Recovery of Grief:

1. Depression continued abnormally
2. General constant sadness
3. Sudden bouts of weeping
4. Sadness of countenance (change in previous demeanor)
5. Preoccupation with departed loved ones (death grief)
6. Preoccupation with departed associates (grief in life losses)
7. Anger towards God
8. Confusion
9. Lack of organization (change in behavior)
10. Inability to Sleep
11. Loss of appetite
12. Withdrawal (can occur on a variety of levels)
13. Isolation (a pulling away from close associations and/or activities.)
14. Enshrinement of a loved one (ex. keeping a room as was prior to death)
15. Lack of motivation (loss of purpose in living)
16. Thoughts of suicide*
17. Suicidal attempt*
18. Talks of being with loved one (death grief)*
19. Unusual behavior, i.e., visiting the grave, talking with dead
20. Physical ailment (psychosomatic manifestation)
21. Fears (ex. of dying)
22. Nightmares/sleep disturbances
23. Gritting teeth (change of behavior)
24. Self medication (begin drinking, etc., as a behavior change)
25. Mental disturbance (psychosis)
26. Refusal to deal with death
27. Denial of reality

* *Asterisked items strongly indicate possible need of professional assistance.*

Pastor's Plan

VII. Grief Recovery/Follow Up

Laying A Foundation in the Course of Gospel Ministry

Therefore being justified by faith,
we have peace with God through our Lord Jesus Christ:
By whom we also have access by faith into this grace wherein we stand,
and rejoice in hope of the glory of God.
And not only so,
but we glory in tribulations also;
knowing that tribulation worketh patience;
And patience, experience;
and experience, hope:
And hope maketh not ashamed;
because the love of God is shed abroad in our hearts by the Holy Ghost
which is given unto us.

Romans 5:1-5

Too often, preaching is looked at as preparing people for heaven or warning them from hell. Enough evangelical time is not spent preparing people for life and warning them from the pitfalls of simply living. We focus on tribulation as something that happens during the millennium to those who are not raptured out, or is visited on the saints because of the testimony of Jesus Christ, and we ignore the frequent meaning given to it in scripture as what occurs in the normal experience of living. In the Parables of the Sower, our Lord distinguishes between the tribulation of merely living and the persecution that comes because of the Word. (Matthew 13:21)

However, the cults and the positive thinker false teachers have not neglected to reach out and approach people in the area of their need for things they can apply to their lives. This is precisely why so many have been lead down this perilous path away from the faith in which they were raised. Old fashioned discipleship needs to be rediscovered in our modern churches, and the pastor, who takes the forefront and brings the word of God into application in the challenges of our world, develops believers who weather the storms and experience grief in a positive and God glorifying manner.

When the Lord chose the Parable of the Sower to express the great truth regarding the spread of the gospel message, his choice was very deliberate. He never did anything carelessly. His expressions regarding the sowing of seed can be related to by farmers and gardeners, easily. It would be good that every pastor had experience in this aspect of life. There are some things that every gardener knows that relate to the parable. Some key points about the business of dealing with soil need to be observed:

1. The wayside, which is a trodden down path, is hard land. Often, brick hard. Nothing can be grown where people walk. There is an old saying, "grass is grown by inches and killed by feet." That is why seed sown in such places is ready feed for birds. It simply lays on top of the ground.
2. Stony places may not have much earth, but stony places can be developed. Rocks can be moved. Earth can be dug and manured. All kinds of needed nutrients can be brought to the land and pretty soon rocky soil can be some of the best. Because in rocky soil, after the big rocks are moved, the little rocks that remain help hold moisture in the land so it does not dry out. Another advantage is that when enough rocks are moved and piled on the sides a barrier is formed that allows no intrusion of animals and such that you don't want in your garden.
3. Thorns can be dug out, too. They really take a lot of work. They prick the fingers, just as difficult believers prick the heart, and every root has to be search and sifted. But, while that is being done, the soil is being loosened and aerated, so that its potential is improved.

In short, two out of three kinds of unfruitful soil can be turned into some of the best kinds of soil. Most of the sermons that are preached on the subject of the parable wind up being discouraging or, at best, encouraging to complacency in outreach, but, I suggest the Lord never intended it to be such. People are like gardens. Very few of them start out with the very best soil. Most take a lot of work to develop. But all that effort pays off in productivity, proportional to what has been put into it.

One of the big criticisms sometimes directed at Bible Studies and Sunday School curriculums is that they do not make it relevant to their lives today. It's a shame, because a key point of the Gospel message is what God can and will do in your life, now, besides "punching your ticket for heaven." While in most churches, pastors do not choose the Sunday School teachers and other teachers in the church, they can certainly take the lead in teacher development and in setting standards in teacher selection. It is not always easy to change or re-educate a church staff to accomplish all that needs to be done in developing a ministry, but the pastor can take the forefront first of all in how he directs his own work, and how he goes about bringing the rest of church leadership into an appreciation of his vision.

Simply hearing the pastor speak of the types of life crisis that will confront people is a warning that will be recognized by a few in the congregation. Others will respond to his teaching about what is Christ honoring in relationships and what is not. Some people will grow to place their dependency on the Eternal God for their Significance and Security by being afforded genuine and deep worship experiences within the Body of Christ. All of this requires more than simply warnings about hell and warm fuzzies about heaven. I believer in hellfire and brimstone preaching, but that does not minister to the Saints. It is appropriate to Evangelical preaching, not pastoral preaching. Pastoral preaching leads beside the still waters (which run deep) and restores the soul (which has been challenged by the world's system).

So many people get mad at God for the routine tribulations that fall to us, because we live in a world under the curse of original sin, and we are in a flesh, which left to itself, commits sins against God. The results of these sins are that we must bear the brunt in living out our lives in the flesh. Why does God let these things happen? Because in fertile ground, difficulties can develop in us the wonderful attributes of patience, experience, hope, and boldness in Christ, of which no amount of easy life can produce. We often miss the fact that Job, in spite of a self righteous twinge, did emerge a better man in the end, and was elevated above his fellow men for their good by God.

Scripture does remind us that no difficulties in this life are comfortable or desirable to us, but we can be certain of their beneficial effect for us. An expression I learned years ago was "the devil meant it to me for ill, but the Lord Jesus allowed it for my good." If we can cultivate that thought in the people we serve, we have accomplished in their lives a great benefit. For it will mean they have turned from worldly systems for the definition of who they are and that their dependency for Security and Significance now resides in the Person of the Living God.

How wonderful it is to realize that the one who framed the heavens and the earth cares for us in a deeply personal manner. It is reassuring to think that His eyes are ever watching, that He *"neither slumbers nor sleeps."* The depth of His concern for His creation is so great that He notices the fall of sparrows, yet so much deeper for us that He *"numbers the hairs upon our head."*

If we do not catch the wonder of all this, surely recognition that we are being used as object lessons for angels in the great *"mystery of the fellowship"* should stir us. That His angels are assigned for ministering spirits on our behalf, and will one day be subject to our judgment, should really fill us with awe. But, for all this there must be a preparation, and great things require great challenges for the accomplishment thereof.

When we begin to see what we experience in the light of the eternal purpose, the tribulations of this present life do seem small, don't they?

> *My son,*
> *if thou wilt receive my words, and hide my commandments with thee;*
> *So that thou incline thine ear unto wisdom,*
> *and apply thine heart to understanding;*
> *Yea, it thou criest after knowledge, and liftest up thy voice for understanding;*
> *If thou seekest her as silver,*
> *and searchest for her as for hid treasures;*
> *Then shalt thou understand the fear of the Lord, and find the knowledge of God.*
> *For the Lord giveth wisdom:*
> *out of His mouth cometh knowledge and understanding.*
> *He layeth up sound wisdom for the righteous:*
> *He is a buckler to them that walk uprightly.*
> *He keepeth the paths of judgment, and preserveth the way of His saints.*

Then shalt thou understand righteousness, and judgment, and equity, yea,
every good path.
When wisdom entereth into thine heart, and knowledge is pleasant unto thy soul;
Discretion shall preserve thee,
understanding shall keep thee:
To deliver thee from the way of the evil man,
from the man that speaketh froward things;

Proverbs 2:1 thru 12

Pastors' Plan

VII. Grief Recovery/Follow Up

Laying A Foundation in Death Grief

When the pastor has the privilege of presiding at the funeral services of a person who has died, he has a marvelous opportunity to lay the groundwork for healthy recovery of those who must grieve the loss. This can be done only within the frame work of ethical ministration of your duties, however. It will consume a significant amount of time with the hurting members during this time, but it really pays off in doing what you hope to accomplish in their lives and in your relationships for the future.

Notification of loss comes in many ways, but when it does come, the pastor should always respond to the hurting person or family as quickly as possible. If your personal attention must be delayed, cut the delay to a minimum and dispatch your associate pastor and/or deacon(s) to the grieving members. Make sure they let them know you are unavoidably delayed, but will be present as soon as possible. Your presence is generally all that is truly needed at this time. It is marvelous how ladies of the church respond initially to do supportive things at such times, even with those uncomely members who are less appreciated than some.

When you arrive, your initial purpose is simply to be there, whether you are asked to tend the funeral rites or not. Listen to people talk. Hold those most severely affected, whether they need to grasp a hand or literally to lean against you and cry. Let them do the talking. All the listening is yours. They do not need your words, so much as your presence. You convey the aura of the rock in times of distress that Jesus truly is. You may have occasion to observe among the mourning party those who are particularly quiet or withdrawn. It is not necessary to engage them in conversation, unless they choose to do so, but taking the time to sit with them and simply be available has a wonderful effect.

For about three years, I attendend or conducted funeral services of many people that I wasn't acquainted with. The conclusion is that all too many pastors squander their credibility for future deliverance of the gospel message and the hope of assisting recovery at the graveside. Many a vile man or woman has been preached into heaven by the well meaning incompetent and his progeny lost to the gospel, thereby. Also, a key moment in death grief recovery has been lost by the failure to focus on the future.

It is good to laud the fond memories we have of a saint departed, but saint or sinner, I always point out that their work on earth has been finished. All they might do in this life has been done, whether for good or ill. Before us lies our own lives. We, the living, yet have the choice on what we should do with our futures . And with confidence, I deliver the one message that I am sure both departed saint and sinner would proclaim, if they had the opportunity. That message would be that those who are yet alive and remain should, in the conduct of their tomorrow's, "remember the Lord" and not to leave Him out of the affairs of this life.

Your observations of the conduct of the members at the time of group mourning may give you clues to who will need special attention in the future. In this regard, it is difficult to say that some particular action is a hard and set indicator of future trouble. One would think that a lack of emotionalism would be a sure indicator of locked-in feelings and recovery difficulties in the making, but this isn't necessarily so. One particular prominent South Carolina family was remarked upon, concerning their coldness when the beloved patriarch died. However, the old gentleman had lived his life in God's word and had raised children of a similar stripe. So firmly entrenched was the family's belief in the resurrection and rejoining of the saints, the departure was more the farewell to one who had gone on an extended journey, but with whom reunification was sure. Needless to say, grief recovery did not become an issue with them.

I shall go to him
but he shall not return to me.
2 Samuel 12:23b

When the pastor does speak, he should confront death boldly. Phrases like "passed on" and "gone on" are too indefinite for those already moving in a cloud of unreality. We do not fear death, so words like "dead, death, and died," are not something to be tiptoed around, and they bring home to the hearer a sense of the permanence of the transition that has occurred. How many times does the bereaved say something like, "I expect him to walk through the door for supper any minute." Use reality words. Help them to "dialogue with death." It can be done without being either rude or crude, and it enhances your own position of being a rock in a sea of uncertainty.

> *O death, where is thy sting?*
> *O grave, where is thy victory?*
> *The sting of death is sin;*
> *and the strength of sin is the law.*
> *But thanks be to God,*
> *which giveth us the victory through our Lord Jesus Christ.*
> ***1 Corinthians 15:55-57***

On the final note of laying the foundation in death, the onerous burden, imposed by too lavish funeral arrangements, must be noted. Many a family has been severely strained by the desire to give their very best to the empty remnant of a lost loved one. Their lavishness has come back to haunt them when the funds expended in grief are needed to ease the burden of the living. If you see such a possibility, or if you are asked to assist in the arrangement, point out that it is possible to be tasteful without being ostentatious. Sometimes a word to someone in the family is sufficient to guide this process. Funeral homes have the interest of their income at stake. Do not depend on them to be seeking to sell their cheapest. I have heard the expression, "a cheap coffin and a good vault", haven't you? The truth is, even a vault is only good for delaying the sinking of the ground as deterioration occurs. Keep it simple. Lessening financial worries decreases the burden, as the cycle of depression related to recovery, is passed through.

Pastor's Plan

VII. Grief Recovery/Follow Up

Remembering the Child In Grief

G. Campbell Morgan, in his book *Studies in the Prophecy of Jeremiah,* correctly point out the provision of God for children even in this sin cursed world. It is true, as we have pointed out, that a child is early acquainted with grief, but it is grief that he can bear. It is amazing that even when exposed to outsized emotions, children have this wonderful provision and protection from God.

Recently, in a murder case, it came out in court that of the two children present when their mother was brutally murdered, only the elder had actually observed the event. In the provision and protection of God, the younger slept through the whole thing, and the awareness of the reality of his mother's death was something he comprehended only in accordance with his age, not as an adult. The elder child, in spite of all the child psychologists and experts warnings that he would be traumatized if he came to court and testified about his mother's murder, reported that through testifying he actually felt better about his mother's death. He had finally been able to do something. His problem in her death was that he had felt helpless to do anything to help his mother at the time. Giving testimony gave him release from that feeling. This would have been denied him had the so-called experts been listened to.

Morgan used as his example the story of a tragic train crash in South Wales where a child was found alive, protected in the folded over body of his dead mother. The child smiled at his rescuers, unaware of his loss. It was not until, in checking him for injury, a bag of candy was pried from his fingers, that he protested with tears. It was correctly pointed out the child would later in life mourn the loss of the mother, long after the bag of candy was forgotten. *

There is no doubt that "experts" intrusion in times of tragedy have probably precipitated emotions that God would have dealt with in accordance with his provision for children, had they not been forced prematurely upon the child. It is very important that one be careful to realize that, while God may well use you as the instrument of assisting the child in facing his experience of loss in grief, the expectation of a child's loss, being defined as an adult might imagine, is inappropriate.

**Studies in the Prophecy of Jeremiah by G. Campbell Morgan published by Fleming H. Revell, of Grand Rapids pg. 92.*

It is, therefore, incumbent to go carefully, but to discover where the child is in his thought processes.*

If you already have a relationship with the children in the church, it is easier to ask them if they know what is going on, without being alarming, during times of grief such as death or grave illness. If they tell you in adult terms, it probably means they have been listening to adults talk. Ask them, "what does that mean?," if you think they are merely parroting adults. Often, you will get a shrug that may mean I would like you to define it for me, or I'm not sure it's real important to me. In either case, the truth at its simplest level is sufficient.** If more is needed, they will let you know. Most of the time though children are involved in being children, and they realize that the adult world intrudes on their world, some, but they refuse to allow it to dominate them. We should appreciate that God in His goodness has made it so. Without this resilience, the protection and development of happy well adjusted children would be an impossibility.

One of the best ways to have laid the foundation for interaction with the child, as you go about pastoring, is through occasional "children's sermons". Best presented before the adult message, the use of objects, little knickknacks that can be given as gifts afterwards, helps the pastor to convey to children that he thinks they are important. Children are responsive to the minister who shows just a little attention to them. If the parents have referred to you in positive ways in private, it will cinch such positive experiences, giving you an open road for ministering to and evangelization of the child.

> *O thou afflicted, tossed with tempest, and not comforted, behold,*
> *I will lay thy stones with fair colours, and lay thy foundations with sapphires.*
> *And I will make thy windows of agates, and thy gates of carbuncles,*

and all thy borders of pleasant stones.
And all of thy children shall be taught of the Lord;
and great shall be the peace of thy children.
Isaiah 54:11-13

It is often very appropriate to give children a role in the funeral rites, to allow them a healthy recovery. In conversations with children, they can be asked what they would like to do and some simple gesture might be named, such as giving the lost loved one a picture or a favorite possession such as a stuffed toy. Some have allowed older children to walk with the pall bearers, and so forth, but children have little patience with adult ritual and it is advisable to consider that when making arrangements. What is appropriate in working with children is to always consider what is appropriate for the child.

**Scripture contains a body of references to the thought processes of children. For instance I Corinthians 13:11 refers to the distinct manner inwhich a child speaks, understands, and thinks. **Studies inthe Prophecy of Jeremiah by G. Campbell Morgan published by Fleming H. Revell, of Grand Rapids pg. 92.*

Pastor's Plan

VII Grief Recovery/ FollowUp

Celebrating the Crisis of Life

Within the practice of Hebrew faith under law, provision was made for observing the various life crisis human beings must endure in this world. These observances had both practical and emotional purpose. With the separation from Judaism that was forced first by persecution of Christian believers and then by the naming of a false messiah preceding the cataclysmic fall of Jerusalem in 70 A.D., a process away from those observances were begun in the church. This movement became more pronounced in Christianity, as it became more and more dominated by the gentile believer. In every type of Christian observance, the awareness of the transitions in people's lives has received some measure of a nod of recognition, but overall has been inadequate to thoroughly minister to people.

With the decline of discipleship within the church and the subsequent loss of institutions within the church that ministered to needs, the lack of church observance of life crisis has become even more pronounced. Each individual group is best qualified to speak of such things within the context of their own denominations and institutions, but it is a fact that every part of Christendom is suffering loss of participation within the life cycles of their constituents in some areas, if not all.

Another generalized observance is that there exists a general dissatisfaction with ministers, and pastorates have become shorter and less successful throughout Christendom. Apart from the general rebellion of the age, credit must be given to the fact that people are focusing their dissatisfaction with the churches response in meeting needs on the pastors.

Similar observances can be made within other forms of Christian institution. In short, the point is that while church focus and emphasis on opportunity to recognize and observe needs is already small, it is declining. Some programs are coming into a few churches that sound some positive notes. For instance, there are programs like AWANA and Golden Age groups that are a hopeful sign. We must remember, however, they are seeking to replace what was already perceived as inadequate. They are not new movements that are seeking to meet needs, and unfortunately, they too, have their shortcomings. For instance, Golden Age groups often do more to minister to women in what they offer than they do to men. This is partly because more women, than men, reach the age group, but this does not negate the needs of men in the group.

So, the question is what can be done to minister to life crisis within the church to forestall situations where the grief being experienced in transitions gets out of hand? The answer to that is much. But each church will have to work out its service by determining how far it will go in various areas.

Some suggestion I would offer would be:

1. Churches with congregational forms of policy, where all members are accorded equal status, I would recommend for all new members of the church to go through a special class taught either by a deacon, associate pastor, or the pastor. This would minister to the transition of moving into a new church for the older Christian. And for the convert, it would minister for the change encountered moving into a believer's lifestyle. It would elevate the status of church membership as they worked toward the day of being received into "full fellowship" of the church.
2. Within those same churches, a child's membership within the congregation is often held on equal status with an adult's, as far as voting is concerned. I am hoping that the many new Messianic Congregations that are now being formed by saved Jews will not follow their gentile brethren in this. We need to have our own Bar and Bas Mitzvah forms of observance where children who are entering into teenage years can prepare for and celebrate a transition of status within the church. Establishing peer helping programs that recruit budding teenagers as assistants are worthwhile endeavors.
3. I enjoy and promote infant dedication observances, when they are conducted right. By this, I mean the parents present their new infant before the church in special ceremony and in ritual form acknowledge their responsibilities to the infant before God and to the church. Then, the church rises to recognize the new addition within its family and as a church, recognizes their responsibility to the child and the couple.

4. Recruitment of people, who are retiring, into service within the church is an idea whose time has come. Many large employers actually give their retiring employees extra retirement incentives for embarking on volunteer service projects. The advantage of their worthwhile service to the church, as it helps them handle stresses related to job loss, cannot be overemphasized. This is one area where churches often reap a direct profit in their attempt to minister. Whether you get a carpenter, secretarial help, or graphics aid, the place for each person, going through transition to see a worthwhile niche to fill, exists.
5. Job losses within the community can often serve as the point in which the church has an opportunity to expand its service and ministry. For instance, factory layoffs can provide a Christian labor force to start a Christian Day Care center within the church. Retiring teachers can help a Christian School come into being, and so forth. In these ways, life crisis get ministered to, and the work of the church in touching lives for Christ grows.

Of course, we have only touched on the surface of what can be done. But in every situation things can be that really help people through the tribulations of life and glorify Christ. It requires work, ingenuity, and resilience, but the good news is that these things can develop a life of their own and become self perpetuating in large part. Short term challenges, even to finances, yield long term profits as tithes, gifts, and incomes go up, but most important, the church grows a body of willing, even excited Christian workers.

> *He that gathereth in summer is a wise son:*
> *but he that sleepeth in harvest is a son that causeth shame.*
> ***Proverbs 10:5***

Pastor's Plan

VII. Grief Recovery/Follow Up

Doing Follow Up or Not Dropping the Ball

From the section on Celebrating the Crisis of Life, it should be clear that the church should note passages in a person's life, even take advantage of them. The problem with much grief is that people are present around the obvious parts, but disappear shortly after, and that is when people can suffer the most. This is precisely why in "Celebrating" I point to long term activities. However, people need personal relationships because they can get awful lonely in a crowd when experiencing grief. Nobody is better equipped to minister than the pastor at this point in the grief cycle.*

Loss of life is a good example of how the sense of abandonment happens. At the time of loss, people come around. In our area people bring food and gather in what are called by terms such as visitations, wakes, sittings, and so forth. People are everywhere. But after this initial flurry, people are nowhere to be found and the world comes crashing in. After the initial loss, what is sometimes called rationalization of loss must take place.

Case History

People who lose spouses, children (even unborn), and parents all have experiences of reconciling what has occurred, just as those who experience other types of loss, such as, lost professions. According to the severity of the challenge, you must gauge response. On one occasion I made a point of dropping by to see a retired man, who had lost his wife, at least twice a week for several weeks after his wife died. It turned out that he also needed to talk through the yet unreconciled loss of his occupation as a truck driver, even though he had been retired over fifteen years. His wife's death had resurrected his earlier unfinished grief of retirement with a vengeance. It was not a burden to visit with him. His life was full of many interesting facts and anecdotes. I learned much about the old time days of trucking before the modern highway system came into being. I came away with a better appreciation for him and his wife, as people. In short, by helping him I prospered. Follow up work could fill many diaries with information that would be of value to people who come behind us as well.

It is too easy to presume everything is okay in following up. Since people often do not understand themselves in grief, they often try to disguise or cover over what they are experiencing. Meeting them on their own territory (in the homes) has a way of breaking down the barriers. Pastors are still in the business of making house calls, I hope. Getting grief recovery accomplished, within the norms of their design by the Creator, is important to defusing the time bomb grief represents in the human life. You will never regret the investment you make in follow up care of your congregation.

Pastor's Plan

VII. Grief Recovery/Follow-up

Resources

Video Recommended:	*Love Is A Choice*
Featuring:	The Doctors of the Minirth Meier Clinic
Published by:	Thomas Nelson Nashville, Tennessee

In this video, Dr. Robert Hemfeldt, Ed.D., Dr. Frank Minirth, and Dr. Paul Meier, discuss codependency issues in relationships. During the discussion, they repeatedly go into the subject of codependency relationships to grief issues. The insights this film offers the pastor will increase with repeated viewings.

It is possible that the pastor will find this worthwhile to show those who come for help, as well. As in all materials, the user will have to select the subjects for which it is appropriate.

Book Recommended: *Recovering from the Losses of Life*

Written by: H. Norman Wright

Published by: Revell Publishers

It has been said that everything H. Norman Wright writes is good. Not having read everything I cannot vouch for that, but I can say with certainty that this is the premier work on this subject.

Added to this is a "A Curriculum Resource on Recovering from the Losses of Life" published by Christian Marriage Enrichment of Tustin, California. This will provide you with materials to accomplish some of the work discussed in our text.

You will find another writer referred to in these who is worthy of being added to your library. His name is Max Lucado. It is suggested you begin with "No Wonder They Call Him Savior." You will have no trouble finding him in good Christian Book Stores or catalogs.

Notes:

Section Three

Pastor's Referral Resource System

(PRRS)

PRRS

Section Three Index

Pastor's Plan

Pastor's Referral Resource System

The Importance of Networking

We all agree that Moses was a man that God made great. But this great man knew, in the very midst of his ministry, deep despair. In the presence of God, he said:

> *I am not able to bear all this*
> *people alone, because it is too*
> *heavy for me.*
> ***Numbers 11:14***

He wanted to die. The problem was that he had been doing it all himself. Some things he needed to turn over to others. What did the Lord do? He told Moses to select seventy elders. After Moses did that, the Lord God picked out two more for good measure.

In Acts, chapter six, the Apostles were faced with a similar dilemma in which decisions had to be made concerning what was appropriate to entrust others with in their situation. They gave themselves to prayer and the ministry of the Word, leaving the rest to men God had raised up for such a time as that. Later, a recognition of divisions in the ministry of the Word is acknowledged in the statement:

> *I have planted,*
> *Apollos watered;*
> *but God gave the increase.*
> ***1 Corinthians 3:6***

Counseling is part of the Ministry of the Word. It is central to the Pastoral Ministry.

Today, some churches and denominations are experiencing a phenomena called Lay Renewal. This event is resulting in lay persons being utilized in areas of ministry to individuals. Where this is effective, members of churches get more individual attention, and those who are hurting can be more readily identified to the pastor. The pastor can, if he is prepared, minister to those needs beyond the scope of the layperson, who has brought his hurting brother to their pastor. However, the wise pastor realizes he does not know all things or excel in all things. For a variety of reasons a pastor sometimes needs a couple more resources before God gives the increase. This is where good networking of resources pays off.

We must minister to the needs of our own Christian family. If we fail to aid our own, who need us, where will they go to seek help? Perhaps some place where the result will not be honoring to the Lord. What a tragedy!

Failure to network (enlist helpers in the ministry) means that ultimately a pastor finds himself overloaded with problems to the point he can no longer handle the load. Or, he is discouraged from counseling because he encounters problems beyond his scope and does not know what to do with them. A pastor can be overwhelmed by ministry to the point that he, like Moses, wants to die! Then he needs counseling!

Usually what happens is that pastors who fail to network, who fail to introduce an orderly plan into their counseling ministry, draw back from counseling before they get their feet wet. Many wind up being pulpiteers instead of pastors.

As with everything else we do, the main thrust of our labor, even in counseling, is to bring a person to Jesus and into a more intimate relationship with Him. Counseling is, by far, one of the best instruments to win persons and families to Jesus. After all, who knows they need Jesus more than those who are hurting and seeking help for their pain?

The pastor's authority to counsel is not by permission of our world's system, but by the authority of God. In order to carry out this part of your ministry successfully, you have to understand what you need, and then gather what you need together. This is a principle taught in the Book of Nehemiah. Remember also what Paul said to Timothy:

> *And if a man also strive for masteries,*
> *yet is he not crowned,*
> *except he strive lawfully.*
> ***2 Timothy 2:5***

Now you understand why networking is important. It is not only important, it is Biblical. So, what are you waiting on?

As we have therefore opportunity,
let us do good unto all men,
especially unto them who are of the household of faith.

Galatians 6:10

Pastor's Plan

Pastor's Referral Resource System

How To Find Resources

It is very hard to gather people who can help if you do not know where help is. How to start is a big question.

Your National Resource Guide is a great place to start. It is very small now, but it will grow with time as you make additions tailored to your needs. National resources may be able to recommend people in your area who might be useful to you. By their very nature, they exist by building relationships all around the country. So, a national organization that specializes in a need can very well know more about what is available locally than you do, if you have never needed that type organization.*

Another contact that might be informative is the Secretary of State where you live. If you minister near state boundaries, the adjacent state's official might also be worth contacting. Not only can they tell you about state agencies, but they can also tell you about organizations that have incorporated in your state.

State Representatives for the areas your ministry touches can also prove useful. Not only can a good relationship promote special assistance if you do need help with the governmental system, but they should be willing to provide comprehensive blocks of information on state agencies that serve the public across a broad spectrum of human services. Of course, you will want to use these types of services very selectively, but you need to know about them when considering options.

The local sheriff(s) or similar law enforcement officers are also great men to know. Often, they can expedite entry into places like detox centers for your client. They can also provide insight into some of the people who come to you for help.

Probate Judges also have an unique feel for the area they work in. The office is connected with marriage, birth, and death records. You will need this contact for more than just your counseling ministry. The Probate Office has assisted me in helping older citizens resolve retirement problems.

Every good investigator knows the value of the Yellow Pages of the phone book. Do not neglect looking in that area when seeking out what may be available. Virtually every service, even Christian ministries, need phones to function. They list themselves for you to find them. The phone book will also provide you with information on medical, legal, daycare, and nursing home facilities. In short, if you miss the phone book, you've missed three-fourths of you initial local area input.

Research Christian papers, magazines, mail-outs, etceteras. Since networking is essential to proper counseling, you will be constantly looking for the variety that will provide the right resource at your fingertips. That is part of the way you prepare to meet the need that has not yet knocked on your door. We are constantly looking, even now, to see what might be available that didn't used to be around.

If you advise us of a good resource among national groups, it will earn you honorable mention in subsequent editions of this manual. You see, we are really about working together to go forward with counseling.

Another thing to be considered for your directory is those things available through your denomination. If they have a hospital or hospital system, what services can be obtained through it? Does any of the areas of Denominational Resource have programs that will assist in possible counseling encounters? Almost every large denomination has a section that focuses on cults. Information available from them might assist in dealing with Codependency and other issues relating to cult membership. This is just one possibility out of many, but it shows the value of the denominational resource. When you begin to know the agencies, their interests, special phone numbers and addresses, you open up a goldmine of benefits to your church.

Talk with counselors and pastors in your local area. Develop relationships. People like to be consulted, naturally. Those who have a commitment to their area of service have additional impetus to respond positively to your questions. The newly arrived pastor cannot only get a head start on his ministry, but can create valuable relationships, even friendships, by letting the old guys know that the new kid on the block values their counsel. A word of caution is interjected here. If you have not already realized it, not all pastors are apt to counsel. Some have developed techniques and resources without realizing or acknowledging counseling as the central activity they are participating in. Other pastors are a good place to start practicing communication skills.

Contact and talk with counselors, mental health practitioners, state, county, and local health agencies, medical doctors and other medical field persons/agencies you anticipate using one day. Find out about their procedures for gaining admission and, most importantly, the basic philosophy that drives them. Attain and file as much material, brochures, etceteras, on potential resources as you can. Visit facilities. Little things can mean a lot when your looking for the best way to help someone. A visit to a local facility can tell you a lot, and your interest is encouraging to people.

Nobody expects that you would take a month or two off from your other duties and just concentrate on building your directory. You do this as you work at other things in your Christian ministry. The Great Commission given to the whole of Christendom is "as you are going," literally. That is how you build up your Pastor's Referral Resource System (PRRS). Too many pastors throw away or neglect material that comes to them that could prove beneficial. Now you have something to do with it that is constructive. Once your interest becomes known to organizations, they have a way of keeping you updated. In a sense, they are working for you. Too often we just complain about the amount of information we get and mislabel it junkmail, some of that junkmail is more useful than for starting fires. It might help you put one out.

Let's discuss for a few moments how we can know whether or not we have found a resource. Not everything is useful. The best resources are those that are Christ oriented. We don't want them to just be Christian in name, but Christian in perspective. Some of these can be very subtle. For instance, those groups that seek to bind burdens of civil law and regulation upon Christian counseling, forcing it into a secular mold need to be rejected outright as on a par with the Judaizers recorded in the New Testament. Association with groups that are allied with such movements is like giving aid to your enemy. In the long run, you'll be sadly disappointed. It is very good for you to find out what is going on behind the scenes in the field of counseling in your state.

In the introductory section you were presented with a Theology of Christian or Pastoral Counseling page. Secular models of behavior modification, and so forth, are a far cry from the Christian standard. The Christian standard does require more than just an improvement in the way people feel and is not passive in its approach. Our standard is to set people on the road to conformance with the image of Christ, whom, we agree with Watchman Nee, is the example of what is a normal Christian life. While it may be necessary to use some non-Christian organizations in order to accomplish everything a hurting member needs, the very best resource is one completely Christ oriented.

When using a non-Christian resource you must be careful that their philosophy of function does not work to oppose the goals of Christian Counseling in a hurting member's life. No matter who you use, they must be able to be effective in doing what you need them to accomplish as part of your Pastor's Plan. It's important to have a feel for how good they are at their job.

Two things go hand in hand. Is your potential resource interested in knowing about you and your ministry? Are they willing to discuss themselves and their organization? Christian groups particularly should be interested in knowing who they are dealing with for a multitude of reasons, but any professionals who truly are committed to their work should be interested in those who might play a role or have an impact in what they do. They should be wanting to assess the value of your opinions in the conversations that might take place in the future. People who are unwilling to talk about what they do are either not committed to their work, do not value your interest or opinion, or have something to hide. You should always be very leery of people who seem interested in having you make a commitment to them, but do not want to inform you or discuss with you what it is they are about.

This brings us to the question, can a basis of relationship be established with a potential resource? One should not go about with their feelings on their sleeve, as the saying goes, but you need for anyone you utilize to respect you as a professional and cooperate with you. The person you are trusting to them may very well be a member of the church body you serve, or at the very least, a member of the community you are a witness to. They are being consulted by you to play a particular role in this person's recovery process. Because the referral comes through you and the church and comes back to you and the church, you will have the ongoing role in that life. Paul told Timothy not to let people despise his youth, we tell you for the same reason not to let people despise your position. You are God's representative.

A final word of advise in this segment is to beware of New Age oriented groups. Counseling has proven particularly vulnerable to these kinds of groups. You need to be on the look-out for them. Sometimes they go so far as to pretend to be Christian. An organization that pretends to be Christian, but works to a different perspective, is the most dangerous to a person experiencing difficulties in life. If you do not have a solid grasp of the New Age phenomenon, you are already behind in your ministry. Good material is out there. You can probably get help in catching up fast through your denomination's Interfaith Witness program and by consulting a knowledgeable Christian book store operator.*

*Enough cannot be said about the Pastor being knowledgeable concerning the New Age Movement and alert to its encroachment. It is like a vast spiderweb that has attachments in what are sometimes very unlikely places. Its influence extends even into government, so you must always be on guard that you do not surrender your sheep to a determined, Christ-hating enemy.

Pastor's Plan

Pastor's Referral Resource System

How The Pastor's Referral Resource System Works

You will notice that the Resource Section is divided into several categories of resources. Several reproducible forms are in each section. They list specific resources that we recommend be identified, if available, in your area. Then, you are given a reproducible blank form for that category of resource to use to document other resources you might identify. This is designed to keep you organized by helping you keep your resources accessible. The forms are a resource to you; a reusable resource. You keep your original book section intact by filling in photocopies and placing them in your working locator. You will never need to replace this book.

The intent in building your customized resource listing is to file resources within a section alphabetically, because you are the person who determines how many pages are going to be in each section of your resource directory. Also, the alphabetical filing system makes it easier to find the right resource in your listing easily.

Except for the National Groups Listing, every part of your Pastoral Referral Resource Directory will be unique to your area.

If your resource sections become extensive, which is likely to occur over time, each section will lend itself to easy indexing by you. Everything is designed to keep order in your ministry, because your time is valuable. The resource is so simple, going to the extra trouble of putting the information into a computer is probably a waste of time.

Let all things be done decently and in order.
1 Corinthians. 14:40

Pastor's Plan

Pastor's Referral Resource System

Using the Resource Investigation Checklist

The Resource Investigation Checklist is a very general investigatory guide to assist you in selecting resources that can aid in accomplishing the counseling portion of your ministry. It is intended to be a flexible reminder of things you will want to know.

Not every item on the checklist applies to every type of group you will want to investigate. Look at your checklist before beginning to question a possible resource and determine what is appropriate. A highlighter pen can prove useful in planning your inquiry.

You might want to have some notebook paper handy to record other possible questions, as well as, additional information you might gather. Everything you find out is important. Make your notes and hang on to them. You can file your notes and the checklist with literature your resource sends you.

From what you record on the Investigation Checklist, ancillary notes, and information sent to you, a determination can be made whether an appropriate resource has been discovered or at least whether or not they deserve further consideration. An appropriate resource is one that you decide can be used with confidence, should the need arise. That is why every potential resource should be considered prayerfully.

If you decide to list a resource, and have followed these steps, you now have the information needed to enter it into your personal directory. If you reject the resource, the notes in your file will remind you why that decision was made later on if the question comes up. Since you are too busy to remember everything, you have written it down and will not duplicate work reconsidering the possible resource, if it is readily apparent that the situation has not changed.

The danger of using checklists is allowing them to become your master instead of your servant. The Resource Investigation Checklist is not here to command, but to assist. Modification is always appropriate to meet your needs. Remember, the checklist is not a final work, but a tool to help you accomplish your mission in the Lord's Service.

An Appropriate Resource:
One you can use with confidence, should the need arise

Resource Investigation Checklist
(general checklist)

Name & Address of Organization_______________________________

____

Phone Nos.____
Provides acute care services? Y___N___ Christian? Y___N___
Alcohol/Drug detox/other________________________________

____

Provides general medical care? Y___N___In___ Out___ Patient?
Age restrictions on entry?_______________________________
Other restriction?______________________________________
Length of stay allowed?__________________________________
Fees? Y___N___ private funded___ insurance___
non-profit___ contribution___
government___ flat fee ___ amount ______
other ______________________________________

____

Has agreed to send literature Y___N___
Affiliation____

____

Source of knowledge about resource ________________________

____

____

Name & Phone No. of possible contact person or person contact for information _______________________________________

____

Location(s) of meetings/dates & times ______________________

____

____

____

Special rules of organization _____________________________

____

____

____

Basis of cooperation with your ministry _____________________

____

____

____

Procedures, requirements and policies ______________________

____

____

____

Admission Procedures______________________________

____

____

____

____

____

____

notes:

Alphabetical Phone Listing of Charitable Organizations

ALZHEIMER'S DISEASE & RELATED DISORDERS ASSOCIATION	800-621-0379
AMERICAN CANCER ASSOCIATION	800-562-2623
AMERICAN COLLEGE OF ALLERGY & IMMUNOLOGY	800-842-7777
AMERICAN COUNCIL OF THE BLIND	800-424-8666
AMERICAN DIABETIC ASSOCIATION	800-232-3472
AMERICAN KIDNEY FUND INC	800-638-8299
AMERICAN LEPROSY MISSIONS	800-543-3131
AMERICAN LIVER FOUNDATION	800-223-0179
AMERICAN SUDDEN INFANT DEATH SYNDROME INSTITUTE	800-232-7437
BETTER HEARING INSTITUTE	800-327-9355
CANCER RESEARCH INSTITUTE	800-223-7874
CENTER FOR DISEASE CONTROL	800-729-6686
CHEMICAL EMERGENCY PREPAREDNESS PROGRAM HOTLINE	800-535-0202
CHILD FIND	800-292-9688
CHILDHELP NATIONAL CHILD ABUSE HOTLINE	800-422-4453
CHILDREN INCORPORATED	800-538-5381
CHILDREN'S WISH FOUNDATION	800-323-9474
800 COCAINE INFORMATION	800-262-2463

COMIC RELIEF	800-528-1000
DEAFNESS RESEARCH FOUNDATION	800-535-3323
DIABETES RESEARCH INSTITUTE	800-321-3437
EPILEPSY FOUNDATION OF AMERICA	800-332-1000
FAIR HOUSING-EQUAL OPPORTUNITY DEPT OF HOUSING & URBAN DEVELOPMENT	800-424-8590
FATHER FLANAGAN'S BOYS' HOME	800-448-3000
HEARING AID HELP LINE	800-521-5247
JUVENILE DIABETES FOUNDATION	800-223-1138
LACTAID INC (FOR LACTOSE INTOLERANCE)	800-257-8650
MAKE A WISH FOUNDATION OF AMERICA	800-722-9474
MEDIC ALERT FOUNDATION	800-344-3226
MISSING CHILDREN HELP CENTER	800-872-5437
NATIONAL AIDS HOTLINE	800-342-2437
NATIONAL BLACK UNITED FUND INC	800-223-0866
NATIONAL CHILD SAFETY COUNCIL	800-327-5107
NATIONAL COUNCIL ON COMPULSIVE GAMBLING INC	800-522-4700
NATIONAL DOWN SYNDROME CONGRESS	800-232-6372
NATIONAL DOWN SYNDROME SOCIETY	800-221-4602
NATIONAL EASTER SEAL SOCIETY	800-221-6827

NATIONAL KIDNEY FOUNDATION INC	800-622-9010
NATIONAL REYE'S SYNDROME FOUNDATION	800-233-7393
NATIONAL RUNAWAY SWITCHBOARD HOTLINE	800-621-4000
NATIONAL SOCIETY TO PREVENT BLINDNESS	800-221-3004
NATIONAL SPINAL CORD INJURY ASSOCIATION	800-962-9629
NIDA DRUG-FREE WORKPLACE HELPLINE	800-843-4971
PARKINSON EDUCATIONAL PROGRAM	800-344-7872
RESEARCH TO PREVENT BLINDNESS	800-621-0026
RETINITIS PIGMENTOSA ASSOCIATION INTERNATIONAL	800-344-4877
RUNAWAY HOTLINE	800-231-6946
SAINT JUDE CHILDREN'S RESEARCH HOSPITAL	800-877-5833
SPINA BIFIDA ASSOCIATION	800-621-3141
STD HOTLINE	800-227-8922
STUTTERING FOUNDATION OF AMERICA	800-992-9392
SWEET N LOW	800-231-1123
TOURETTE SYNDROME ASSOCIATION	800-237-0717
UNITED CEREBRAL PALSY	800-872-5827
UNITED CHILDREN'S FUND	800-458-8683

US CONSUMER PRODUCTS SAFETY COMM	800-638-2772
US FEDERATION OF SMALL BUSINESSES	800-827-5722
US NATIONAL HAZARDOUS MATERIALS	800-752-6367

12 Step Support Groups

Notes on support groups:

You may want to list more than one group of a particular type. More than one operating organization may be in your area and worthy of consideration. Utilization of one group over another may be indicated by a variety of factors. These factors will depend on the type of needs that the member you are trying to help has within the particular general disorder indicated. You must weigh and decide which group fits the need. You may desire to list more than one acceptable organization in a particular area, simply because information about their operation locations may become deciding factors in planning which organization to choose, or because other variations may present a preference over another under some circumstances. Variations, such as the method of approach to the individual, could mean you would use one group to meet the needs of one person and another group for an individual with a different personality type. If you have the luxury of choice, know what the differences are in the groups you can choose between.

(A) Alanon Spouses of Alcoholics/Drug Abusers

Address:____

____

____

Telephone: ____

Contact person________________________Ph____________

Location of meetings______________________________

Time & days of meetings ____________________________

Christian ___ non-Christian ___ support group

Literature on file? Y___N___

Under title______________________________________

Other related groups listed____________________________

Other information:__________________________________

 (AA) Alcoholics Anonymous

Address:____

Telephone: ____

Contact person________________________Ph____________

Location of meetings________________________________

Time & days of meetings ______________________________

Christian ___ non-Christian ___ support group

Literature on file? Y___N___

Under title____

Other related groups listed______________________________

Other information:____________________________________

Address:____
____
____

Telephone: ____

Contact person______________________________Ph______________

Location of meetings____
____
____
____

Time & days of meetings ______________________________
____
____
____

Christian ___ non-Christian ___ support group

Literature on file? Y___N___

Under title____

Other related groups listed______________________________
____
____
____

Other information:____
____
____
____
____
____
____
____

Address:____
____
____

Telephone: ____

Contact person__________________________Ph_____________

Location of meetings______________________________________
____
____
____

Time & days of meetings ____________________________
____
____
____

Christian ___ non-Christian ___ support group

Literature on file? Y___N___

Under title____

Other related groups listed__________________________________
____
____
____

Other information:______________________________________
____
____
____
____
____
____
____

Address:____
____
____

Telephone: ____

Contact person____________________________Ph______________

Location of meetings____
____
____
____

Time & days of meetings ____________________________________
____
____
____

Christian ___ non-Christian ___ support group

Literature on file? Y___N___

Under title____

Other related groups listed__________________________________
____
____
____

Other information:____
____
____
____
____
____
____
____

 (NA) Narcotics Anonymous (Drug Dependency)

Address:____
____
____

Telephone: ____

Contact person____________________________Ph_____________

Location of meetings____
____
____
____

Time & days of meetings ________________________________
____
____
____

Christian ___ non-Christian ___ support group

Literature on file? Y___N___

Under title____

Other related groups listed________________________________
____
____
____

Other information:________________________________
____
____
____
____
____
____
____

Address:____
____
____

Telephone: ____

Contact person__________________________Ph____________

Location of meetings______________________________________
____
____
____

Time & days of meetings ___________________________________
____
____
____

Christian ___ non-Christian ___ support group

Literature on file? Y___N___

Under title____

Other related groups listed_________________________________
____
____
____

Other information:____
____
____
____
____
____
____
____

Address:____

____

____

Telephone: ____

Contact person____________________________Ph______________

Location of meetings____

____

____

____

Time & days of meetings _______________________________________

____

____

____

Christian ___ non-Christian ___ support group

Literature on file? Y___N___

Under title____

Other related groups listed____________________________________

____

____

____

Other information:____

____

____

____

____

____

____

____

Support Group General Form

Address:____
____
____

Telephone: ____

Contact person__________________________Ph______________

Location of meetings______________________________________
____
____
____

Time & days of meetings _________________________________
____
____
____

Christian ___ non-Christian ___ support group

Literature on file? Y___N___

Under title____

Other related groups listed________________________________
____
____
____

Other information:____
____
____
____
____
____
____
____

Professional Counselor Listing

Name & Address of Organization______________________________

____

____

Phone Nos.____

Toll Free____

Is the organization Christian?____non-Christian?____

What are the business hours?______to______on days____________

______to______on days____________

Method of payment: private funded____ insurance____

non-profit____ contribution____

government____ flat fee____amount____

Other____

____

Contact person____________________phone no.______________

Christian____non-Christian____

Who recommended?____

Basis of cooperation with your ministry_______________________

____

____

____

____

____

____

Literature in file Y___N___under title_______________________

Other notes on resource______________________________________

____

____

____

____

____

____

____

____

Name & Address of Organization______________________________

____

____

Phone Nos.____

Toll Free____

Is the organization Christian?____non-Christian?____

What are the business hours?______to______on days___________

______to______on days___________

Method of payment: private funded____ insurance____

non-profit____ contribution____

government____ flat fee____amount____

Other____

____

Contact person____________________phone no.______________

Christian____non-Christian____

Who recommended?______________________________________

Basis of cooperation with your ministry_______________________

____

____

____

____

____

____

Literature in file Y___N___under title______________________

Other notes on resource___________________________________

____

____

____

____

____

____

____

____

Sex Therapist

Name & Address of Organization________________________________

____

____

Phone Nos.____

Toll Free____

Is the organization Christian?____non-Christian?____

What are the business hours?______to______on days____________

______to______on days____________

Method of payment: private funded____ insurance____

non-profit____ contribution____

government____ flat fee____amount____

Other____

____

Contact person____________________phone no.______________

Christian____non-Christian____

Who recommended?______________________________________

Basis of cooperation with your ministry________________________

____

____

____

____

____

____

Literature in file Y___N___under title________________________

Other notes on resource__________________________________

____

____

____

____

____

____

____

____

Name & Address of Organization______________________________

____

____

Phone Nos.____

Toll Free____

Is the organization Christian?____non-Christian?____

What are the business hours?______to______on days____________

______to______on days____________

Method of payment: private funded____ insurance____

non-profit____ contribution____

government____ flat fee____amount____

Other____

____

Contact person____________________phone no._______________

Christian____non-Christian____

Who recommended?____

Basis of cooperation with your ministry_______________________

____

____

____

____

____

____

Literature in file Y___N___under title_________________________

Other notes on resource______________________________________

____

____

____

____

____

____

____

____

Name & Address of Organization______________________________
____
____
Phone Nos.____
Toll Free____________________ ___________________________
Is the organization Christian?____non-Christian?____
What are the business hours?______to______on days____________
______to______on days____________
Method of payment: private funded____ insurance____
non-profit____ contribution____
government____ flat fee____amount____
Other____
____
Contact person____________________phone no._______________
Christian____non-Christian____
Who recommended?_______________________________________
Basis of cooperation with your ministry_________________________
____
____
____
____
____
____
Literature in file Y___N___under title_________________________
Other notes on resource___________________________________
____
____
____
____
____
____
____
____

Name & Address of Organization______________________________

____

____

Phone Nos.______________________________________

Toll Free____

Is the organization Christian?____non-Christian?____

What are the business hours?______to______on days____________

______to______on days____________

Method of payment: private funded____ insurance____

non-profit____ contribution____

government____ flat fee____amount____

Other____

____

Contact person____________________phone no.______________

Christian____non-Christian____

Who recommended?________________________________

Basis of cooperation with your ministry______________________

____

____

____

____

____

____

Literature in file Y___N___under title________________________

Other notes on resource___________________________________

____

____

____

____

____

____

____

____

Psychologist (Ph.D, Ed.D, Psy.D.)

Dr.'s name:_______________________________phone_______________
Address:__________________________________Christian Y___N_____

____

Clinic/Center name:______________________________________

Bus. Hrs: from________to______days______________
from________to______days______________

Contact person__________________________phone______________
Christian Y___N___ Relationship to Dr.___________________________
Specialty or General Practice:_______________________________
Child___ ______________________________________
Marriage___ ______________________________________
Sexual___ ______________________________________
Other___ ______________________________________
Procedure to receive treatment:________________________________

____

____

____

Fees:____

____

____

Payment: Part Pay____ Medicare/Medicaid(specify) Insurance__
Other:____

____

Recommended by:________________________phone______________
Basis of cooperation with your ministry___________________________

____

____

____

____

____

____

Other notes:____

____

____

____

____

____

____

____

____________________ Counselor
(general form)

Name & Address of Organization____________________________
____
____

Phone Nos.____
Toll Free____
Is the organization Christian?____non-Christian?____
What are the business hours?______to______on days____________
______to______on days____________
Method of payment: private funded____ insurance____
non-profit____ contribution____
government____ flat fee____amount____
Other____
____
Contact person______________________phone no.________________
Christian____non-Christian____
Who recommended?____
Basis of cooperation with your ministry________________________
____
____
____
____
____
____
Literature in file Y___N___under title__________________________
Other notes on resource____________________________________
____
____
____
____
____
____
____
____

Medical Listing

Psychiatrist (M.D., D.O.)

Dr.'s name:______________________________phone______________
Address:________________________________Christian Y___N_____

____

Clinic/Center name:____

Bus. Hrs: from_______to______days______________

from_______to______days______________

Contact person________________________phone______________
Christian Y___N___ Relationship to Dr.________________________
Specialty or General Practice:_________________________________
Child___ ________________________________
Marriage___ ________________________________
Sexual___ ________________________________
Other___ ________________________________
Procedure to receive treatment:______________________________

____

____

____

Fees:____

____

____

Payment: Part Pay____ Medicare/Medicaid(specify) Insurance__
Other:____

____

Recommended by:______________________phone______________
Basis of cooperation with your ministry_______________________

____

____

____

____

____

____

Other notes:____

____

____

____

____

____

____

____

Medical Doctor (M.D.)

Dr.'s name:____________________phone__________
Address:____________________Christian Y___N____

____

Clinic/Center name:________________________

Bus. Hrs: from______to_____days__________
from______to_____days__________

Contact person__________________phone__________
Christian Y___N___ Relationship to Dr.________________
Specialty or General Practice:____________________
OB/GYN ____________________________
Cardiology ____________________________
Internal Medicine __________________________
Procedure to receive treatment:____________________

Fees:______________________________

Payment: Part Pay____ Medicare/Medicaid(specify) Insurance__
Other:____________________________

Recommended by:__________________phone__________
Basis of cooperation with your ministry________________

Other notes:____________________________

Pharmacist

Name:______________________________phone______________
Address:______________________________Christian Y___N_____

____

Business name:____

Bus. Hrs: from_______to______days______________

from_______to______days______________

Basis of cooperation with your ministry_______________________

Notes on relationship:____________________________________

NOTE:

When someone comes to you for counseling that is using prescription drugs, it is often worthwhile to know what side-effects the chemicals they are using might have, or even how they might inter-react with one another. It is not reasonable for a minister to try to keep a current Physicians Desk Reference at hand. Besides that, a Pharmacist is able to provide more current information. In fact, the Pharmacist probably knows more on this subject than most MDs. Most Pharmacists will gladly share information when you call, but where relationships are built, extra attention is available when needed.

Alcohol and/or Drug Treatment Facility

Name of Center:______________________________

Address:____________________Phone____________

____

Contact person:__________________Phone____________

____

Type of Facility: Christian___ Secular___
Governmental________
Other______________________

Care: In-patient___ Out-patient___
Ambulatory only___ Non-ambulatory___

Paid: Insurance___ Self-pay___
Gov't funded____ Non-profit___

Notes on facility ops/procedures/funds________________

Notes on personnel______________________________

Support Agencies

Pastor's Referral Guide

Home Health Care

Name of agency____
Phone____________________Contact person____________________

There are a number of home health care organizations that are now very prominent and there are a few that exist in local areas only. While the larger organizations do have their own standards and control processes, it does not follow that they are always uniform in quality wherever you go. All care agencies are required to meet whatever standards that are enforced in the state they reside as well as some federal guidelines. How they go about doing that makes all the difference.

The individual who comes in contact with your client is the most important factor in whether the service agency is going to meet their needs. The quality of that individual is made up of several factors:

What are the qualifications of the individual?

____
____
____

How well is the person paid in comparison to others in similar or lateral occupations with the same employment requirements? When you assess this in places where qualification requirements are lower, remember that quality of pay, even for lesser skilled persons, is a strong factor in holding the best who can improve their own circumstances elsewhere, if their economic position is uncomfortable. For these people, medical and health benefits are something they are even more conscious of than the average folks. So figure that in when you look at remuneration.

____
____
____

How long has the average care giving employee been with the organization? This will give you a clue to whether internal problems will affect care.

____

____

If possible, try to meet the individual who would be assigned to your client.
Many agencies assign home care patients to Care Givers by area. Y___N___
Others assign Care Givers to home care patients by the type care needed. Y___N___

The Individual Care Giver

Name________________________________Phone________________
What is this person's relationship with the Lord Jesus Christ?
____
____

What special qualifications do they have that meet the needs of your client?____
____

How long have they been with the agency?______________________
____

Do they have any bad habits, like smoking, that would adversely affect your client's health?
Note: Even the odor on clothes can adversely affect people whose constitutions are weak.
note____
____

Are you aware of any personal problems that might affect their ability to perform?
____
____

Is their personality likely to be compatible with the person for whom you are making inquiry? Y___N___How about with the members family? Y___N___

Equipment
Note: Many Home Care agencies require the Care Giver to furnish their own transportation.
What types of equipment do the home Care Giver carry with them routinely?
____
____
____

Does the Care Giver have to provide any of their equipment or are they equipped by the agency? Y___N___Try to see what kind of condition equipment is in; how it appears.
____
____

If your client has special needs, will any problem exist in getting those things and having them available?

____

____

You might consult with any oversight agency in your state. Has any complaints been lodged against the local home health care agency. If so, when and why was the complaint filed? What is the status today? Document this on separate paper and attach.

Pastor's Referral Guide

Nursing Homes/Extended Care Facilities

These types of facilities are owned by individuals and organizations. The owners have gotten into this type of work for reasons of their own:
A. Some religious organizations are in it because they see this as an extension of ministering to people and also a way of spreading the gospel, or taking care of their own.
B. Other religious organizations see this solely as a means of generating profits for their organizations. Many such facilities are cult owned, because they are a place where cash can be invested and where the results of that investment can also be rolled over into a non-profit status, and further their purposes.
C. Occasionally people or organizations have come into existence because the founder had experiences in their own lives and families that led them to invest in such work

You can see that knowing who is behind an extended care institution, and why they are in the business, can be important.

Very often, the people who work in these homes are underpaid and overworked. Where pay and benefits are minimal, the extended care facility is congenitally understaffed. Sometimes, the quality of care is further impacted by some of the people who are employed there. Where poor pay exists, some staff persons are inclined to also give poor performance, making it harder on workers trying to meet their resident's needs. They are kept on as employees because the facilities need certain numbers of employees, in ratio to the patients, to meet many states standards, as well as a certain quality of care, within the facility. Employee numbers can be checked by a person reading a report from their office. Quality of care review requires a personal visit from inspectors that are preferably unannounced. These do not happen ver often.

Visit
One of the best ways to see what really goes on in an extended care facility is to begin by walking in during the day. In most places you can come right in the front door and walk around without anyone bothering you. If someone asks who you are and why you are there, tell them.

They should be glad you care enough to come down and see what is going on. If they do not want you there, ask them why? An unsatisfactory answer should result in you making your visit and its results known to the state oversight agency. Something is badly wrong.

When you walk into an extended care facility, breath in. What does it smell like in there? You might whiff localized bad odors just as one may in a hospital. People in extended care frequently have many physical problems that result in odors. When a facility has reached the point where it has pervasive odors, you know that the level of personal attention required to maintain the health of those they are supposed to tend has failed.

Go to the activities board and see what types of activities are planned for the residents through the month. A nursing home or extended care facility is not merely a place for warehousing infirm individuals till they die. It should be a place where they reside and experience as much of life as possible.

Observe the employees. Do they smoke on the job. Many such facilities provide places for employees to take smoke breaks. But remember, these facilities care for people who pretty much are dependent on others. Workers may smoke off duty, but they should come to work without the smells upon them and they should not participate during the shift. Even though some residents might smoke, chew, or dip, and do so within the institution, these caregivers tend to many residents whose comfort and well being is the object of the facilities purpose. If a management has a diminished standard or turns a blind eye in this area, the likelihood exists that they are doing so in others.

Try to observe staff interaction with residents. How do they behave toward them? Consider if that were your mother, father spouse that they were having contact with. How would you or they feel about what you are seeing? Even in those homes where residents require lesser amounts of personal care and attention, people reside there who need reassurance of their worth and to receive love and respect from others. This is particularly true where they have been abandoned by family or are all alone in the world. Staff are in nursing homes and extended care facilities to give to their residents those things.

Visit the dining room. Watch meals being delivered to rooms. Observe what happens with the people that need to be fed by someone else. Many times residents might complain about food served in a long term care facility. The reason might be that they are not used to the blander balanced diet prepared in a place where many who live there have sugar and salt problems. Also, residents in such places sometimes lose track of time and think they have not eaten for long periods. Added to this some, older residents might have feelings of hunger, continually, in spite of the fact they are eating regularly. In your visit to dining, ask yourself the following:

1. Are the people getting adequate portions for their state of activity and age?
2. Is any considerations being given to patient preferences?
3. What kind of environment do residents get meals served in?
4. Do residents who have meals served in rooms get adequate time to eat before trays are collected?
5. Are trays being left in room too long?
6. Those residents who have to be hand fed need servers who are patient. They need people who allow them enough time to masticate food and prepare for the next bite. Does this happen or are they rushed and forced fed?

Talk to ministries

Most nursing and extended care facilities do not have resident chaplains, but they do allow volunteer chaplains and various ministries to come in to provide services. Contact these people and talk with them about the situation they have experienced within the facility. Often they have strong relationships with the sharper residents and know a great deal about the intimate details of the place. Sometimes, they do not realize how much they actually do know and it is up to you to ask specific questions that they can respond to and expand upon. You can use the knowledge supplied to you here as the basis for accomplishing that. But one thing that can be very telling is whether they move the ministry around a lot inside the institution or whether they are always certain where they are going to meet. Another telling point is whether the management has ever, or how often, they have canceled religious meetings. If they did, was it coordinated with the ministry or did the ministers find out about the change when they showed up?

Talk to families

Find out what people who already have family members in the home think of it. The best source here is those families who are resident within your congregation. If you do not have any in the church, the nursing home or extended care facility should be willing to supply you a number of references. But remember, they would not give them to you if they were uncertain of the persons feelings toward them.

A final note

These kinds of organizations do change. Once you have established this resource, do not depend on it to be the same five years later. Keep abreast of what is going on within the care supplier.

Facility name____________________Date visited________________
Owners___________________________Type______________________
Level of care given____
Contact person___________________________Phone______________
Special information useful to know:

Pastor's Referral Guide

Anti-Abortion Hotline/Pro-Life Clinic

An anti-abortion hotline, like a Pro-Life Counseling Clinic, must be Christian oriented if they are to be effective. But the qualifications do not stop there. Currently some Christian clinics have become dominated by charismatic groups that have gone into activities that are not Christian. To add to the problem, they are now recruiting for their movements from people coming for help. So, it behooves the pastor to know the clinic and what they are doing. This requires the pastor to have a familiarity with their function that goes beyond what they say in their statement.

The following questions apply:

Who sponsors the Anti-Abortion/Pro-Life
Hotline?____
What hours is it staffed?______________________Are call monitored
Y___N___
How are they trained? Use a separate page if necessary

____

____

What churches do they represent?____________________________

____

____

____________________________add space if necessary
Is there a statement of philosophy?__________________________
Who are they?____

____

____

____

____

Do they refer to the church nearest the caller? Y___N___
Are there standards for referral? Y___N___

What are they?____

____

____

____

(attach page if necessary)

Who sponsors the Pro-Life Clinic?__________________________
What is their statement of belief?

____

Name of supporting pastors and churches______________________

____

____

____

____

Consult with pastors and record on an attached sheet what they tell you.

What hours is the clinic staffed?____________________________

Do they provide pregnancy testing? Y___N___
Do they have professional counselors to make referral to? Y___N___
Who are they?

____

____

____

____

How are the staff trained?_________________________________

____

____

What churches do they represent? You will need to record this on a separate page.
Do they present the Plan of Salvation to each client?Y___N___
Do they refer the client to the church nearest the caller?Y___N___
Do they have standards for church referral? Y___N___

What are they?____

____

____

____

____

____

____

Pastor's Referral Guide

Suicide Counseling Hotline

If you have a locally available suicide counseling hotline, it would be very good to know the following about it:

1. Who sponsors the suicide hotline?____________________________

2. How is it staffed?____

3. How are they trained?______________________________________
   ____
   ____

4. Is there follow-up with callers who identify themselves? How is this accomplished?

____
____
____
____

5. Other information

Name of contact____________________________Phone____________

Address____
____

additional notes:

Pastor's Referral Guide

Funeral Home Name______________________________

Director______________________Phone____________

Contact person__________________Phone____________

Basis for good relationship______________________

____

____

Observe several funerals being conducted by the agency.
Try to see a variety of their staff people at work.
Do they demonstrate an awareness of family relationships?
Y___N___
Do they try to avoid situations where family stresses might cause a scene? Y___N___
Do they try to facilitate the work of ministers? Y___N___
Do they rush at any point during the observances? Y___N___

Note these points:______________________________

____

____

Will they include the ministries fee in their billing?____

Basis of billing agreement:________________________

____

____

____

____

Other information_______________________________

____

____

____

____

____

Pastor's Referral Guide

Law Officers
Sheriff or County/Parish Police

You will want a minimum of two contacts in this department. One person will be needed who is part of the functioning enforcement division, and another will be needed within the detention area. These divisions have unique and varying responsibilities and needs. Deputies and Detention Officers are each going about their own responsibilities and overlap only when people come into arrest, booking, and transport phases of their encounter with the law. This means that they are each acutely aware of their own world, but minimally affected by their counterparts concerns.

One of the first questions you will want to have answered is does your department have a Police Chaplain? You can find this out without intruding into the department by going to the County or Parish Commissioner's Office with the question.

Chaplain's name________________________________
Duty phone ________________________________
Full time? Y/N Officer? Y/N Responsive? Y/N

Mailing address________________________________
A contact with the Chaplain might yield the following:

Home adress____________________Phone__________

If no Chaplain exists, a letter to the Sheriff, letting him know you are available anytime his department has need, is in order. As a minister, you are, of course, available to all who have need, but people do not always realize this, especially those who sometimes feels most often under public critical scrutiny. You might be invited to go on a "ride along" or to participate in some special service as a result of the letter. The chief policeman of your area might not respond at all, but you will have built tremendous good will.

Enforcement Division Contact:

Name________________________________Duty phone____________
Position______________________________Christian? Y___N______
Special needs this person has

____
____
____

Detention Division Contact

Name__________________________Duty phone_______________
Position________________________Christian? Y___N___
Special needs this person has_________________________________
____
____
____

Prison/Detention/Jail Ministries

It is very possible that each one of these areas has different or even multiple leadership. Talk to your local ministerial association to find out all they are aware of. Then discuss the works going on in each facility with your contacts that you have developed. In some Detention Centers and Jails all ministers allowed to enter the facility must be cleared through the locally approved ministry. This is a security measure that departments, who practice this, have put in place to insure that phony ministers do not manage to slip in with contraband materials. It is a good idea to establish your credentials and relationships, early, in the very real likelihood that you might need to visit someone in prison.

Make yourself a sheet on each ministry including information about the director and any staff people you know. Do any within these ministries come from your church? Maybe it would be a good place for a preacher within you congregation to serve. If this comes about, make it known that he is part of your Pastoral Staff assigned to serve in that capacity, thus you will validate his ministry and bring the whole church into awareness of human needs in this area.

Police Department

In a small police department it is a very good idea to know everyone possible, from the chief down to the newest RTO (Radio Telephone Operator). Regular visits are in order. They will assist you at funerals and in emergencies as part of their job, but they will do so happily when they know you have an ongoing interest in them. Mailing lists at the special times of the year are a minimum effort that can pay off greatly. If you have law enforcement within your congregation, observe law enforcement day each year. Send cards to your various departments on that day. Check with your local newspaper about writing an article extolling the blessing of good protection in a free society or include something in the church column.

Probation Parole Officers

In a large office there might be a secretary who keeps things organized and going who can be invaluable to you. In some cases, because of the things they encounter, they may be leery of you initially. Take your time and get to know these people. You can be a real blessing in their lives and they can be useful to you when you are counseling with someone on probation or parole or when you are dealing with a family member.

Always remember that these people are strongly affected, and to some degree, ruled by the various privacy acts. Also, they have ethical considerations that govern their responses. They live under several guns, so to speak. It takes time to network in law enforcement divisions effectively. But in the process you can make firm and true friends, as well as, bless many people's lives.

Pastor's Referral Resource

Children's Home

Name____

____

Address______________________________________

____

Phone numbers/at the desk of: _______________________

____

____

Children's Homes are operated by a number of different organizations. All have to be State certified in order to be operating legally.

What authority (parent agency) operates the children's home?

____

____

Address ______________________________________

Other directory information: people/phone numbers/chain of authority

____

____

____

What is the status of their certification? Are they on probation as a care facility? Has there been any complaints lodged with the state regulatory agency?

____

____

____

Type of services offered by the facility: abused children/drug cases/abandoned children/foster care/

____

____

Someone you know in the agency or have the possibility of establishing a good relationship with:

____

____

Notations:

Food and/or Clothing Assistance Organization

Many local organizations that deal in food or clothing assistance handle both. They are usually operated by church or benevolent organizations that are part of the local community. Compared to government agencies, they are more efficient in supplying short term rapid response to a need since they do not have the bureaucratic cogs to slow things down. Usually these local organizations are more flexible than the government agencies, being able to adjust or bend their rules to meet special and unique needs. Developing a relationship with the people who administer these programs is the key to having a need met, especially when the need is somewhat out of the ordinary. This is not difficult to do since the people you wish to cultivate are usually the very people you are seeing at ministerial meetings and various functional get togethers.

The local group can really help out in the short term so people can survive till the government agency can catch up. They are generally unequipped for long term benevolence.

Name of program: ________________________________

Address ________________________________

____

____

Contact________________________ phone ____________

Notes on contact: ________________________________

____

____

Procedures, requirements, and policies for assistance:

____

____

____

Christian ___ government ___ state ___ county/parish ____ other

____

Information on file under: ______________________________

Notations:

Pastor's Referral Resource

General Listing

The following are kinds of resources you will need to have knowledge of from time to time:

Adolescent Care Facilities[1]
Emergency shelters[2]
Battered Women's Home[3]
Unwed Mother's Home[4]
Home for AIDS Victims[5]
Half Way Houses (post alcohol, drug care) women, men, and youth facilities[6]

Government Operated Institutions

Mental Institutions
Youth Detention Facilities[7]
Commission Office[8]
Education Office[9]

[1]See Children's Homes format/Admission Procedures and length of stay allowed needed.
[2]What agency operates/Length of stay allowed/Counseling services available/Pastoral Privilege factors in using a shelter.
[3]Similar to Emergency Shelter Concerns/Security considerations
[4]Similar to Battered Women's Homes/Medical resources even greater concern.
[5]Homosexual groups are the issue here. What goes on inside? What are the medical resources?
[6]These facilities should be gender specific. Many can provide only limited help medically.
[7]Sometimes these specialize in various behavioral problems, violence etc.
[8]Becomes more and more important to protecting the church generally.
[9]This is important for problems related to youth disorders as well as the fact the minister needs to have input into education.

* menopause and thyroid problems are good examples of hormonal imbalance.
* The pressures of bad mental health on digestive systems frequently means that the beneficial bacteria dies in the stomach. Members who come in with mouth ulcers may be in such a state.
* Notice that all our quotes are in the Authorized text. It is the pinnacle of ministering in the Word; none other can compare in caring for the hurting. We suggest, when it is possible, that you choose a book which quotes from this text.
* A careful study of the context of this passage shows that more happens than prayer.
Both the (1) earnest request for help must come from the person in need, and (2) the confession of sins.
* Exploring the place witnessing has in the member's life can also help the member to realize the tremendous power that is backing him up. Or, it can also reveal insights to reasons for depression being in the life. For example: Stumbling through the motions of doing the Christian thing might reveal an erroneous image of God in his life which robs him of the joy in relationships, not only with his Lord, but with others.
** Burdened by the concerns of the world or by desires for material things may rob the heart of joy in the blessings of God. We know that some of the most important blessings are often those we take for granted. The unthankful heart must be taught to consider these things and realize that which the flesh sets its desires upon are of least importance.
* While acknowledging the devil is alive and well on Planet earth, we reject those extremists who see a demon inhabiting every situation or every person who has a problem. These people actually do harm to legitimate instances of direct evil influence.
* Sometimes depressed people need new kinds of friends.
** The key is to have contacts. Limitation of duration of individual contact may be indicated.
* Depression is often symptomatic of self esteem issues, and vice versa. Your evaluation must discover which comes first. In short, either can be the cart or the horse. You get the cart behind the horse for ministering to the need.
* Two groups of people who are routinely victims of legal medication without their knowledge are women being medicated for imbalance affecting their emotions and, war traumatized soldiers. These are not

the only two; victims of legal medication can come from all walks of life.

* You have already been introduced to the book Healing Relationships, by Stephen Grunlan and Daniel Lambrides. Hopefully, you added it to your counseling resource library. Table 9-1, beginning page 136 contains the Holmes-Rahe Social Adjustment Rating Scale. Use of this simple scale can help you determine what problems are most likely to have the greatest impact in a person's life. Not only that, the cumulative total points of depressive events can give you a handle on the severity of depression.
* The emphasis that must be placed on counseling cooperatively with an attending physician who specializes on weight control issues is here made. I cannot express to you strongly enough that a physician that is unsympathetic to the patient, even if he practices in the weight control area, is not acceptable as your resource. But always to counsel the dieting client, you must require physician participation to protect the health of the client.
* By neutral, we suggest a place where well meaning family or friends cannot influence him to say or do something he really does not mean.
* The argued purpose in this definition is to make medical treatment possible through various insurance programs.
* The expression pastors and teachers, while plural, clearly belongs to one person.
So each pastor must be a teacher by virtue of the function of his office.
* Dr. Larry Crabb has some very positive things to say about the role of the church in counseling. Audio tape interviews with Dr. Crabb can be procured through the American Association of Christian Counselors.
* Deacons and elders are invaluable where they are actually involved in ministry.
* The American Association of Christian Counselors publishes a National Registry of members with affiliations. Membership in this organization is worthy of the Pastor's consideration.

Barry Keaton holds the Master of Theology, Doctor of Ministry, and Doctor of Philosophy degrees. He is founder of Comfort Care Ministries, Inc., a non–profit Christian outreach for people who are hurting and in need of care. He also serves as pastor of Holly Springs Baptist Church in Rockmart, Georgia. He is married to Linda Allen Keaton, and they have three children, Haley, Cass, and Justin.

Printed in the United States
63336LVS00001B/7-66

9 781414 107271